The Myth of Civil Society

The Myth of Civil Society:
Social Capital and Democratic Consolidation in Spain and Brazil

Omar G. Encarnación

THE MYTH OF CIVIL SOCIETY
© Omar G. Encarnación, 2003.

First published 2003 by
PALGRAVE MACMILLAN™
175 Fifth Avenue, New York, N.Y. 10010 and
Houndmills, Basingstoke, Hampshire, England RG21 6XS.
Companies and representatives throughout the world.

PALGRAVE MACMILLAN is the global academic imprint of the Palgrave Macmillan division of St. Martin's Press, LLC and of Palgrave Macmillan Ltd. Macmillan® is a registered trademark in the United States, United Kingdom and other countries. Palgrave is a registered trademark in the European Union and other countries.

ISBN 1–4039–6226–X hardback

Library of Congress Cataloging-in-Publication Data

Encarnación, Omar Guillermo, 1962–
    The myth of civil society: social capital and democratic consolidation in Spain and Brazil/by Omar G. Encarnación.
        p. cm.
    Includes bibliographical references and index.
    ISBN 1–4039–6226–X
        1. Civil society—Case studies. 2. Democratization—Case studies.
3. Civil society—Spain. 4. Democratization—Spain. 5. Civil society—Brazil. 6. Democratization—Brazil. I. Title.

JC337.E53 2003
300'.946—dc21   2003051793

A catalogue record for this book is available from the British Library.

Design by Newgen Imaging Systems (P) Ltd., Chennai, India.

First edition: September, 2003
10 9 8 7 6 5 4 3 2 1

Printed in the United States of America.

Contents

Preface and Acknowledgments

These are heady days for "civil society," broadly understood to represent the broad and diverse universe of voluntary associations created by individuals to advance mutual interests and objectives. In recent years this alluring concept has found its way into everyone's lips, especially in discussions of how to revitalize democracy both at home and abroad. The rise in popularity of civil society is intimately linked to the unprecedented, worldwide spread of democracy since the mid-1970s. Arguably, the most compelling and enduring image of the drama of democratization as staged in nations as diverse as Spain, Argentina, Poland and South Africa is that of ordinary citizens acting collectively on behalf of democracy. These struggles for democracy were the catalyst for the emergence of multiple forms of civil society activism and organization—from student groups, to trade unions, to neighborhood associations. Through both discreet and overt means, these organizations created the conditions that made possible the establishment of a free political system including eroding the legitimacy of authoritarian institutions and in some cases literally hollowing out an entrenched tyrannical leadership.

Within the academic, policy-making and philanthropic communities, the popular mobilizations for democracy highlighted above have encouraged the notion that if an invigorated civil society can bring about a democratic transition it can consolidate democracy as well. Decades into what is generally regarded as the largest expansion of democracy in human history, it is clear that the view of civil society as the engine behind the consolidation of democratic regimes—currently an established conventional wisdom in democratization studies—is deeply flawed and in need of reconsideration. Civil society in many parts of the democratizing world has failed to sustain the vigor obtained in the fight against dictatorship, leading many observers to worry about a "post-transition civil society recession" that could threaten democratic consolidation. More importantly, much of the theorizing that sees a strong civil society as a prerequisite or a must-have for the consolidation of democracy lacks a firm empirical foundation in the real-life politics of democratizing societies. Democracy is struggling in nations possessing some of the most vibrant civil societies in existence and thriving in some lacking the requisite civil society. Explaining these apparent contradictions is the main task of this volume.

In the course of preparing this book, I have accumulated numerous debts that I am happy to acknowledge here. The first are to my academic mentors at the department of politics of Princeton University, where this project was born nearly a decade ago as a doctoral dissertation. While a graduate student at Princeton, I was very fortunate to benefit from the wisdom and guidance of Nancy Bermeo, Atul Kohli, Ezra Suleiman, Paul Sigmund, Michael Doyle and Kathleen Thelen. Among this distinguished roster of scholars, Nancy Bermeo's contributions to my professional and intellectual development deserve special recognition. She taught me comparative politics, sparked and nurtured my interest in the study of democratization, and encouraged me to challenge established conventional wisdom.

Second in line are a number of organizations and institutions that contributed materially to the completion of this project. Research stays in Europe and South America were made possible by grants and fellowships from the Council of European Studies, the Fulbright Program, the Princeton Program on Latin America, the Program for Cooperation between the Spanish Ministry of Culture and United States' Universities and the Bard College Faculty Research Fund. A 1997–1998 Ford Foundation/National Research Council Postdoctoral fellowship afforded me a year away from teaching to focus on the transformation of my research from a dissertation into a book. At various stages of the research and writing of this book I was affiliated with a number of institutions including the Center for Advanced Study in the Social Sciences of the Juan March Institute in Madrid, the Department of Government of Georgetown University and the Carnegie Endowment for International Peace in Washington D.C. The gracious hospitality and the intellectual stimulation that each institution provided is gratefully acknowledged.

Over the last few years I have also benefited from the generosity and insight of many colleagues on whom I imposed the task of reading portions or the entire draft of the manuscript. They include: Sonia A. Alvarez, Michael Baum, Sheri Berman, Nancy Bermeo, Thomas Carothers, Richard Gunther, Kathryn Hochstetler, David Kettler, Edward Malefakis, Sebastián Royo, Ben Ross Schneider and several anonymous reviewers. I am also thankful to the organizers and participants of the Brazil Seminar at the Institute for Latin American Studies of Columbia University and the Iberian

Studies Group of Harvard University's Center for European Studies for providing stimulating settings for the discussion of the ideas underpinning this project. My gratitude also goes to my friend and colleague James Chace, who as editor of the *World Policy Journal* published my first essay on the subject of civil society and the politics of democratization (*WPJ*, Vol. 17, Spring 2000), and to the Academy of Political Science, publishers of *Political Science Quarterly*, for allowing me to reprint a substantial portion of my essay "Civil Society and the Consolidation of Democracy in Spain" (*PSQ*, Vol. 116, Spring 2001). Thanks are also extended to Karen Homan for her assistance with the charts and tables found in the index, to Jorge Schwartz for his hospitality during my stay in Brazil and to Denise Durand Kremer for supplying the cover photo of the Brazilian demonstrations for direct elections of 1984. Of course, all errors and misrepresentations remain my sole responsibility.

On a final personal note, I wish to thank my partner, John E. Kinney, for his emotional support during the long gestation of this project, and Amos, my rambunctious Italian Greyhound, for his many distractions. Last but not least, I thank my parents Guillermo B. Encarnación and Gladys M. Encarnación for their love and understanding.

PART I

The Intellectual Terrain

CHAPTER 1

Introduction

The transition to democracy of dozens of nations once thought condemned to authoritarian or totalitarian rule may well be the most important political happening of the last three decades. How many of these new regimes will succeed in securing democratic governance remains an open question. Previous waves of democratization can be read as a cautionary tale of how difficult and protracted the path toward a consolidated democracy can be. But the debate about what it will take for the world's newest democracies to grow into efficient and stable polities appears to have been settled, at least for the time being. Almost irrespective of the geographic setting (whether it is Africa, Latin America or the former Communist world), the likelihood that any political opening can evolve into a consolidated democracy appears to depend upon one indispensable condition: the emergence of a vibrant and robust civil society. According to the prevailing conventional wisdom, a strong civil society lies behind successful democracies while a weak civil society is the root of failed or flawed democracies. This axiom about the relationship between civil society and democracy is projected by a large and diverse scholarship covering virtually every country in which the trend toward democracy has taken hold.[1] It also permeates policy debates within the international aid community about the most effective way to fortify fragile and fledging democracies abroad.[2]

At the risk of creating a caricature of what in reality is a complex and serious attempt to place cultural traditions and social habits at the root of the functioning of democracy, the prevailing discourse surrounding the importance of a strong civil society can be compressed into several interrelated points. First and foremost is the capacity of civil society to furnish a national stock of "social capital" that can serve to protect society from the state's inherent authoritarian tendencies, grease societal collaboration on behalf of democracy and improve the performance of political institutions. The concept of social capital, as employed by leading civil society theorists such as Robert Putnam, refers to a culture of trust, tolerance and reciprocity that allows nations to engage in a wide range of collaborative endeavors for the benefit of democracy and social and economic development.[3] The key dimension of this culture is "trust," both "inter-personal," the trust that individuals place upon each other, and "generalized," understood to represent a social endowment of trust.

The particular components of social capital, especially trust, are thought to emanate from the face-to-face interaction afforded to ordinary citizens by civil society associations. Virtually all of them count—from a trade union to a choral society to a bird-watching club—as long as they are voluntary in nature and created outside the family, the state and the marketplace for the purpose of advancing mutual values and objectives. In these sites of social organization citizens are believed to be trained to become good democrats by learning to work with one another and ridding themselves of selfish and authoritarian behavior, and by forging integrated ties of solidarity that transcend many social cleavages including class, gender and race. This social-ization provided by civil society works in democracy's favor by spilling onto the political sphere, where civil society imparts its democratizing effects. Among them are affording the citizenry practical skills (both organizational and deliberative ones) that can be applied to the betterment of governance, underwriting various aspects of democratic culture such as tolerance for pluralism and dissent and increasing public spiritedness.

Any new paradigm seeking to explain the mystery of what makes democ-racy possible deserves serious inspection, and the felicitous association that has been made in recent years between strong civil societies and healthy democracies is no exception. Despite its allure and widespread popularity, civil society must be greeted with the same critical eye applied to other high-profile concepts whose explanatory power once seemed so promising and are now resting comfortably in the social science graveyard.[4] In the case of civil society, there are compelling reasons to suspect that the current faith in its capacity to affect the consolidation of democracy has been overestimated and that the precise manner of how civil society interacts with the democratiza-tion process has been misunderstood as well. Indeed, the prevailing view of civil society as an infallible democratic miracle worker is arguably the most problematic conventional wisdom to be attached to civil society in the last few years. It amounts to a myth.

For a start, the widely held assumption that a vibrant and robust civil society is either a prerequisite or a precondition for the successful consolidation of democracy does not hold up to rigorous empirical scrutiny. In fact, it brazenly flies in the face of mounting evidence from a wide range of national experiences spanning various historical timeframes. Recent research into the rise of democracy in nineteenth-century Europe, a time of significant expansion of both civil society and democratic governance, finds that "the idea that a dense associational landscape is more likely to be a democratic one appears highly questionable."[5] The study arrives at this conclusion by juxtaposing nineteenth-century dramas of democratization that succeeded in erecting stable democracy: Britain, France, the Netherlands and Belgium, with those that descended into communism, fascism, corporatism and other political evils: Germany, Italy, Russia and Portugal. In all of these cases, the particulars of the constitution of civil society proved to be a poor indicator for predicting the development of democracy. Rather ironically, some of the nations in possession of the densest civil societies in the nineteenth century (such as Germany and Italy) found it most difficult to develop effective and enduring democratic institutions in the twentieth century.

Democratization in the contemporary period poses no less of a challenge to prevailing assumptions about civil society, as suggested by the evidence gathered in the present study from what Samuel Huntington has famously termed "the Third Wave" of democratization.[6] Begun in earnest in the mid-1970s in the Iberian Peninsula with the collapse of long-standing authoritarian regimes in Portugal and Spain, the Third Wave intensified throughout the 1980s with the demise of military regimes in Argentina, Brazil and Uruguay and the creation of numerous political openings in Asia and Africa. It crested in the early 1990s with the stunning disintegration of Communism in Eastern Europe and the former Soviet Union. The spate of new democracies born out of this democratic revolution demonstrates that a stable democratic public life can in fact be attained lacking most of the conditions usually attached to a vibrant and robust civil society. Moreover, it suggests that a strong civil society does not in and of itself guarantee democracy, much less a consolidated one. Quite the contrary, a flourishing civil society can actually be a hindrance to democratization, particularly if surrounded by weak and inefficient political institutions.

Civil society as a paradigm for understanding the consolidation of democracy also stands on very shaky theoretical grounds. Indeed, the virtuous cycle of how a thriving civil society promotes social capital and how social capital in turn aids democracy, however alluring and compelling, is deeply flawed and in serious need of reconsideration. It is questionable, for instance, whether the mere involvement of citizens in the various endeavors of civil society actually yields the many pro-democratic socializing functions ascribed to it, a point underscored by many critics of civil society and social capital theories.[7] Sheri Berman's probing analysis of the politics of the Weimar Republic compellingly illustrates how a very vibrant associational life did little to prevent Germany's slide into Fascism.[8]

Another central theme for the rapidly growing chorus of critics of civil society is that associationalism of the very kind praised by civil society advocates engenders all kinds of social behaviors, including many that are hardly beneficial to the maintenance of a democratic public life. Scores of studies point to the manner in which voluntary associations (even civic-minded ones!) can poison the hearts and minds of the citizenry and the public sphere by fostering apathy, mistrust and intolerance.[9] These attitudes and behaviors fall squarely under the category of what some scholars have referred to as "unsocial" or "non-communitarian" social capital.[10] Needless to say, the effects of such negative forms of social capital upon democracy can be highly pernicious if not downright devastating.

Further problems emerge when many of the assumptions about civil society are employed to understand the politics of democratic consolidation in post-authoritarian democracies, where theorizing about the virtues of civil society has been especially intense in recent years. It remains unclear, for instance, what the connection might be between levels of social capital within society and the decision of authoritarian elites to give up power or the decision of their adversaries to cooperate with them for the sake of attaining the consolidation of a new democratic regime. Nor is it obvious how the values and attitudes generated by civil society at the grassroots level (such as generalized trust) ascend to the top of the political arena, where political actors and institutions forge the compromises required for democratic consolidation. Finally, it is doubtful that civil society organizations can produce a system-level property such as democratic consolidation when their agenda tends to be rather narrow, their ties to the general public often weak and their ability to incorporate and represent the population limited. These contentions are especially relevant in connection to social movements, which are often cast by civil society enthusiasts as potential replacements for political parties. While social movements may in fact find it easier than parties to mobilize the public, it is questionable that they have the capacity to aggregate societal interests and offer effective political representation to a wide range of social actors.

In sum, the sunny and uncomplicated view of civil society as the linchpin of democratic consolidation is fraught with multiple empirical and theoretical problems. This conundrum, in turn, throws the field of democratization studies, democratic consolidation in particular, into a sort of theoretical limbo. For starters, if a flourishing civil society is not the foundation for the launching of a successful democracy—as we have been led to believe lately—then what is? Moreover, since it appears that civil society is capable of both aiding and hindering the process of democratic consolidation, what are the social conditions that determine each of these political outcomes? Finally, and most importantly, what can ensure that civil society as a political actor plays a positive, supportive role in the consolidation of democratic institutions? These are the questions addressed in this study.

The Arguments

Seeking to help fill the lacunae that plague civil society as a framework for understanding democratic consolidation, the present study offers two interconnected theoretical correctives. The first and most straightforward is that civil society, however vibrant and robust, cannot replace in importance other requirements for democratic consolidation, especially a stable and well-functioning political system. This assertion about the primacy of formal political institutions in the creation and maintenance of democratic regimes has long served to inform the study of mass democracy since its appearance in the nineteenth century.[11] In recent years, however, it has been overshadowed (if not eclipsed altogether) by all the hype surrounding civil society's presumed democratic virtues. Whether intended or not, much of the enthusiasm about civil society leads to the conclusion that democratizing societies would do well to do away with political institutions (or at the very least seriously restrain them) in order for civil society to realize all of the good things ascribed to it. Such assumptions are misguided and even dangerous.

Although political institutions are currently the object of apathy, cynicism and disdain in some scholarly and policy circles (and consequently held in considerably lower esteem than civil society), the government, the agencies of the state and the party system, remain the key players in the game of democratic consolidation. They set the stakes of the democratic game and forge the societal compromises that allow for its functioning and stability. More specifically, political institutions perform two critical and unique functions in the consolidation of democratic regimes that rest beyond the capacities of civil society, regardless of its strength and reach. The first is "social integration," a task that involves aggregating interests across many societal divides and forging a broadly based consensus on the rules of the democratic game. The second is "political representation," a task that entails affording societal actors institutional means for channeling their demands through the political system and for accessing the state and the policy-making arena.

The second and most important argument of the present study is that the principal reason why the role of civil society in the study of the consolidation of democracy has been inflated is because the prevailing analytical narrative regarding the concept of social capital has been misconstrued. While civil society theorists have correctly identified social capital as a key ingredient in the consolidation of democracy they have erred in locating the main source of its production. I contend that social capital is more likely to emerge as the result of the constitution and performance of political institutions (in other words the political context) than from participation of the citizenry in the endeavors of civil society organizations. This contention stands in direct opposition to the prevailing view of civil society as the exclusive domain of social capital formation. As indicated previously, the civil society revival is premised on the consideration of voluntary groups (e.g. civil society) as the sole producer of social capital. But this perspective is very impoverishing to say the least. It neglects to account for the many ways in which government action, public policy and state structures can serve to foster and protect the values and behaviors conventionally understood to constitute the metaphor of social capital. Moreover, it fails to recognize the crucial role that political institutions (political parties in particular) play in providing the organizational channels through which social capital can be gainfully employed to facilitate the process of democratic consolidation.

We should expect social trust, networks of reciprocity and other components of social capital to thrive in an environment in which the political system is effective, by which I mean responsive to the needs and desires of the public, and well-institutionalized. In connection to democratizing societies, such a political–institutional context includes a government that is committed to the values and practices of democracy, a credible and coherent state apparatus and political parties with deep roots in society. These conditions provide the best prospect for the general well-being of the polity in terms of both political stability and socioeconomic development, which in turn provide the ideal foundation for increasing the capacity of individuals to trust each other and engage in collaborative efforts on behalf of democracy. They also facilitate trust in the political system, a critical requirement for political institutions to successfully execute the integration of society around the project of democratization and offer social actors effective means for political representation. By contrast, we should expect the formation of social capital to be undermined if not altogether stalled by inefficient or poorly developed political institutions. Indeed, mostly negative forms of social capital (e.g. mistrust and cynicism) are likely to emerge from such a political context.

These arguments underscore several lessons about civil society and the politics of democratization. The first and most obvious is that democratic consolidation depends for its success upon efficient and stable political institutions rather than vibrant and robust civil societies. At best, civil society plays an auxiliary role in the consolidation of democracy that consists primarily of supplementing the work of political institutions. This is, to be sure, an important role for civil society in the process of democratic consolidation since it serves to bolster the legitimacy and stability of democratic institutions. But it falls short of the starring portrayals found in the works of leading civil society theorists, which make civil society a leading rather than a supporting actor in the various stages of the drama of democratization.

Another lesson is that we have misplaced or misunderstood what matters most about civil society in connection to the process of democratic consolidation. Instead of focusing on civil society itself and more specifically on organizational features such as the density of voluntary associations and levels of civic engagement, we are better served by shifting our analytical lenses toward the performance of the political system, its legacies and institutional design. It is the external political shell surrounding the organizations of civil society rather than their internal configuration that fundamentally determines the political coloring of civil society and whether this actor as a collective social force will have beneficial or perilous influences upon the emerging democratic system.

In the right political context (e.g. a stable and efficient political system) civil society is likely to become a partner of political institutions in the legitimatization of the new democratic regime thereby facilitating the tasks of social integration and political representation. In the absence of such a context, however, the likely end result of the process of democratization is a stalled or unconsolidated democracy. More worrisome yet, when surrounded by unstable, failing or underdeveloped political institutions, civil society is likely to remain outside of the realm of political bargaining and crafting that makes democratic consolidation possible and a potential threat to the stability of the new democratic regime. It can undermine representative institutions, institutionalize an antisystem and anti party political culture, radicalize demands against the state and encourage the rise of opportunistic and personalistic leaders willing to exploit the failures of the political system for their own personal benefit.

The Empirical Setting

From the many democratic transformations launched by the Third Wave of democratization, the present study focuses on the experiences of Spain and Brazil. These two landmark cases of democratization provide exceptionally rich laboratories that vividly bring to light the inquiries and arguments that animate this study.[12] For a start, Spain and Brazil share the status of pioneers among newly democratic nations having begun their democratic transitions almost simultaneously in the mid-1970s. Thus, unlike the more recent democratic transitions of Eastern Europe and the former Soviet Union, the politics of democratization in Spain and Brazil afford expansive historical timeframes in which to examine prevailing assumptions about civil society and democratic consolidation. More important, however, is the manner in which each case pointedly challenges the positive connection that has been made between a thriving civil society and success at consolidating democratic institutions and practices.

The case of Spain can be deemed a crucial testing ground for any theoretical assumption about what makes democratic consolidation possible in formerly authoritarian states. Juan Linz and Alfred Stepan, the deans of democratization studies, observe that post-Franco Spain "has emerged as the paradigmatic case for the study of democratic transitions, almost as the breakdown of the Weimar Republic has been for the study of the fall of democracies."[13] This privileged standing for Spain in the comparative literature on democratization mirrors the widely shared impression among scholars of Spanish politics that the country's experience since it abandoned authoritarian rule in 1977 amounts to "a successful and relatively unproblematic consolidation of democracy."[14] It also conveys the sense that Spain's new democracy is not only fully consolidated but also a model that other nations are seeking to emulate. In Adam Przeworski's characterization, "the banner of new elites and the peoples of Eastern Europe is democracy, the market and Europe, and the optimistic scenario is to retrace the steps of Spain."[15]

The success of democracy in Spain, however, stands in striking contrast to the very impoverished nature of civil society as the country undertook to democratize, the consequence of delayed modernization, multiple ethnic and regional cleavages and the problematic legacies of social organization and political participation left behind by the Franco dictatorship. Consequently, few scholars intimately familiar with the contours of Spanish political history would posit a vibrant and robust civil society as the foundation of the country's successful democratization. Quite the contrary, a dominant theme in the study of post-transition politics in Spain is the acute civil society deficit that afflicted the nation during the consolidation of democracy.[16] This civil society deficit is suggested most notably in the low level of civic engagement found in Spanish associational life. As shown in the appendix, among Iberian-Latin societies, Spain ranks near the bottom in terms of the percentage of citizens that belong to a voluntary association. This percentage is also lower than those found in many post-Communist European societies, where civil society was obliterated by decades of totalitarian rule.

The experience of Brazil, like that of post-Franco Spain, turns the received conventional wisdom about civil society and democratic consolidation upon its head. Among major cases of re-democratization in Southern Europe and South America, Brazil is often held as the paradigm of civil society resurgence in the aftermath of authoritarian rule.[17] Frances Hagopian's discussion of the proliferation of civic associations in post-transition Latin America notes that "perhaps nowhere in Latin America was the resurrection of civil society more dramatic and the rise of social movements more pronounced than in Brazil."[18] The roots of the resurgence of civil society in Brazil can be located in the long struggle for democracy (the longest among South American nations), the many sites for social organization left open by the authoritarian regime and the energetic and unparalleled role of the Catholic Church in organizing Brazilian society against military rule. Not surprisingly, as suggested by the data reviewed in the appendix, Brazil leads the Iberian-Latin world in participation by the citizenry in virtually all kinds of civil society organizations—from NGOs, to unions, to religious and recreational groups.

A flourishing civil society, however, has not made for a successful experience with democratic consolidation in Brazil. Linz and Stepan's comparative analysis of democratization in Southern Europe and South America deems Brazil's transition to democracy "the longest and most constrained" and its process of democratic consolidation "the most difficult."[19] Experts of Brazilian politics confirm this evaluation by qualifying the Brazilian democratic transition as "the most ambiguous and questionable of all of Latin America's new democracies."[20] Harsher still is their judgment of the politics of democratic consolidation. A recent review of politics in Brazil concludes that since 1985 "democratic deepening has lagged appallingly."[21] These assessments of Brazilian democratization explain the speculations of a democratic breakdown that swirled around Brazil's new democracy during the early 1990s, as well as recent discussions about a crisis of democratic consolidation.[22] Ironically, among the conditions preventing the consolidation of democracy in Brazil are some of the very problems that a vibrant and robust civil society is meant to solve or at the very least help alleviate. Chief among them are: unrestrained state control and violence, weak support for democracy from the masses, corruption and clientelism, a poor conception of citizenship and widespread social and economic inequities.

The cases of Spain and Brazil also point to political institutions rather than civil society organizations as the key facilitating sources of social capital and its incorporation into the process of democratic consolidation. Despite the overall weakness of its civil society, an ample supply of social capital permeated the crafting of a new democratic regime in post-Franco Spain, including an impressive capacity by the citizenry and all kinds of social groups to engage in trust-based political interaction for the benefit of democracy. This is best appreciated in what the Spaniards refer to as *concertación social* (social concertation), a process of societal consultation and negotiation erected during the peak years of democratic transition and consolidation (1977–1986). It is widely regarded as the linchpin of democratic consolidation in Spain.[23] In this study, I attribute the social capital that underwrote the rise and institutionalization of "social concertation" in the form of "social pacts" to the performance and constitution of the emerging democratic political system. In particular, the present analysis highlights the democratic commitment and competence displayed by public officials, the social and economic transformations engineered by state agencies during the decades preceding the democratic transition that lifted living standards and moderated a previously radical political culture and finally, left-wing parties with deep roots in society. These conditions allowed for the efficacious integration of social forces in Spain at critical phases in the process of democratization. Moreover, they permitted civil society to bolster the legitimacy of the emerging democratic system and enhanced the capacity of its organizations to advance multiple political and economic goals.

The picture of social capital production in Brazil stands in striking contrast to that provided by the Spanish case. Despite possessing a civil society that exhibits many of the signs traditionally attributed to a thriving civil society including, most notably, an impressive level of engagement by the citizenry in voluntary groups of almost every kind and purpose, social capital is in very short supply in Brazil. For instance, the cross-national survey data reviewed in this study portrays Brazil as a veritable dessert of social trust, the key empirical indicator of social capital. This is perhaps not altogether surprising given the poor performance of Brazilian governments in the post-transition era and the institutional decay that has afflicted the country's political system in the last decades.

Since the inception of democracy, Brazil has operated under mostly erratic (and at times illegitimate) political leadership with a highly ambiguous commitment to the democratic process, discredited state institutions emanating from staggering social and economic failures (including an enormous gap between rich and poor and rampant crime and corruption) and a poorly institutionalized party system with shallow connections to society. These conditions explain the absence of effective means of social integration and political representation in Brazilian society as the nation undertook to democratize. Furthermore, they tell us much about the rise within Brazilian civil society and the general public of values and behaviors antithetical to democracy such as apathy, cynicism and mistrust; thereby depriving civil society of its potential for aiding in the legitimation of the new democratic order and undermining its capacity to affect political change. This in turn has compromised a wide range of democratization tasks, including securing an expedient transition out of military rule, extricating the legacies of authoritarianism, gaining mass support for democratic values and alleviating economic and social ills.

The Organization of the Book

Part I, opened by this introductory chapter, offers an analytical and historical overview of the renewed interest in and appreciation for the role of nonpolitical, voluntary groups in creating and sustaining democracy. It continues with chapter 2, which is devoted to charting the social and political developments underpinning the revival of civil society and mapping out its various intellectual agendas with emphasis on the consolidation of democratic regimes. In regard to the latter task, chapter 2 first discusses the prevailing understanding of the concept of civil society and the dominant model employed to gauge levels of civil society vibrancy and robustness. It then summarizes the causal links believed to exist between a strong civil society and the creation and maintenance of democracy, as embedded in so-called neo-Tocquevillean theories of civil society. Chapter 2 closes with a summary of my own critique of the application of theories of civil society to the study of contemporary democratization.

Parts II and III incorporate chapters 3–6 and flesh out the arguments outlined for this study in light of the experiences of Spain and Brazil. An important caveat worth noting from the onset is that the historical narrative of democratization politics in Spain and Brazil contained in these chapters is not comprehensive. Instead, it is highly selective and exclusively designed to illustrate the manner in which each case pointedly contradicts the received conventional wisdom about civil society and democratic consolidation and to prove my arguments about the importance of political institutions to democratic consolidation and the formation of social capital. The data utilized in these chapters is culled from an extensive review of the secondary literature and my own published and unpublished original research about civil society and democratization in Spain and Brazil.[24]

Part IV (chapter 7) assesses the implications of the present study for the debate about civil society in the contemporary study of democratization. It emphasizes, above all, the need to recast the role of civil society in the politics of democratic consolidation. Currently regarded as nothing short of an infallible democratic miracle worker, the role of civil society in the consolidation of democracy is best understood as conditioned by political context and circumstances. Whether civil society is good or bad for democracy depends upon the constitution and performance of the political system. In the right political context we can expect civil society to become an active participant in the consolidation of democracy by bolstering the work of political institutions. In the wrong political context we should expect civil society to remain of relatively limited utility to the actual advancement of democratic consolidation and a potential source of regime instability for the new democracy.

CHAPTER 2

The Revival of Civil Society

At the opening of the new century, few concepts possess as much political currency as that of civil society. The normally restrained *New York Times* reports: "In the world of ideas, civil society is hot. It is almost impossible to read an article on foreign or domestic policy without coming across some mention of the concept."[1] The visibility (as well as the vitality) of the concept of civil society is most prominently suggested by its presence in the rhetoric of political figures who appear to agree on very little else. Indeed, the embrace of civil society and its presumed virtues by both Liberals and Conservatives is nothing short of breathtaking. At the very heart of Hillary Rodham Clinton's contention that "It Takes a Village" and George W. Bush's agenda for a "Compassionate Conservatism," is a plea for greater engagement of civil society organizations in the delivery of social services once deemed the primary responsibility of the state. For both Clinton and Bush, the involvement of businesses, churches and private charities in health care, child rearing and education is premised on the belief that such involvement not only benefits the common good (by empowering local communities as well as national institutions) but also yields greater efficacy in the delivery of public services.

The enthusiastic embrace of civil society by the political class mirrors the concept's current appeal among scholars and political commentators, as demonstrated by the impressive number of books and articles devoted to the subject in recent years. The most celebrated and influential text so far is Robert Putnam's *Making Democracy Work*, a study of Italian regional politics that has been hailed as "seminal, epochal and path-breaking."[2] It prescribes a vibrant and robust civil society as the remedy for the various ills afflicting advanced industrial democracies, particularly the apathy, discontent and mistrust that ordinary citizens feel toward their governing institutions. This work and subsequent writings have brought Putnam considerable fame and endowed civil society with a theoretical importance virtually unmatched in the social sciences. Especially influential in shaping the current debate about civil society was the publication of his essay "Bowling Alone."[3] It portrays American society as gripped by a crisis of civic engagement triggered by a dramatic decline in participation by Americans in secondary associations such as bowling leagues, bird-watching clubs and choral societies, among many others. In Putnam's view, this crisis has negatively impacted American democracy by depleting the national reserves of social trust, generalized reciprocity and mutually beneficial collective action, and only a concerted effort to reverse this trend can assure that the United States will continue to enjoy a healthy democratic public life.[4]

Putnam's central source of inspiration is Alexis de Tocqueville's *Democracy in America*, widely recognized as the first social science book to link a vibrant and robust civil society with a successful democracy.[5] This 160-year-old treatise on American political culture in the postcolonial era posits the well-known and time-honored thesis that a flourishing civil society is the bedrock of American democracy.[6] In Tocqueville's view, American democracy was sustained by the richness and diversity of its voluntary associations—from religious groups, to neighborhood associations to commercial enterprises. Through their various functions and operations, these organizations held the nation together in the absence of a monarchy and a highly centralized federal structure. More importantly, voluntary associations served American democracy by developing the kind of citizenry that is best suited for the maintenance of a democratic public life. Tocqueville observed that citizens' participation in voluntary associations allowed for the tempering of individualism and self-interest for the sake of the common good by instilling "habits of regularity, temperance, moderation, foresight and self-command."[7]

As would be expected, the vigorous renaissance of civil society has made Tocqueville one of the most influential political theorists of the new century (a point vividly illustrated by the renown of so-called neo-Tocquevillean scholars such as Putnam) and *Democracy in America* something of a bible for civil society enthusiasts. "Tocqueville was right: Democracy is strengthened, not weakened, when it faces a vigorous civil society," asserts Putnam seeking to validate his claims that when democracy is anchored upon a strong civil society it thrives, while in its absence it languishes.[8] "Tocquevilleanism," notes another scholar, "is the most promising intellectual development to fill the gap left behind by the demise of Marxism."[9] For their part, the editors of the *Journal of Democracy*, whose tenth anniversary issue is devoted in its entirety to canvassing Tocqueville's influence upon recent scholarship on democracy in the United States and around the world, observe that "as we enter the millennium, one may say with little exaggeration: We are all Tocquevellians now."[10]

Notwithstanding its importance to contemporary debates about the travails of American democracy, it is in connection to discussions about how to aid in the development of democracy abroad that the concept of civil society has made its biggest splash. Prior to the 1990s, the term civil society was not only largely relegated to arcane discussions in political theory and philosophy but also virtually without a history with regard to the academic thinking about political development and the work of international development agencies. It is telling that the landmark social science work on political development ideas and foreign aid in the postwar era, Robert A. Packenham's *Liberal America and the Third World*, does not register a single citation for the term civil society.[11] But at the present time, references to civil society have become almost obligatory in any academic or policy discussion about development regarding either politics or the economy. Indeed, in recent years theorizing about the virtues and potential contributions of civil society organizations to the advancement of political and economic development has reached a frenzied pitch of seemingly unrestrained proportions.

A review of the multiplicity of claims currently being attached to a strong civil society leads to the almost inescapable conclusion that civil society can rightly be regarded as nothing short of a panacea for the developing world. Just within the last decade, numerous academics and policy experts have come to view civil society as the ideal vehicle to dislodge authoritarian, corrupt and incompetent governments,[12] to fortify civil liberties and human rights,[13] to promote good governance and economic prosperity,[14] to improve health and general well-being,[15] to deter nationalism and ethnic conflict[16] and to consolidate fledging and fragile democratic institutions and practices.[17] Among these many positive claims about the virtuous powers of civil society, none is more heralded and widespread than the capacity to facilitate a successful passage from authoritarian rule to a stable democracy. Whether the focus is on Argentina, Russia or South Africa, newly democratic nations are being urged to beef up the civil society sector as the first step toward attaining "democratic consolidation," understood as the process through which democratic institutions and practices become fully rooted and widely accepted by the public.[18]

Leading the way in promoting civil society as the engine behind the successful consolidation of democracy is the so-called democracy aid industry, the cadre of scholars, political activists, social movements and international aid organizations directly engaged in promoting democracy abroad.[19] In its eyes, a vigorous civil society and a successful democracy go hand in hand. Representative of this perspective is the work of Larry Diamond, arguably the most authoritative voice among scholars concerned with the role of civil society in contemporary situations of democratization and ways to encourage its development in foreign lands. He writes: "Democracy—in particular a healthy liberal democracy—requires a public that is organized for democracy, socialized to its norms and values and committed not just to its myriad narrow interests but to larger, common, civic ends. Such a public is only possible with a vibrant civil society."[20]

Diamond's faith in the capacity of civil society to bring about democracy is loudly echoed in the endeavors of international donor agencies, which in recent years have embraced civil society as a programmatic priority. At the present time, civil society assistance features prominently in the portfolio of every major international development agency, including the United States Agency for International Development (USAID), the United Nations Development Program (UNDP) and the World Bank. Global spending by these and other international aid organizations on civil society assistance topped US$4 billion by the mid-1990s, or 8.6 percent of total official aid flows to the developing world of $46.5 billion.[21] Admittedly, this is a small percentage as a proportion of the overall aid budget, but what is striking about civil society assistance is how rapidly it has come to dominate the agenda of international donors. Since the early 1990s, support for civil society initiatives within USAID has grown steadily and significantly, going from $56.1 million in 1991; to 118.1 million by 1993; to 164.7 million by 1995; to 181.7 million by 1998.[22] This aid is being employed to support a vast network of NGOs, which the international aid community regards as synonymous with civil society and critical to the boosting of social capital. It incorporates grassroots social movements, trade unions, a free media and a wide range of organizations involved in promoting such causes as human rights, governmental transparency and the environment.

Explaining Civil Society's Return

No single factor explains the seemingly sudden burst of interest in civil society in the context of both mature and emerging democracies. Behind the current popularity of civil society stands a somewhat messy and incoherent story; one in which unrelated and overlapping ideological and historical happenings have converged in multiple settings to create a true global phenomenon engulfing the worlds of academia, policy-making and international development. Explaining civil society's red-hot popularity is made the more difficult still because it could not have been easily predicted. Indeed, to some extent the revival of civil society currently underway is quite puzzling. While the publication of *Democracy in America*, the *locus classicus* for contemporary students of civil society, brought Tocqueville considerable celebrity, especially in the United States, his reputation suffered a precipitous decline beginning in the late nineteenth century, from which it did not recover until fairly recently. For its part, the concept of civil society was on the brink of oblivion barely a decade ago: an *idée passée* and the object of cynicism and even outright hostility.[23]

In the broad context of Western democracies, factors of a nonideological nature are often relied upon to explain the widespread appeal of civil society; most notably, the perception that traditional means of socialization now belonging to the past provided for a better and more reassuring way of life. Theda Skocpol and Morris P. Fiorina write that civil society "recalls a time when bowling leagues met regularly and people sat on their porches or played bridge; a time when wives organized dinner parties and neighbors threw themselves into all kinds of community activities."[24] This sense of loss and longing about the past has in turn created a concern about the "civic health" of the United States, a point reinforced by scores of studies highlighting the decline and deterioration of civic engagement among Americans. Such developments are tellingly documented in the *General Social Survey* (*GSS*), which tracks the membership levels of Americans in voluntary associations, from recreational groups, to unions, to parties, to churches. Its findings for the years 1974 and 1994 suggest that Americans were members of about 25 percent fewer voluntary groups in the 1990s than in the 1970s.[25]

Ideological and partisan projects (from both the Left and the Right) in reaction to particular political circumstances have also played a role in pushing along the civil society revival in Western democracies. For Europe's so-called New Left, and the social movements that it engendered (France's "Second Left" and the German Greens, to name just a few), the appeal of civil society rests in the crisis of the welfare state. This embrace of civil society within the European Left developed against the backdrop of the neo-corporatist arrangements that have characterized state–society relations in postwar Western Europe. These arrangements had incorporated the labor movement, employers and parties into institutionalized patterns of governance but had afforded little access to other constituencies such as feminists, ethnic minorities, gays and environmentalists. Civil society was thus conceptualized in opposition to the status quo of this neo-corporatist political settlement and as a means to further democratize society by increasing the access and influence of marginalized voices.

In the United States, the rising stock of civil society is also linked to a crisis of the state, and specifically the disrepute of government, a development that may have culminated, at least symbolically, with President Clinton's declaration after the 1994 elections that "the era of big government is over." Indeed, the sense that government was too intrusive, untrustworthy, wasteful and best kept to a minimum essentially drove the rise of civil society to the top of the agenda of politicians and scholars across the partisan spectrum. While clinging to the notion that government is still relevant to people's lives, in the last decades the political activism of American Liberals has been tempered by the reality of growing resistance from the general public toward the expansion of government.[26] Thus, in embracing civil society the Liberal intelligentsia has hoped to find answers to society's vexing problems (from poverty to racism to sexism) that do not invite further intrusion of the state into the lives of the citizenry. As argued by Fiorina, "liberals appreciate voluntaristic approaches as the principal ones available at a time when popular support for activist government is at a low ebb."[27]

For the Right—whose growth in the United States during the 1980s mirrored the falling fortunes of government—civil society is the key for wrestling control over many of the decisions affecting society from the hands of an overbearing and ever-encroaching state. Civil society is also the vehicle for turning over governmental decision-making to presumably more responsive local and nongovernmental organizations. For Conservatives, however, the virtue of civil society does not depend upon the rise of vibrant social movements and reinvigorated advocacy groups, as is the case for Liberals. Instead, the civil society rhetoric of Conservatives emphasizes the emergence of networks of local and seemingly apolitical citizens' organizations perceived as capable of shouldering a host of social needs as well as cleansing politics of the evils of big government. As contended by Daniel Bell, "the demand for a return to civil society is the demand for a return to a manageable scale of life," one that emphasizes decision-making by voluntary associations, churches and local communities rather than the state and its bureaucracies.[28]

The empowering of local communities extolled by Bell is often premised on the decentralization of the national state, which is generally perceived in conservative quarters as the culprit in the weakening of civil society and the crisis of civic engagement. Michael Joyce and William Schambra write: "The restoration of civil society in America requires nothing less than a determined, long-term effort to reverse the gravitation of power and authority upward to the national government and send that authority back to local governments and civil institutions."[29] These demands for the decentralization of state power have in turn provided the philosophical rationale for the advent of policies aimed at dismantling state enterprises, regulatory and planning functions and welfare services. Such policies began to take center stage in the policy arena in Britain and the United States during the 1980s and throughout the developing world during the 1990s as part of the so-called neoliberal economic agenda.

The Global Democratic Revolution

While interest in civil society in Western democracies has been attributed to a perceived crisis of democracy, in much of the rest of the world this phenomenon is intimately linked to debates about the birth of democracy. More specifically, the debate has centered on how civil society might contribute to democratic consolidation in the aftermath of a prolonged experience with authoritarian or totalitarian rule. This debate was triggered in a dramatic fashion by what Samuel Huntington famously baptized as the "Third Wave" of democratization.[30] Characterized in the democratization literature as "the greatest period of democratic ferment in the history of modern civilization," the Third Wave is credited with creating dozens of new democracies across the globe.[31] By one estimate, between 1974 and 1990, 30 new democracies were established across the globe, and that tally does not include the dozens of attempts at democratization triggered by the collapse of Communism.[32] As a result of this unleashing of democratic fervor, democracy, once confined for much of the postwar era largely to North American and Western European societies, is today a global political commodity.

What accounts for the global democratic revolution of the last three decades remains the subject of some debate. The Third Wave metaphor employed by Huntington and others suggests some intertwined connection among these regime transitions, but this is highly questionable.[33] Although the Southern European democratic transitions served as models for those of Latin America and Eastern and Central Europe; they certainly did not trigger them. Nonetheless, the close temporal agglomeration of these transitions has had a significant impact on how scholars have conceptually interpreted the causes of a democratic transition and what might bring about democratic consolidation. Prominent among them is "the rise of civil society." In almost all the cases of democratization included in the Third Wave, the idea of civil society, both figuratively and literally, resonated very powerfully with the struggle for freedom and democracy waged in dozens of formerly authoritarian and totalitarian societies. In the many locations in which these dramas against tyranny unfolded, resistance leaders and social movements employed the idea of civil society to crystallize projects of social autonomy against dictatorship.

Thomas Carothers, whose work traces the rise of civil society in the programs of democratic promotion of Western donors, reminds us that it was "Czech, Hungarian, and Polish activists who wrapped themselves in the banner of civil society, endowing it with a heroic quality when the Berlin Wall fell."[34] Their struggle against Communist rule posited civil society as something of a "middle way" between the excesses of the East (Communism) and those of the West (Capitalism). For Vaclav Havel, one of the heroes of the Central and Eastern European revolutions, civil society (especially the stirring phrase "civil society against the state") became the means for attaining political freedom and human creativity. More concretely, civil society in Havel's writings and actions represented empowered ordinary individuals working collectively and from below toward forming a parallel polis to that represented by the official Communist totalitarian system and party-state.[35]

A more radical understanding of civil society ensuing from the Central and Eastern European democratic transitions made the concept the embodiment of an "anti-politics" and "anti-state" movement. This approach is exemplified in the work of the Hungarian dissident György Konrád who vividly captured the mood of civil society as a form of societal retreat from the state. In his book *Antipolitics*, civil society is posited as an alternative to the state or, as Michael Walzer puts it, "living with one's back toward it."[36] In Konrád's thinking, the state is "unchangeable and irredeemably hostile," leading him to urge his fellow dissidents to reject the idea of seizing or sharing power and to devote their energies to religious, cultural, economic and professional associations.[37]

The intellectual discourse about civil society flowing from the collapse of Communism was vividly brought to life by many social movements that made civil society the political celebrity of the Third Wave of democratization. A case in point is Poland, where civil society consolidated its reputation as a foundation for democratization. Witness the rise of Solidarity, the symbol of civil society howling out an entrenched totalitarian regime. Solidarity bravely defied the tight grip of Communism and eventually toppled it, compellingly suggesting the power of citizens acting in concert to effect political change.[38] In Michael Bernhard's account, Solidarity was "able to force the party-state regime to recognize the principle of autonomous organization and the boundaries of the public space. Civil society co-existed for a time with an authoritarian regime that tried to stifle it; but when the regime found itself incapable of doing this, it acceded to demands for democratization of the political system."[39]

Civil society also played a starring role in the Latin American democratic transitions of the mid-1980s and the early 1990s. At the height of the repression of the bureaucratic-authoritarian regimes that ensconced themselves throughout the region in the 1960s and 1970s, the intelligentsia embraced the term civil society as a result of the popularity of the work of Antonio Gramsci. His *Prison Notebooks* posited civil society as the antidote to dictatorship. The Latin American adaptation of Gramscian thinking about democracy reflected the struggle against bureaucratic authoritarian rule as well as the widespread realization that politics as usual and its emphasis on parties and legislatures had failed in the past.[40] Civil society in Latin America under authoritarian rule was thus framed "not only as society against a repressive state but also as society in place of the parties."[41] This led to the identification of civil society with "non-political groups" causing many Latin American intellectuals to engineer multiple connections with popular movements that in time would go on to attain iconic status in the civil society lore.

The most emblematic example of civil society activism in Latin America was the struggle of *Las Madres de la Plaza de Mayo*, the group of Argentine mothers that peacefully challenged the political authority of a brutal military regime in their search for justice against the violations perpetrated on their children.[42] Elsewhere in Latin America, the face of civil society took the form of vigorous popular, poor people's movements openly challenging authoritarian institutions and demanding democratic government.[43] In the early 1960s, the Catholic Church in Brazil began to organize and mobilize the poor on behalf of social and political change in a movement that came to be known as the "Christian Base Communities."[44] Mixing classic Catholic teachings about social justice with the struggle against military rule, this expansive social movement provided a compelling picture of forging democracy from below. In Uruguay in the mid-1980s, and several years later in the struggle against the Pinochet dictatorship in Chile, the transition to democracy was precipitated by the emergence of vigorous urban social movements anchored in shantytown organizations.[45] Their agenda included the defeat of dictatorship, better living conditions and respect for human and political rights.

Unpacking Civil Society's Intellectual Agenda

No scholar has yet to make the argument that civil society, by itself, can bring about the consolidation of democracy. But it is quite astonishing how much of the discourse about civil society and its presumed virtues is predicated upon the notion that it can. This is especially the case of neo-Tocquevillean theories of civil society and democratization, which are the focus of our attention. But before unpacking how Tocqueville's work has been reinterpreted and reinvented by contemporary scholars of democracy, a clear understanding of what is meant by civil society must be established. Oddly enough, Tocqueville himself never used the term civil society, preferring instead to write simply about voluntary associations and their impact on democracy. And despite all the attention devoted to civil society in recent years, a consensus on its precise meaning remains highly elusive. A summary of recent writings on civil society notes that just within the concept's current revival, civil society appears to represent at least six different viewpoints: "value, collective noun, space, historical moment, anti-hegemony and anti-state."[46] Complicating matters in the study of civil society and its application to contemporary problems is the elasticity of the concept's ideological appeal. The concept of civil society has been embraced by virtually the entire political spectrum, allowing political thinkers and actors to turn the concept into something of a conceptual grab bag or "analytical hat-stand" suitable for almost any political agenda.[47] Not surprisingly, disentangling the various meanings of civil society has become in and of itself a worthy academic endeavor.[48]

Defining Civil Society

In its current revival, the term civil society stands for "the realm of social life that is open, voluntary, self-generating, at least partially self-supporting, autonomous from the state, and bound by a legal order or set of shared values."[49] This sphere of social organization is distinct from what is usually referred to as "political society," which comprises political parties, state agencies and the government. It is also separate from "economic society," which refers largely to for-profit businesses and firms. Notwithstanding these widely shared notions of what civil society actually is, there remains within the civil society scholarship considerable tension regarding the specific groups that belong inside and outside of civil society's organizational walls.

On the one hand are conceptualizations of civil society so open and elastic that include virtually everything we know as social. A case in point is Michael Walzer's well-known proposition that civil society encapsulates "the space of non-coerced human association and also the set of relational networks formed for the sake of family, faith, interest and ideology."[50] On the other hand are definitions of civil society that equate the concept with a particular cluster of laudable organizations. This is the case of Putnam, for whom civil society is essentially synonymous with a "civic community." The same can be said of Diamond, who insists that civil society is those organizations "whose interests, passions, preferences, and ideas serve to improve the structure and functioning of the state, and to hold State officials accountable."[51] Finally, there are those who see civil society in more neutral terms. Its various components may or not behave in civil ways; also, they may or may not espouse democratic goals, a point that is stressed by other conceptualizations of civil society. Nancy Bermeo's definition of civil society is a case in point. She writes: "The associations of civil society can be good or evil or something else."[52]

Less tension and disagreement exists within the civil society literature regarding what constitutes a vibrant and robust civil society. But what do these terms actually mean? And how can something as expansive, fragmented (and even amorphous) as civil society be effectively calibrated? The dominant model for gauging civil society's strength is provided by Putnam, who takes the density or thickness of the national associational landscape as the principal, empirical indicator of civil society's vibrancy and robustness. Density refers, specifically, to the level of participation by the citizenry in voluntary associations (neighborhood associations, choral societies, cooperatives, sports clubs and the like).[53]

Despite the widespread acceptance of associational density as the main indicator of civil society strength, other scholars have sought to modify this model. This ensues from the recognition that not all the sectors of civil society serve democracy with the same degree of influence and that some may not serve to advance democracy at all. Therefore, many scholars of democratization such as Diamond are more discriminating than Putnam with regard to what organizations within civil society are best suited to facilitate democracy. For Diamond, democratic consolidation appears to demand the construction of a politically minded civil society that possesses the predisposition for democracy generated by the social interactions that civil society affords and also the organizational means to press for democracy. Thus, rather than focusing on the organizations that animate Putnam's analysis (bowling leagues, choral societies, PTA clubs, etc.), Diamond is more inclined to focus on organizations that are likely to assume an advocacy role in the public sphere—women's groups, human rights organizations, civil rights groups and trade unions.

Diamond also emphasizes the institutional features of a strong civil society. He notes that the chances to develop stable democracy improve significantly if civil society does not contain "maximalist, uncompromising interest groups or groups with anti-democratic goals and methods."[54] These groups are likely to incur state repression and radicalize the more democratic elements of society. A second feature is "organizational institutionalization." He writes: "Where interests are organized in a structured, stable manner, bargaining and the growth of cooperative networks are facilitated." A third requirement is the "internally democratic character" of organizations as defined by "decision-making, leadership selection, accountability and transparency." The fourth and fifth requirements are "pluralism without fragmentation" and "density," or participation of citizens in multiple organizations.

To be sure, Diamond's modifications do not stand in opposition to Putnam's model of civil society strength. In fact, to a significant degree, they are quite complementary. The denser the national associational landscape, the stronger the individual components of civil society are likely to be and the more intense collective action on behalf of democracy and other endeavors is likely to be as well. Moreover, the more pluralistic and developed civil society is, the stronger the protection that it can create for itself vis-à-vis the organs of the state.

The Causal Links

Almost invariably, all discussions of the causal association believed to exist between civil society and democracy reflect upon Tocqueville's work. Among the many passages in *Democracy in America* linking a lively civil society to democracy, the following is the most direct and probably the most often quoted. Tocqueville wrote:

> In democratic countries the science of association is the mother of all science … If men are to remain civilized or to become so, the art of associating together must grow and improve among them in the same ratio in which the equality of conditions is increased.[55]

In Tocqueville's view, a strong civil society served to socialize the citizenry in the ways of democracy and to scrutinize state action. Central to Tocqueville's belief in the pro-democratic functions of civil society was the manner in which the social interaction that voluntary associations afforded individual people served to improve their democratic capacities. At the core of such assumptions was the expectation that voluntary associations would reform untrammeled individualism by teaching citizens the virtue of sacrificing one's self-interest for the larger common good. In other words, voluntary associations breed virtuous citizens. Tocqueville argued that "the more individuals get used to the idea of coming together for economic, social, or moral purposes, the more they enhance their capacity to pursue great undertakings in common."[56]

Tocqueville's ideas about the democratic, socializing virtues of civil society have inspired generations of scholars to draw a richer and more complex picture of the causal connections between a flourishing civil society and democracy. Much of the credit in this regard has gone to Putnam, who has become known among academic and nonacademic audiences for attaching democratic virtues to all kinds of voluntary associations including, most famously, bowling leagues. But, as argued by Sheri Berman, Putnam is not alone in having "rediscovered" the great Frenchman, nor even the first scholar to link group bowling and political development.[57] During the 1950s and 1960s, social scientists such as William Kornhauser and Hannah Arendt used Tocqueville's ideas about voluntary associations to help turn the concept of "mass society" into a powerful explanation for the rise of totalitarianism in interwar Europe. These theorists of mass society believed that Europe's slide into barbarism was greased by, among other factors, the collapse of intermediary associations across much of the Continent during this period. Summarizing the ideas of mass society theorists, Berman writes:

> They argued that industrialization and modernization had estranged citizens from one another, leaving them rootless and searching for ways of belonging. Ripped from their traditional moorings, masses were available for mobilization by extremist movements—unless, that is, individuals could develop communal bonds through organizational affiliations and involvement. Civil society, according to these theorists, was an antidote to the political viruses that afflicted mass society. Participation in organizations not only helped bring citizens together, bringing cleavages and fostering skills necessary for democratic governance, but it also satisfied their need to belong to some larger grouping.[58]

The assumptions of mass society theorists were applied most forcefully to the collapse of the Weimar Republic and the advent of Nazism, the twentieth century's most emblematic example of democratic breakdown and totalitarianism. Mass society theorists believed that it was Weimar's "status as a mass society, which made it susceptible to the blandishments of totalitarian demagoguery."[59] In their view, Hitler's supporters were drawn primarily from alienated individuals who lacked a wide range of associational memberships and saw in the NSDAP (the Nazi panty) a way of integrating themselves into a larger community. Implied in this analysis is that had German civil society been stronger, Weimar would not have fallen.

It is to Putnam's work, however, that we must return to unpack contemporary assumptions about the importance of civil society to democracy and its consolidation. In *Making Democracy Work*, Putnam deftly weds the work of sociologist James Coleman on "social capital" with Tocqueville's theorizing about the virtues of voluntary associations. As used by Coleman, the concept of social capital describes the norms and expectations underpinning economic activity that cannot be accounted for from an exclusively economic standpoint.[60] In Putnam's analysis, however, social capital underwrites effective political performance and has correspondingly been overlaid with a broader set of values and properties. More specifically, social capital stands for "features of social organization, such as trust, norms, and networks that can improve the efficiency of society by facilitating coordinated actions."[61] When present in ample supply, we should expect society to exhibit high levels of "cooperation, trust, reciprocity, and collective well-being." In its absence, we should expect "defection, mistrust, shirking, exploitation, disorder and stagnation."

In Putnam's model, "trust" is the key component of social capital for it determines society's capacity to engage in collective action for mutual benefit. According to Putnam, "the theory of social capital presumes that, generally speaking, the more we connect with other people the more we trust them and vice versa."[62] Flowing from this expectation is that the more we trust one another, the higher the probability of the emergence of societal collaboration on behalf of democracy and economic development. Putnam contends that trust lubricates cooperation "such as that required between legislature and executive, between workers and managers, among political parties, between the government and private groups, among small firms and so on."[63] He adds that "the greater the level of trust within a community, the greater the likelihood of cooperation. And cooperation itself breeds trust."[64]

As presented in Putnam's work, trust begins to form at the personal level ("personal trust") and eventually becomes "social trust," (also often referred to as "generalized" trust), which in turn becomes part of the general stock of social capital. Key to formation of trust and its transformation from "personal" to "social" is the face-to-face interaction that voluntary associations afford ordinary citizens. Virtually all forms of citizens' associations contribute to the formation of social capital as long as they are organized in "horizontal bonds of mutual solidarity" rather than "vertical bonds of dependency and exploitation." Horizontally structured groups bring together agents of equivalent status and power, as is generally the case of a recreational group. Vertically structured groups, by contrast, link agents of unequal power into asymmetrical relations of hierarchy and dependency, as is the case of the Catholic Church and the Mafia.

Putnam contends that "membership in horizontally ordered groups like sports clubs, cooperatives, mutual aid societies, cultural associations and voluntary unions should be positively associated with good government" because of the internal and external consequences that flow from them.[65]

He observes that, internally, voluntary associations facilitate democracy by instilling "habits of cooperation, solidarity, and public spiritedness." They do so because voluntary associations, whether their manifest purpose is political or not, tend to engender "a sense of shared responsibility for collective endeavors." Putnam writes: "Taking part in a choral society or a bird-watching club can teach self-discipline and an appreciation for the joys of successful collaboration." Moreover, voluntary associations can facilitate social integration because when individuals belong to "cross-cutting" groups with diverse goals and members, their attitudes will tend to moderate as a result of group interaction and cross-pressures.

Externally, a dense network of secondary associations "contributes to effective social collaboration" of the kind that extends onto the wider polity. Quoting Tocqueville, Putnam writes: "An association unites the energies of divergent minds and vigorously directs them toward a clearly indicated goal." This "intense horizontal interaction" aids democracy by forming the foundation for effective governance and economic development. A dense network of secondary associations not only promotes liberal notions of citizenship, but also allows society to keep their political leaders accountable thereby providing a check on state power. In sum, a dense associational landscape, high levels of social trust and effective democracy are strongly intercorrelated.

To illustrate the relevance of his arguments to democracy and socioeconomic development, Putnam relies upon differences in institutional performance by Italian regional governments since their creation in the early 1970s. The presence of high levels of social capital in Emilia Romagna and other regions of Northern Italy is given as the explanation for the construction of effective governing institutions of regional self-government. By contrast, low levels of social capital in southern regions such as Puglia have allowed for the flourishing of "amoral familism," Edward Banfield's well-known conceptualization of the dearth of social trust among Southern Italians.[66] It accounts, in Putnam's analysis, for the South's inefficient and unresponsive regional governments. Putnam attributes the origins of different endowments of social capital in the North and the South to different historical trajectories. In the North, a high endowment of social capital was made possible by the advent of Republicanism in the twelfth century, a period that coincided with the conquest of the South by the autocratic Norman regime, which turned the region into a feudal yoke.

Putnam's work, as explained later, is fraught with serious analytical problems and, not surprisingly, it has invited multiple criticisms.[67] Nonetheless, it has found considerable resonance in the general thinking about contemporary democratization. The publication of *Making Democracy*

Work coincided with the collapse of Communism, making this work relevant and attractive to many students of the politics of new democracies. Putnam's own work encouraged this by warning post-authoritarian states of the perils ensuing from failing to pay attention to the development of the civil society sector. He writes:

> Where norms and networks of civic engagement are lacking, the outlook for collective action appears bleak. The fate of the Mezzogiorno is an object lesson for the Third World and the former Communist lands of Euroasia tomorrow, moving uncertainty toward self-government. The "always defect" social equilibrium may represent the future of much of the world where social capital is limited or non-existent. For political stability, for government effectiveness, and even for economic progress social capital may be even more important than physical or human capital. Many of the formerly Communist societies had weak civic traditions before the advent of Communism, and totalitarian rule abused even that limited stock of social capital. Without norms of reciprocity and networks of civic engagement, the Hobbesian outcome of the Mezzogiorno— amoral familism, clientelism, lawlessness, ineffective government, and economic stagnation—seems likelier than successful democratization and economic development. Palermo may represent the future of Moscow.[68]

Civil Society and Democratic Consolidation

Discussions of civil society in the context of democratic consolidation mirror a seismic shift in the intellectual agenda of the study of democratization itself. At the present time, scholars appear to be less concerned with such classic questions as what causes the rise of democracy (mass movements or political elites?) and how can transitions to democracy survive its enemies (such as the military), a poorly performing economy and vexing problems such as ethnic conflict. Instead, attention is being devoted to the sturdiness and quality of nascent democratic institutions. At least since the mid-1990s, the question of how to improve the quality of democratic governance in new democracies has dominated discussions about democratization. Such concerns are mirrored in the rise of a vast literature devoted to the subject of "democratic consolidation," generally understood to mark the juncture in which democracy, to use Linz and Stepan's characterization, becomes "the only game in town."[69] This political situation requires the institutionalization of free and competitive elections, and depending on the definition used, a wide range of political tasks including civilian control over the military, mass support for democratic values and respect for the rule of law.[70]

Present-day political realities across the democratizing world explain concerns about the quality of democracy and issues of democratic consolidation. While the vast majority of countries that made the democratic revolution of recent decades a reality appear to have succeeded in accomplishing a formal democratic transition, democratic consolidation remains a work in process, if not an elusive goal. Indeed, surprisingly few new democracies have been declared "consolidated." In Linz and Stepan's comparative study of democratization in the late twentieth century, only the new democracies of Southern Europe (Spain, Portugal and Greece) merit the unqualified consideration of consolidated democracies.[71] By and large, new democracies the world over are limping along chasing after the status of democratic consolidation. This suggests the hard reality that the institutionalization of democratic procedures such as free elections does not guarantee a well-performing democracy. Diamond rightly notes that in many of the world's new democracies, competitive elections have not ensured liberty, adherence to the rule of law and widespread respect for civil and human rights. He writes: "To varying but alarming degrees human rights are flagrantly abused, ethnic and other minorities suffer not only discrimination but murderous violence; power is heavily if not regally concentrated in the executive branch; and parties, legislators, executives and judicial systems are thoroughly corrupt."[72]

In light of the distressing state of democracy in much of the democratizing world it is understandable why Putnam's theorizing about the capacity of civil organizations to improve the performance of democratic institutions has found a very receptive audience among students of democratic consolidation. Little is added to Putnam's virtuous circle about how civil society engenders social capital and how social capital in turn promotes democracy. Instead, its assumptions have been purchased and exported wholesale to a wide range of empirical situations from the post-Communist world to remote villages in Latin America. In the many versions of Putnam's neo-Tocquevillean argument, scholars of democratic consolidation emphasize the socializing role of civil society and its capacity to fortify the social foundations of democracy by enhancing citizenship and stamping out antidemocratic behavior such as corruption and clientelism, among many other tasks.

The broadest acceptance of Putnam's theories of civil society within the context of democratic consolidation can be located in Diamond's work on the "development" of democracy. In his view, a vibrant civil society "is probably more essential for consolidating democracy than for initiating it."[73] This assumption is made largely on the basis of Putnam's theoretical framework and empirical evidence culled from the Italian case, especially the presumed capacity of civil society to socialize the citizenry into the ways of democracy. Diamond observes: "Putnam's evidence suggests that involving citizens actively in the democratic process (in horizontal relations of political equality), both through the electoral process and through civil society is more likely to generate a 'civic culture' of tolerance, trust, reciprocity, and cooperation. This in turn cushions a new democratic system against popular alienation and polarization if government performs well below expectations."[74] Elsewhere, Diamond notes: "Putnam, like Tocqueville, sensitizes us to the importance of the nature and intensity of associational life in general—of social capital—as a crucial cultural foundation of liberal democracy."[75] As for trust, Diamond writes: "If trust is low and expectations of fellow citizens are pervasively cynical, institutions will be mere formalities, lacking compliance and effectiveness, as most people defect from obedience in the expectation that most everyone else would (do the same)."[76]

Diamond is careful to point out that civil society by itself cannot bring about the consolidation of democracy and that we should be realistic about civil society's potential contributions to this process. He writes: "If civil society is to be a theoretically useful construct for studying democratic development, it is important to avoid the tautology that equates it with everything that is democratic, noble, decent and good."[77] But this cautionary warning is basically tossed to the wind when accounting for the many contributions that civil society can be expected to make toward the consolidation of democracy. In keeping with current neo-Tocquevillean fashion, Diamond's analysis regards civil society as the venue for the "socialization" of the citizenry into the ways of democracy, including developing citizenship skills. It also stresses other tasks, however, including serving as a source of "representation" for a wide range of voices within society (especially minority or repressed ones) as well as performing "contestatory" functions by positing civil society as a bulwark against the forces threatening democracy. These additional functions that civil society is meant to serve are tellingly illustrated in the 13 tasks that Diamond suggests allow civil society to promote democratic consolidation.[78]

1 Civil society provides the basis for the limitation of state power, hence for the control of the state by society and hence for democratic political institutions as the most effective means of exercising that control.

2 Civil society supplements the role of political parties in stimulating political participation, increasing the political efficacy and skill of democratic citizens and promoting an appreciation of the obligations as well as the rights of democratic citizenship.

3 Civil society educates for democracy. Participation in community affairs could lead to profound cultural changes, reshaping the way

children are educated and relate to authority, the way they understand their country's political history and their readiness to trust and cooperate with their peers.

4 Civil society serves democracy by structuring multiple channels, beyond the political party, for articulating, aggregating and representing interests. This function is particularly important for providing traditionally excluded groups, such as women and racial or ethnic minorities access to power.

5 Civil society can deepen democracy by affecting a transition from "clientelism to citizenship" at the local level.

6 A rich and pluralistic civil society tends to generate a wide range of interests that crosscut and mitigate the principal polarities of social conflict.

7 A democratic civil society serves to recruit and train new political leaders. Civil society leaders and activists acquire through rising in the internal politics of their organization and through articulating and representing their members in public policy arenas the leadership and advocacy skills that qualify them for service in government and party politics.

8 Civil society has explicit democracy-building purposes such as deterring fraud and enhancing confidence in the electoral process.

9 A vigorous civil society widely disseminates information and so empowers citizens in the collective pursuit and defense of their interests and values.

10 Civil society facilitates democratic consolidation by mobilizing new information and understanding essential to the achievement of economic reform. Such functions in a democratizing society are performed by new actors in civil society such as economic policy think tanks and chambers of commerce.

11 Civil society organizations emanating especially from the religious and human rights communities can develop techniques for conflict mediation and resolution and offering these services.

12 A vigorous civil society can strengthen the social foundation of democracy even when its activities focus on community development and have no explicit connection to or concern with political democracy per se. These activities build social capital by bringing citizens together to cooperate as peers for their common advancement.

13 A vigorous civil society gives citizens respect for the state and positive engagement with it by enhancing accountability, responsiveness, inclusiveness, effectiveness and hence legitimacy of the political system.

Certainly, Diamond's work is not alone in placing considerable faith in civil society as the foundation for democratic consolidation. Francis Fukuyama's massive treatise on social capital (appropriately titled "Trust") and its importance to democracy and prosperity the world over is another notable example.[79] In it he observes: "Today, having abandoned the promise of social engineering, virtually all serious observers understand that liberal political and economic institutions depend on a healthy and dynamic civil society for their vitality."[80] Fukuyama is especially concerned with the state of civil society in many post-authoritarian democracies (especially the post-Communist world) where he finds that levels of social capital are either perilously low or nonexistent altogether. As a result of this situation, successful democratization and economic prosperity remain a great uncertainty, if not exceptionally difficult.

Fukuyama notes that the consequence of socialism in the Soviet Union and Eastern Europe was the destruction of civil society, "a destruction that has hampered the emergence of both working market economies and stable democracies."[81] He notes that by the time of Stalin's consolidation of power in the late 1930s, the Soviet Union exhibited a missing middle: the complete dearth of strong, cohesive or durable intermediate associations. That is, "the Soviet State was very powerful, and there were many atomized individuals and families, but in between there were no social groups whatsoever." In Fukuyama's analysis, these conditions are not unique to the former Soviet Union. He notes that France, Spain, Italy and a number of Latin American societies exhibit "a saddle-shaped distribution of organizations, with strong families, a strong state and relatively little in between."[82] These societies are "utterly different from socialist ones," but like socialist societies, "there has been a relative deficit of intermediate social groups in the area between the family and large, centralized organizations like the Church or the State." The outcome of such a condition is low trust among individuals and potential doom in respect to the formation of social capital.[83]

Echoing the fears of mass theorists of the 1950s and 1960s, Fukuyama notes that in the absence of a strong layer of voluntary associations, individuals cling to their ascriptive identities all the more fiercely and engage in all kinds of nondemocratic behavior including criminal activity. This is the consequence of feeling "atomized, weak and victimized by the larger historical forces swirling around them."[84] By contrast, a strong civil society provides individuals "a source of social identity and belonging." Fukuyama concludes his analysis by laying out the task for the world's societies. He writes: "Now that the question of ideology and institutions has been settled, the preservation and accumulation of social capital will occupy center stage."[85]

Scholarly assumptions about civil society and democratic consolidation provide the scientific rationale for civil society assistance programs. Carothers reports that "boosters of civil society aid often cite Putnam as support for their approach."[86] As a result, "social capital building" has become a key mission of international aid organizations in their efforts to boost the development of civil society overseas. To be sure, many of the civil society organizations being supported by the aid community do not square well with Putnam's world of a strong civil society. Instead of bowling leagues and choral societies, it is civic education clubs, rural cooperatives and other grassroots organizations that tend to get donors' attention. But the expectation of international donors is that the more people come together, the higher the likelihood that these efforts will have the rippling effect of engendering other types of associations thereby assisting in the thickening of civil society. As suggested by Axel Hadenius and Fredrik Uggla, academic advisors to international development organizations, "organizations which are originally established for one specific purpose eventually come to serve other (and perhaps much broader) objectives. Once they are established, then social networks can set a dynamic, self-reinforcing process in motion."[87] Very much influenced by Putnam's theorizing about how civil society promotes a wide range of pro-democratic virtues, Hadenius and Uggla contend:

> An active civil society is a necessary condition for the development of a democratic system of government. Only by joining together in lasting networks of cooperation can citizens gain power and skills necessary for controlling the state that wields control over them. Moreover, only the free practice of democracy found in the civil sphere can promote the development of the democratic popular culture that makes "rule by the people" a feasible option.[88]

Civil Society and Its Critics

The most apparent flaw with the widely spread and celebrated association between a strong civil society and a successful democracy is that it lacks a firm empirical foundation. As shown in the appendix, the cross-national data is quite clear in supporting this association: the countries with the oldest records as stable democracies are those with the highest indexes of civil society density. By contrast, the countries with the lowest indexes of civil society density have enjoyed the shortest existence as democratic societies. Correlation, however, does not imply causality, a point compellingly illustrated by our forthcoming analysis of the Spanish and Brazilian political experiences since the mid-1970s. In both cases, the development of civil society prior and after the advent of democracy is a very poor indicator for explaining the fate of democratic consolidation in each case. These cases are not alone in suggesting this. The cross-national data contained in the appendix suggests that among newly democratic nations, there does not appear to exist much of a close connection between the density of associations and the quality of democracy. Nations in possession of some of the weakest civil societies have produced some of the most stunning democratic successes while nations with some of the most vibrant civil societies appear to be having quite a difficult time in developing stable democratic institutions.

The uncomfortable fit between the size and scope of civil society and the quality of democracy grants current criticisms of neo-Tocquevilleanism considerable credence as well as inviting new ones. At the heart of many scholarly critiques of civil society is the concept of social capital, believed by civil society advocates to be civil society's key currency in facilitating a democratic public life. Indeed, social capital is the lightning rod of most critiques of civil society and its presumed virtues. First among them are complaints about the usage of the term as a heuristic device to understand political phenomena, democracy in particular. Bob Edwards and Michael W. Foley note that Putnam has bastardized the concept of social capital by stripping it of its neutrality (a characteristic of Coleman's original conceptualization) and by adding moral and ethical value to it.[89] In doing so, these critics contend, Putnam has unduly narrowed the concept's analytical usage. In their view, Putnam's understanding of social capital is limited "to the good-stuff."[90]

Edwards and Foley also fault Putnam for casting too broad a net of civil society organizations believed to be conducive to the formation of social capital. They note that all voluntary associations are not all alike with respect to both the amount and the sort of social capital produced and that some kinds of associations are more productive than others.[91] Additionally, Edwards and Foley fault Putnam for aggregating measures that taken as a whole lose considerable explanatory leverage. They note: "To assume that we can simply aggregate social capital to produce some measure of the resources available to society or the polity is to make the same mistake that economists make in using gross national product (GNP) per capita as a valid indicator of national economic development."[92] As it stands, Edwards and Foley conclude, Putnam's conceptualization of social capital and its importance to democracy "becomes little more than a 1990s version of the attitudes, norms and values at the center of the empirical democratic theory of the 1950s."[93]

Other scholars have taken Putnam to task for the analytical ambiguity that permeates his attempt to sort out those organizations that can be expected to contribute to the building of social capital (horizontally organized groups) and those that do not (vertically organized ones). Berman notes that it is not at all clear how in practice one determines whether an organization is a vertically or horizontally organized group.[94] She makes the point that the Boy Scouts are a hierarchically organized group that promotes the very kind of values that neo-Tocquevilleans praise and that almost everyone agrees belong squarely in the civil society camp. On the other hand, Berman notes that militias and other nationalist organizations do not appear to be more vertically or hierarchically organized than other types of civil society associations. Moreover, these groups foster precisely the sense of solidarity, trust and willingness to engage in the collective endeavors that neo-Tocquevilleans celebrate. "The problem is that the skills and relationships fostered by such organizations are used in the service of goals of which most of us would not approve."[95] Additionally, Berman contends that Putnam neglects to take into consideration that the sociability of the "capital" generated by civil society organizations is not set in concrete since even the most harmless of civil society organizations can be turned to antidemocratic purposes. In support of this point she cites the Nazi infiltration of German choral societies and bird-watching clubs.

Other critiques of social capital challenge the assumption that civil society organizations have the internal capacity to produce and sustain the social trust and networks of reciprocity, cooperation and solidarity (e.g. social capital) thought to assist citizens to overcome parochial interests and conceptualize the common good. For many scholars, the endeavors of civil society are quite mundane and narrow-minded and thus of little consequence to democracy. As argued by Berman, increased league bowling and bird-watching may enhance social life but that does not translate into an effective democracy. She makes this point in light of the experience of the Weimar Republic, one of the densest civil societies in Europe during the interwar years.[96] During this period Germans threw themselves into their clubs, voluntary associations and professional associations but this vibrancy and robustness in the constitution of civil society did not prevent Europe's most emblematic case of democratic breakdown.

More problematic for social capital theories is the hard reality that the endeavors of many civil society organizations, even highly civic-minded ones, often promote values and activities that are antithetical to those associated with social capital and democracy. Throughout history, many civic organizations in the United States and elsewhere have served to produce what has been termed "unsocial social capital" by systematically excluding women and racial and ethnic minorities and actively promoting racism and other social pathologies.[97] This point has been conveniently glossed over in Putnam's reconstruction of civic life in America during the 1950s and 1960s. As noted by Jean Cohen, it is bizarre to present the adult generation of the 1950s as a paragon of civicness or the 1950s and early 1960s as an era of the generalized trust that makes democracy work since this period was the heyday of McCarthyism, institutionalized racial segregation, exclusion of women from a wide range of economic and political institutions and associations.[98] She adds that "civil privatism, authoritarian cultural and social conservatism would seem a more apt characterization of that period than civic virtue."

Laurence Whitehead, whose critique of civil society is situated within the context of the public life of new democracies, echoes Cohen's concerns.[99] He contends that often overlooked by social capital enthusiasts is the fact that emerging civil societies in newly democratic settings are by definition "incipient and untested." As such, we should not expect many of the civil society organizations that dominate the public sphere in neo-democracies to behave in ways that will favor democracy (such as the creation of democratic institutions) because they were not socialized or schooled in the norms of civility. Whitehead writes that "in many neo-democracies some of the most vibrant organizations lack a tradition of commitment to the norm of civility and/or permit very little deliberation over their internal affairs. There is, therefore, in general, no particular reason to expect an elective affinity between a vigorous civil society and electorally successful political parties." He adds that in some cases a broadly based civil society is followed by the establishment of democratic political parties; but equally plausible is the emergence of an antagonism between the architects of civil society and successful party leaders and a compartmentalization of both spheres.[100]

Another critique of particular relevance to our study is whether civil society enthusiasts have identified the correct setting for the production of social capital. Theda Skocpol has noted that even in nations such as the United States, where levels of civic engagement are exceptionally high, relatively few sectors of civil society generate the kind of intense face-to-face interaction that Putnam and others see as contributing to the building of social capital.[101] Specifically, she questions how civil society organizations can be credited with promoting a generalized social trust as well as networks of solidarity, cooperation and collaboration when many of them rarely bring citizens together in an intimate fashion. She cites the case of advocacy organizations and citizen groups, such as the American Association of Retired Persons (AARP), the fastest growing type of voluntary association in postwar America. Participation by the citizenry in these so-called checkbook organizations is often limited to holding a membership card and/or paying an annual membership fee. Thus, while these organizations may contribute to pluralist democracy "they have little, if any, impact on social capital."[102]

A related and final point is raised by Kenneth Newton, who wonders whether ordinary people spend sufficient time engaged in the endeavors of voluntary associations to produce the virtues of social capital and/or to be influenced by them. He writes: "It seems implausible to ascribe voluntary organizations a crucial role in effecting behavior when they account for only a few hours a week of life, and even then for only a small minority of activists."[103] This leads him to ask whether other spheres of social organization are more influential in shaping the character and behavior of individuals than voluntary groups. He writes that participation in school, family, work and community are likely to have far stronger internal effects on the behavior of individuals than voluntary associations.[104]

Rethinking the Formation of Social Capital

Other problems for social capital theories arise when the concept is transported to the study of contemporary democratization politics, where references to social capital have become quite common but where challenges to it are relatively few and isolated. For a start, a very convincing argument can be made against trust, the chief empirical indicator of social capital, as the foundation of democracy or democratization. Mistrust, confrontation and even violence by a wide range of social movements rest at the heart of the making of democracy in the United States and many other countries. This point is powerfully echoed in Ruth Collier's recent work on the role of working-class mobilization in forcing democratic openings in Western Europe and South America.[105] Yet, even the most skeptical of observers looking at we have come to know as social capital would have to agree that its various components are important ingredients to the crafting of democratic regimes. In fact, though not explicitly stated, the importance of social capital is a central theoretical message of some of the most influential scholarly works on democratic transitions to have appeared in recent years. They sustain the core argument that it is the capacity of political actors to compromise with one another and engage society into cooperating with them that matters most to the advancement of democratic consolidation.[106] Democratization is therefore viewed as a political game whose outcomes are largely determined by the choices and decisions made by individual political actors entrusted with the historical task of building a democratic regime. "Democracy has to be chosen by real live political actors who have plenty of room for making the wrong and right decisions," writes Philippe Schmitter, one of the pioneers of what some have called "transitology."[107]

Thus, the central questions about social capital with respect to democracy in post-authoritarian societies confronting scholars today are: how does it develop and what can be done to promote it? In the present study, I question the widespread assumption that social capital is the product of the face-to-face interaction that civil society provides ordinary citizens. Instead, I contend that it is most likely to be the product of the constitution and performance of political institutions. A number of factors lead me to this theoretical proposition, all of them related to the uncritical manner in which neo-Tocquevillean theories of civil society have been embraced in the study of contemporary democratization. My sense is that scholars that stress the importance of civil society in the consolidation of democracy have neglected to determine the multiple ways in which political institutions affect the values and behavior of society as a whole including those thought to make up the culture of social capital. They have also purchased wholesale the many assumptions being made about civil society without considering how they relate precisely to the specific benchmarks of the democratization process.

Even if we buy into the notion that civil society is responsible for the production of social capital, it remains unclear how this property manages to impact the particular dynamics of the process of democratic consolidation. For starters, no empirical thresholds, benchmarks or timeframe are suggested for indicating at what point sufficient social capital has been stored away to reach democratic transition or consolidation. Thus, the work of scholars such as Diamond, which makes ample use of Putnam's theories to make its case about the importance of a robust civil society to democratic consolidation, leave us clueless to wonder how much social capital needs to be produced to achieve a consolidated democracy.[108] Neo-Tocquevillean theories of civil society as employed in the democratic consolidation literature also buy us very little explanatory power in helping us understand the behavior of the societal actors that figure most prominently in the consolidation of a new democratic regime.

For instance, how does the availability or lack of social trust impact the actions of the departing authoritarian elite and its democratic opposition? Presumably, the busier the citizenry is (or has been prior to the democratic transition) in forming associational links the more likely that society will succeed in collaborating toward the common goal of achieving a consolidated democracy. But this presumes the ability of ordinary citizens to work together in a myriad of grassroots-level settings found throughout civil society, itself a very varied and fragmented organizational landscape. It also presumes that societal collaboration at the grassroots level can somehow undergo a metamorphosis into networks of solidarity and collaboration at the elite, political level, where the compromises of democratic consolidation are forged, be it a political pact or a new constitution. These social contracts are only possible if political institutions have the capacity to organize and represent society across class and other social cleavages. Civil organizations, however vibrant and robust, are simply unfit to fulfill this function. While very good at mobilizing the public for a wide range of causes, their capacities to aggregate and represent interests at a large scale, access the state and impact the policy process is rather limited and not always in the interest of democracy. Civil society engagement in politics is often ephemeral and, more importantly, it offers few if any means of accountability to the citizenry.

Surprisingly, the argument that political institutions matter to the production of social capital has received scant empirical attention in the civil society literature. Newton concludes his analysis of social capital theory by noting that "an empirical task for social capital research is to explore the connections, if any, between government policies and structures and social capital."[109] Consequently, the role of political institutions with respect to the production of social capital remains largely undertheorized and empirically under-determined. This is especially the case in the context of post-transition democracies, where the production of social capital (and expert knowledge about it) appears to be most urgently needed.

In the forthcoming analysis of democratization politics in Spain and Brazil, I seek to demonstrate how the performance of political institutions plays a decisive role in fashioning the conditions that are favorable and unfavorable to the creation of social capital. More specifically, I examine the impact of the behavior, design and legacies of the political system on the development of what is conventionally understood to represent social capital, especially social trust. This exercise in comparative political analysis is inspired largely by much of the theorizing surrounding what has been termed "historical institutionalism." It contends, in a nutshell, that institutions and their legacies matter to politics by structuring preferences, interests and values in society.[110] In sum, I aim to show how political institutions determine the creation of social capital.

In particular, my analysis looks at the configuration and performance of political institutions and their connection to the production of social capital along three distinct but related dimensions. The first is government action and public policy regarding the democratization process itself, with emphasis on the commitment of the government and its institutions to democratic practices and principles. This is best suggested by the willingness of democratically elected leaders to confront antidemocratic forces such as the military; their disposition to work and collaborate with the democratic opposition in dismantling the old authoritarian order; their support for representative institutions and other features of the democratic system; and their skill at handling the problems that converge around a transition to democracy. My sense is that the particular outcomes of these actions and policies have a significant impact in affecting the development of social capital, especially the readiness of citizens to cooperate amongst themselves and engage in collaborative efforts with the political system on behalf of the various endeavors of democratic consolidation.

A second focus is the configuration of the state as determined by its credibility, competence and overall legitimacy as suggested by the legacies of state institutions in meeting societal needs and demands. We should expect the state's historical record on a wide range of issues (from the economy, to labor and industrial relations, to human rights) to have a significant impact on the capacity of citizens to trust each other and the government throughout the process of democratic consolidation. Of special interest to our study is the general well-being of the nation as suggested most clearly by levels of socioeconomic development. This concern echoes recent research that links material wealth to levels of interpersonal trust in society.[111] A hypothesis that ensues from this contention is that the more positive the social and economic legacy of the retreating authoritarian regime the higher the likelihood that trust and reciprocity will permeate the consolidation of democratic institutions. Conversely, the more onerous the legacy of the authoritarian regime the more likely the prospect that confrontation and negative social capital values such as cynicism and mistrust will dominate the behavior of civil society and its interaction with the government.

A third and final analytical concern is the capacity of the party system to integrate and represent society, as conditioned largely by the individual parties' links to groups within civil society. I contend that political parties (especially those fully anchored in society) are especially relevant to the production of social capital. One the one hand, because of their capacity to integrate and mobilize the general public, parties play a central role in molding the proclivities of the citizenry and the actual behavior of civil society. On the other hand, as formal members of the political system, parties can provide citizens and social groups with access to the policy arena thereby giving voice and leverage to civil society vis-à-vis the state. These functions are especially important after the transition to democracy has been secured.

At that point, strategies of confrontation and mobilization (which are often required to dislodge the authoritarian regime) are replaced in importance by strategies of cooperation and moderation. The latter are needed to reach consensus on the rules of political behavior and to forge the political settlements that facilitate the stability and endurance of democracy. These tasks can only be successfully accomplished in situations in which the party system has significant capacities for social integration and political representation.

PART II

Spain: Weak Civil Society, Strong Democracy

CHAPTER 3

Spanish Civil Society in Transition Politics

A t the very heart of Spain's democratization is the apparent puzzle of how this country, a paradigm of democratic consolidation among so-called Third Wave democracies, managed to accomplish this seemingly elusive feat in the absence of the civic traditions usually attached to strong civil societies. More impressive still is that since the demise of the Franco regime in 1977, Spain has consolidated democratic institutions and practices at a faster and more meaningful pace than almost any other society that in recent decades has abandoned authoritarian rule and embraced democratic governance. This long and varied roster of cases includes nations (such as Brazil) widely noted for the expansive and highly mobilized nature of their civil societies. Yet, at least within the context of the Iberian-Latin world, few nations have undertaken to consolidate democratic rule with a civil society deficit as egregious as that found in Spain. As illustrated in this chapter, neither from an historical standpoint, nor especially from a contemporary one, does Spain resemble in any significant way the models of civil society strength developed by civil society theorists.

The Civil Society Landscape

By all the conventional measures used by scholars to gauge levels of civil society development, we must conclude that Spain embraced democratization with an impoverished civil society. This state of affairs of Spanish civil society is hardly novel for it mirrors the historical underdevelopment, fragmentation and even retardation of the social organizations and movements usually grouped under the rubric of civil society. It is not surprising that the weakness of civil society has long been a central preoccupation for students of Spanish political development.

The sociologist José Amodia writes that "throughout their modern history, going back to the early days of liberalism in the nineteenth century, Spaniards have shown a great weakness when it comes to organizing themselves into units or groups that will together form a stable social pattern capable of withstanding the tensions and struggles normally generated within the boundaries of any nation."[1] Amodia's words are echoed in Linz's historical review of interest group politics in twentieth-century Spain. Linz concluded that in Spain, "partisan cleavages are more important than interest conflicts. The articulation of interest groups on a permanent and continuous basis is therefore delayed and in part unsuccessful."[2] He adds that this does not mean that interest, economic and social groups do not exercise a decisive influence on the policy-making process but that "their institutionalization and legitimization is less successful than in other countries."

The conditions highlighted by Amodia and Linz are faithfully reflected in the configuration of civil society that consolidated in Spain as the country exited nearly 40 years of fully institutionalized authoritarian rule and advanced through the processes of political liberalization, democratic transition and consolidation. The official awakening of Spanish civil society took place with the passage of the 1976 Law of Political Reform, the first real step toward the dismantling of Franco's dictatorship. It guaranteed the right of free association, denied by the Franco regime since its inception at the end of the Spanish Civil War in 1939. However, while Spaniards certainly welcomed these signs of democratization with considerable gusto, during the democratic period begun with the elections of 1977 they have persistently shown very little enthusiasm for building the kind of civil society that most scholars would describe as vibrant and robust. This is most telling suggested by the very low levels of civic engagement in the post-Franco era.

Associational Density

According to the *World Values Survey*, Spain is one of the least-prone nations to generate the kind of associational life attached to vibrant and robust civil societies (for a broader view of this survey see the appendix). The study finds that among the 43 nations included in the survey, only Argentina had a lower rate of participation by the citizenry in 16 different types of voluntary associations generally thought to represent civil society than Spain. The national organizational membership cumulative percentage given for Spain is 15, just behind Argentina's 3 percent. More revealing is how abysmally low the level of participation by the citizenry in voluntary associations is in Spain when compared to the leaders in this category. The Netherlands, Norway and the United States register organizational membership cumulative percentages above 180.

A richer and more recent portrait of Spanish civil society is provided by the study on the cultural dynamics of democratization in Spain by Peter McDonough, Samuel Barnes and Antonio López Pina.[3] At the heart of their research agenda is explaining "the puzzle of participation in Spain," and more specifically, the low levels of participation of Spaniards in voluntary associations, civic and otherwise. The opening paragraph of the study captures the bewildering nature of what is described as the "striking deficit in civic engagement across the Spanish public."[4] The authors observe that while democratic procedures have been solidly institutionalized in Spain, civic engagement has stagnated. "Only about one-third of Spanish adults belong to any voluntary association, and more than two decades after the passing of Franco the fraction of the public identifying with a political party of any stripe stand at about the same level as in Eastern Europe after the fall of Communism. Civic anemia appears to be endemic in Spain."[5] The authors add that civil engagement—defined as closeness to neighbors, membership in voluntary associations and conventional political participation—has held steady at a low level in Spain from the onset through the consolidation of democracy.

To illustrate how exceptionally low Spain's patterns of associational life actually are, McDonough et al. incorporate into their analysis data from other newly democratic nations, namely Brazil and Korea. In contrast to the finding that in Spain only about a third of the public belongs to any voluntary association, it is reported that in Brazil only about one-third of the citizenry fails to belong to voluntary associations.[6] The comparison with Korea is even harder on Spain. Nearly nine out of ten Koreans claim to be members of some sort of voluntary organization.

Levels of participation in particular civil society groupings provide a clearer picture of the dearth of civic engagement in democratic Spain.[7] (Comparative data for Brazil and Korea is provided in chapter 5 and in the appendix.) Only 1 percent of Spanish females and 2 percent of Spanish males belong to a student association. Only 1 percent of females belong to a political party while 4 percent of males do. Only 3 percent of females claim membership in religious groups while only 2 percent of males do. As for professional groups, the rates are 3 percent for women and 6 percent for men. For trade unions, the rates are 2 percent for women and 8 percent for men. For neighborhood groups, the rates are 7 percent for men and

10 percent for females. The highest percentages are reported for athletic clubs, with 5 percent for females and 13 for men.

Advocacy and Grassroots Groups

Perhaps a reflection of the traditionally low disposition of Spaniards toward joining and/or participating in voluntary associations of any type, the landscape of social movements in post-authoritarian Spain provides further evidence of the weakness of the country's civil society before and after the democratic transition. Victor Pérez-Díaz, Spain's foremost observer of civil society during the democratic transition, offers one of the most accurate descriptions of the state of social movements and advocacy groups in Spain as the country undertook to democratize. He observes that "the fact that in Spain all types of associative links have been historically tenuous meant that at the very moment of the transition, the experience of the population with voluntary association was scanty. This was true not only for those connected with industrialists and workers, but also for those representing the interests of farm-workers, consumers, professionals, cadres, students, etc."[8]

The conditions highlighted by Pérez-Díaz ensured that in Spain, in contrast to other experiences of democratization with which Spain is often compared (Chile, Uruguay, Argentina and Brazil), the return of democracy was not accompanied by burgeoning social movement politics. To be sure, the country did witness the rebirth of organized labor as a major political force as well as an agitated urban grassroots movement, especially in Madrid. And as a result of these developments, the years that preceded Franco's death saw significant mobilization of the masses, mostly in the form of spontaneous strikes and demonstrations. But as we shall see next, the mobilization of the masses in Spain during the transition to democracy was an ephemeral affair limited largely to the period of political liberalization. Furthermore, grassroots groups and the labor movement suffered from a host of organizational and institutional problems, including low levels of membership, and both went into precipitous decline as the consolidation of the new democracy got underway.

Neighborhood and housewife associations represent the most notable form of grassroots activism in Spain during the transition to democracy. This movement made its appearance in Spain in the early 1970s, encouraged by the sense that the end of the authoritarian regime was imminent.[9] Mostly an urban phenomenon, the vast majority of these organizations flourished in the working-class sections of Madrid. It is reported that in one Madrid shantytown the neighborhood association grew from only 6 residents in 1970 to over 1,400 families in 1977.[10] By that same year, it is estimated that the number of neighborhood associations in Madrid had reached 110 with a membership base of approximately 60,000. Their agenda was twofold: to improve the quality of life in working-class enclaves (especially housing) and to promote the country's return to democracy.

Despite an auspicious beginning, the neighborhood movement in Spain did not live to see the success of the democratic transition since it died a very early death. Right before the 1977 elections, neighborhood associations went into rapid decline and a period of acute crisis. Among the reasons cited for the movement's collapse was the inability to expand its membership base as well as the incapacity to develop the means to mobilize the masses on a large scale. It is reported that after the elections of 1977, the neighborhood movement "abandoned its former tactic of confronting the authorities directly through street protests and demands."[11]

The Labor Movement

At the inception of democracy, the art of association initially flourished among Spanish workers, making the labor movement the largest, strongest and best-organized component of civil society as the nation underwent democratization.[12] In 1977, more than 400 national and about 2,400 regional unions registered during the euphoria that surrounded the legalization of trade unions.[13] But despite this obvious sign of associational vitality, the configuration of the post-transition labor movement in Spain does not fit conventional definitions of strength in any meaningful way, especially in the organizational sense.[14]

Due to the longevity and essentially repressive nature of the Franco dictatorship, the once vigorous trade unions of the pre-Franco years, the Socialist *Unión General de Trabajadores*, UGT (General Workers' Union) and the anarchist *Confederación Nacional del Trabajo*, CNT (National Confederation of Workers), "had declined to the point of relative insignificance."[15] Of the UGT it is reported that at the inception of democracy this organization stood for little more than "some historical initials" with a few thousand members concentrated in the Basque country and Asturias.[16] In significantly better shape was *Comisiones Obreras*, CCOO (Workers' Commissions), a trade union illegally formed in the early 1960s. It was controlled by the Spanish Communist party, which successfully turned the union into civil society's main opposition to the Franco regime and its principal tool for fighting the authoritarian state from within its very structures.

During the decades leading to the democratic transition, the CCOO began to penetrate Franco's vertical syndicate (created in 1939 to tame the radical unions of the Second Republic) from which the organization launched a massive mobilization of the working class. Beginning with the Barcelona transport strike of 1951 and lasting through the early 1970s, rising workers' militancy began to make its presence felt in Franco's Spain. This development served to make the years of democratic transition (1975–1978) the most intense period of workers' mobilization in Spain since the end of the Civil War in 1939. Working hours lost through strikes in Spain rose from 1.5 million in 1966, to 8.7 million in 1970, to 14.5 million by 1975.[17]

As the number of strikes rose, so did the political character of the workers' struggles. It is estimated that between 1963 and 1967, political demands represented about 4 percent of all strikes, whereas between 1967 and 1974, the proportion of such demands rose to 45.4 percent.[18] This vigorous mobilization of the workers became civil society's principal tool to delegitimize authoritarianism and to accelerate the demise of the Franco regime. Indeed, more than any other action of civil society, strikes helped convinced the Francoist leadership of the unfeasibility of "Francoism without Franco." José M. Maravall's authoritative study of activism by workers and students in the late Franco period states that the popular pressure from below exerted by the workers' movement was "a causal factor in the Francoist crisis."[19]

Despite its impressive mobilizing capacity around the time of Franco's death, in the new democracy the CCOO operated more as a movement than a formal union. Coming out of the democratic transition, the CCOO experienced a wrenching period of reorganization in which many of its early leadership abandoned the organization once the decision was made to become a conventional union. Many of them would further fragment the labor movement by creating new unions thus making collective action among the various unions more difficult to attain. During the consolidation of democracy, the CCOO, as well as the rest of the unions, also suffered from an acute shortage of workplace leaders. This situation hindered their ability to gain a foothold in many factories, to recruit new members and to elect their own candidates to the works' committees, the system of factory councils created by the Franco regime in the early 1960s to replace union representation in collective bargaining. As late as 1980, it is estimated that the percentage of Spanish workers in firms that had the option of voting for union representation in collective bargaining was between 52 and 57 percent.[20] In the remainder of firms, with more than 40 percent of the eligible labor force, there was no leadership and no union presence.

The labor movement in Spain also entered the democratic period financially strapped and direct financing from the government kept many unions from folding while simultaneously compromising their independence from the state. Official financing of the unions by the state began in 1982, with the infusion of 800 million pesetas (US$5 million), a practice that would become a fixture in the national budget.[21] Labor's financial troubles were exacerbated by internal competition since the unions have kept affiliation dues artificially low as a way to attract new members. For example, in 1986, nearly ten years after the democratic transition, the required monthly contribution by UGT members was eight-tenths of 1 percent of the minimum monthly wage, a very low subscription by European standards.[22] This problem is compounded by the high incidence of non-payment among union members. It is reported that in 1983 only 58 percent of the membership of the UGT was paying dues and 34 percent for CCOO.[23]

A final contributing factor to the poor institutional condition exhibited by Spanish labor during the process of democratization was a very low-affiliation base, a compelling reflection of the aversion of Spaniards to participation in voluntary associations. Spanish workers fled the unions created in 1977 almost as fast as they joined them. The CCOO's membership fell from 1.6 million in 1978 to 500,000 by 1985, while the UGT's membership dropped from 1 million in 1978 to 663,000 by 1985.[24] This decline in union affiliation rates is faithfully mirrored in the dramatic drop in the percentage of Spaniards choosing to belong to a union. Rather ironically, as democracy began to consolidate in Spain and workers could chose to belong to any of multiple trade unions, membership in Spanish unions virtually evaporated.

Having reached over 30 percent during the euphoric years of political liberalization, when millions of workers rushed to join all kinds of workers' associations, the national rate of union affiliation descended to 6 percent by the early 1980s.[25] This rate is one of the lowest in the industrialized West and among recently democratized nations. To find comparable levels of union affiliation to those found in Spain, one has to look at the post-Communist world. As suggested by Philippe Schmitter, only post-Communist countries, "where the association of previous unions with the Communist Party had severely discredited this form of collective action," have lower union affiliation rates than Spain.[26]

Uncivil Movements

Further complicating the picture for civil society as democracy began to consolidate in Spain was the country's historical propensity toward political conflict, extremism and violence, especially in times of political liberalization. Not surprisingly, perhaps, some of the most vociferous and politically charged groups that left their mark on the politics of democratic transition in Spain belong squarely to a category of social movements described by

Diamond as "maximalist and uncompromising groups with anti-democratic goals and methods."[27] The presence of such groups in any polity, as Diamond reminds us, is not a sign of a healthy civil society, despite their popular appeal. Social movements that espouse violence and an anti-system agenda can hinder and even cripple democratic consolidation. In an attempt to contain their influence, government can resort to repressing civil society, thereby compromising civil and political freedoms.

The prevalence of violence and extremism in Spanish politics is deep-rooted and is most memorably remembered during the life of the brief and tumultuous Second Republic (1931–1939). It is worth recalling that associational life during the 1930s in Spain, while quite vibrant in many regards (at least when contrasted to that of the post-Francoist period) was dominated by organizations whose commitment to democracy was at best suspect and whose political agenda did not extend beyond narrowly conceived interests.[28] A leading force behind the creation of mass organizations during the years of Republican government was the Catholic Church in its attempt to battle the anticlerical policies of the Second Republic.[29] Especially influential was the *Confederación Nacional Católica Agraria* (CNCA), which organized thousands of farm laborers in north-central Spain, and which was a supporter of the *Confederación Española de Derechas Autónomas* (CEDA), the most important Catholic, right-wing party of the 1930s.

During the Second Republic, Spain also developed a highly radicalized labor movement. Just prior to the creation of the Republic, Spain became "the only land to produce a mass worker movement of anarcho-syndicalism."[30] Bypassing more "conventional" unions such as the Socialist-affiliated UGT (which itself became increasingly radicalized as a result of the workers' preference for revolutionary activity) thousands of workers in pre-Franco Spain flocked to join the CNT, the principal institutional embodiment of anarcho-syndicalism in interwar Europe. Founded in 1911, and outlawed until 1914, the CNT grew rapidly into an organization of more than 15,000 members by 1914 to just under 1 million by the time the Second Republic was inaugurated in 1931.[31] The tactics of labor terrorism that characterized the strategies of the CNT "left many employers in a state of panic and shock and traditional structures of industrial control and authority were considered under mortal threat."[32] Consequently, during the turbulent years leading to the Civil War, relations between employers and unions descended into a full-fledged violent struggle, as radicalized unions terrorized employers by enacting a massive wave of seizure of business property. Business groups, with the assistance of the repressive branches of the state, and the approving eye of the Catholic Church, declared war on the unions and their leaders.

In the democratic period begun in 1977, Spain's complex legacy of political violence threatened to derail another project of democratization. Among the maximalist and uncompromising groups that surged during Spain's democratic transition, few proved to be as difficult to accommodate into the framework of the new democracy and/or as threatening to its consolidation than those espousing a radical, nationalist and separatist agenda. The political transition in Spain created an exceptional political opening for the rise of a variety of subnationalist movements eager to assert their demands for political independence. These movements had been harshly repressed by the old authoritarian regime, which was fully committed to the idea of a culturally monolithic Spain. Prominent among them was *Euskadita Askatasuna*, ETA (Basque Homeland and Freedom), the armed branch of the Basque separatist movement, which in the aftermath of the demise of the Franco regime sought nothing short of the establishment of an independent Basque homeland.

At least until the late 1960s, ETA violence was restricted to acts of vandalism such as blowing up monuments and setting up bombs in front of Civil Guard stations. With the assassination of Prime Minister Luis Carrero Blanco on December 20, 1973, and Franco's death in 1975, however, the organization's terrorist tactics would be dramatically transformed. Throughout the years of political liberalization and then of democratic transition and consolidation, ETA imposed a veritable regime of terror and violence upon the Spanish people. Between 1973 and 1982, the critical years of democratization, ETA is responsible for 371 deaths, 542 injured, 50 kidnappings and hundreds of bomb explosions and other acts of violence and terror.[33]

Counterviolence from extreme Right groups (such as the *Grupo Revolucionario Antifacista Primero de Octubre*, GRAPO), which got started with the official end of the Franco regime in 1977, served to worsen the situation. Right-wing groups are responsible for 39 deaths in 1979 and 30 in 1980, as well as a long list of assaults, kidnappings and disturbances in major Spanish cities.[34] Perhaps the most symbolic period of violence during the transition was the so-called *Semana Negra* (black week) of January 23–28, 1977. In a series of violent events that vividly brought back the ghosts of the Civil War, two students, five lawyers from the Communist party and five policemen were assassinated in Madrid.

The mayhem generated by ETA and the far Right put the new democracy in great peril since it directly threatened the nation's geographic constitution and the capacity of the newly created democratic government to maintain the social order and guarantee civil liberties and other constitutional protections.

Unsurprisingly, the perceptions that the nation was coming apart at the seams, that new democratic government could not guarantee the social peace and that, as Franco had argued decades ago, Spain could not handle itself in a civilized manner under a democratic system, triggered the failed military coup of February of 1981. It aimed at derailing the project of democratization by shutting down democratically elected institutions. The hijacking of the Spanish Parliament by the coup-makers for a few tense hours dramatically underscored this point. But, paradoxically, the failed coup was the critical test for the new democracy.[35] The refusal of the political class to cave in to the military's demands and the unambiguous support for democracy shown by the public in massive street demonstrations signaled that by 1982 democracy was already on firm footing in Spain.

Explaining Spain's Civil Society Deficit

There is no shortage of explanations to account for the problematic nature of Spanish civil society. Indeed, any scholar looking into this issue is confronted with an embarrassment of explanatory riches. This is perhaps not that surprising since the study of Spanish civil society, whether implicitly or explicitly, goes to the very heart of scholarly efforts to understand some of Spain's most intractable and emblematic problems including the country's traditional socioeconomic backwardness and the propensity toward authoritarian rule, political violence and ideological extremism. The prominent role that civil society is thought to have played in Spanish political development is also mirrored in the diversity of approaches and views that scholars have brought to the task of unpacking Spain's arrested civil society development; they range from cultural explanations built around perceptions about the national character of the Spanish people, to the many ethno-linguistic cleavages that fragment the nation, to the very nature of the dynamics of the transition to democracy.

Cultural and Sociological Explanations

Perhaps the best-known factor afflicting the development of civil society in Spain (especially low participation by the citizenry in voluntary associations) is offered by political anthropologists, and makes reference to the proverbial individualism of the Spanish people.[36] Similar conditions have also been found in other Catholic-Latin societies, especially southern Italy. For the proponents of this view, pervasive individualism is rooted in lack of trust within society, ensuing from the failure of individuals to develop social ties and moral obligations to join groups outside of the nuclear family.[37]

In discussing these issues with reference to Spain, Francis Fukuyama has noted that "excessive individualism, a narrow radius of trust and the centrality of the family have long been characteristic of Spain."[38]

Another intriguing set of explanations come from sociologists, some of whom regard the apparent aversion of Spaniards toward joining formal organizations as a reflection of unique patterns of socialization found in Spanish culture. A number of studies suggest, for instance, that Spaniards have substituted membership in organized associations for informal means of socializing found outside the home.[39] This observation is supported by evidence that indicates that "Spaniards spend more time than other Europeans 'schmoozing'—taking to friends in bars, casual (not to say anarchic) socializing, 'Mediterranean' lounging, and so on."[40]

The study of political participation in Spain by McDonough, Barnes and López Pina offers more persuasive explanations for the low level of associationalism found in Spanish civil society. Their analysis emphasizes structural factors including, first, the high rates of unemployment that afflicted Spain throughout the process of democratization and which gave the nation the most extreme condition of high unemployment among OECD countries by the mid-1980s. Spanish unemployment soared from 415,000 in 1977 to nearly 2 million by 1985, and among the contributing causes for this crisis was a program of industrial restructuring that gutted many of the state enterprises that Franco had created with the purpose of achieving full employment.[41] High unemployment was especially hard on the unions, whose core membership was located in the sectors most directly affected by industrial reform.

The late entry of females into the workforce is another factor suggested by McDonough et al. In contrast to most of Europe, as well as Brazil and Korea, Spanish women are less likely to work outside the home and thus less likely to partake in voluntary associations, especially those of a professional nature such as unions.[42] These authors also focus on the very nature of the transition to democracy, especially the moderation and pragmatism imposed by the legacies of previous attempts at democratization. They note that the style of democracy that took hold in Spain represented not only "a refutation of authoritarianism" but also "a rejection of maximalism," and with it attempts to impose a "substantive, programmatic democracy that goes beyond the formal, procedural variety."[43] Presumably, the emergence of such a democracy is likely to encourage the rise of an activist and highly organized civil society.

Finally, McDonough et al. focus on what they deem is the most important variable in accounting for the difference in levels of civic engagement between Spain and much of the democratizing world: "the exceptionally lukewarm attitude of the Catholic Church toward mass mobilization." They observe that in most cases of democratization in Eastern Europe, Asia and Latin America, the Church played a critical role in mobilizing and organizing the masses. In Spain, by contrast, the Church sat out the democratic transition by assuming a neutral stance.[44] They note that the Church did not oppose democratization, but it stopped short of spurring the faithful to mobilization against the authoritarian system and it declined to back efforts to organize a confessional party. "The result was to leave the link between popular devotion and political abstention intact."[45]

Historical Explanations

Other explanations for the problematic nature of Spanish civil society in Spain delve deeper into the nation's history and, particularly, its agonizing process of modernization and state building. Linz has argued that Spain's failure to generate vigorous social movements of the like that emerged in Western Europe prior to World War II is rooted in the country's historic economic backwardness.[46] He notes that whereas in 1930 only 10 percent of the population in the United Kingdom depended on agriculture, 22 percent in Germany and 27 percent in France, it was 55.2 percent in Spain. With the exception of a few areas of the country such as the Catalonia and the Basque country, industrialization would not arrive in Spain until the early 1960s. Consequently, throughout much of the twentieth century, Spain lacked the conditions that are thought to have facilitated the growth of organized interest groups in other European countries, including the "Western urban social structure of professional and bureaucratic middle classes, and of commercial activity and incipient industrialization." In its place, the nation developed into "a large agrarian and under-developed society in which organized interest groups were less important than the personal and family links between the political class and large landowners, bankers, railroad magnates and many new industrialists."

Another weighty issue addressed by Linz is the multicultural and multilingual character of Spanish society. In Spain, the state developed before the age of nationalism and since the turn of the twentieth century found itself increasingly challenged by emerging peripheral nationalisms in regions like Catalonia and the Basque country. This historical context has no parallels in Western Europe and cannot be ignored when accounting for the delayed and retarded development of organizations in Spain, especially those of a national character. To peripheral nationalism we can add a string of other political ills that have frustrated the growth of civil society in Spain, especially at the national level. As noted by the sociologists Salvador Giner and Enrique Sevilla, the list of cleavages that have thwarted group formation in Spain is both lengthy and complex. They write: "Spain's endemic cleavages such as industrial vs. agrarian, periphery vs. center, hegemonic nationalism vs. peripheral nationalism, clericalism vs. anti-clericalism, and despotism vs. anti-despotism have crossed the ideological, class and political composition of Spain for a long time and in such a manner that they have fragmented and undermined the functioning and expansion of other forms of social cohesion and coalescence, especially those which foster the growth of organized groups."[47]

The Legacies of Francoism

Finally, a full understanding of civil society's weakness in Spain since the transition to democracy must be mindful of the political legacies of the preceding authoritarian regime.[48] As contended by Pérez-Díaz, at the inception of democracy the legacies of Francoism "inhibited civil society's capacity for initiative, individual responsibility, self-organization and collective action."[49] Seeking to cure what Franco referred to as the "familiar demons" of Spanish society, "individualism, lack of solidarity, and extremism," from its very inception in 1939 the Franco regime rejected pluralist forms of interest representation and organization.[50] Instead, it fully embraced a project of social integration as dictated by the rigid doctrine of the "organic-corporatist" state.[51] Above all, the doctrine of organic corporatism afforded the state the right to grant and withhold legitimacy to social organizations, political and otherwise. This, in turn, meant the sudden death of the flourishing but problematic civil society organizations born with the Second Republic.

After 1939, the Franco regime banned all political parties and jailed, murdered or sent into exile many Republican leaders. It also passed a number of laws aimed at regulating associational life. In 1945 the state recognized "the right of all Spaniards to associate freely for licit purpose," but the limits of the law were "so narrow as to make the creation of any political organization unthinkable."[52] As a substitute for a free associational life, the Francoist state sponsored an artificial, compulsory project of civil society building.[53] Unique among Iberian-Latin countries (at least for the extent to which it became part of the identity of the regime as well as its longevity) this project can be credited with engendering considerable apathy within the public with respect to membership in groups. The task of organizing "civil society" in Spain under Franco was assigned to the Catholic Church, a staunch ally of the authoritarian regime at least through the early 1960s, when many church-created organizations began to support workers' strikes. Notable organizations from this period are the *Hermandades Obreras Católicas* (Brotherhood of Catholic Workers) and the *Juventud Obrera Católica* (Catholic Workers' Youth) created to carry out pastoral activities among the students and workers. The regime also created a number of schemes to promote students' associations. Until 1965, all university students were required to belong to the *Sindicato Español Universitario* (Spanish University Syndicate), "a falangist union founded in the thirties, and adopted as a means of control and indoctrination."[54]

Given the fact that class warfare was a central component of the Spanish Civil War, the state's attempt to "corporatize" society under the Franco regime reached its apex in the realm of industrial and labor relations. Upon usurping power, the Franco regime declared illegal all the independent syndicates of the Second Republic and attempts by labor leaders to organize the workers in the new regime were harshly punished. In place of independent trade unions, the Franco regime created a vast and complex system of compulsory "vertical syndicates" grouped around the *Organización Sindical Española*, OSE (Spanish Syndical Organization), that united workers by profession and occupation and that also incorporated the nation's employers.[55] Its official purpose was to create a harmonious environment of labor relations in keeping with the corporatist belief that there is no inherent conflict in the relations between capital and the working class. In reality, however, the purpose of the OSE was to subjugate, domesticate and depoliticize the working class. This mission remained the *raison d'être* of the OSE until its dismantling in 1977.

A Model of Democratic Consolidation

The weakness of civil society in Spain at the juncture of transition to democracy seems to suggest that the country's attempt at democratic consolidation was destined to fail or at the very least would be difficult to predict. Interestingly enough, this was the very sentiment embedded in the many predictions issued around the time of the transition. It is now largely forgotten that scholarly and media assessments of the country's future around the time of Franco's death in 1975 were filled with ominous scenarios. The more optimistic ones envisioned a Latin American–style democracy prone to authoritarian vices, such as a meddling military establishment. The more pessimistic ones foresaw the advent of another civil war of the like that claimed the lives of nearly 1 million people during the turbulent interwar years. "In the political future of Spain I see a great deal of darkness and hardly any light: my forecast must be pessimistic, although never did a forecaster wish to be proved wrong more sincerely than I," wrote Amodia following Franco's death in 1975.[56] Even Linz, the keenest of political observers of contemporary Spanish politics, seemed quite pessimistic when assessing Spain's democratic future. As Spain began to lurch toward democracy he warned about "an impending crisis of legitimation" brought about by the polarization and fragmentation of many actors in Spanish society.[57]

These statements stand in striking contrast to the actual outcome of democratization in Spain. A quarter of a century into the global democratic revolution unleashed by the Third Wave of democratization it is possible to sort out the winners, losers and also-rans. And among the winners, no other case shines brighter than post-Franco Spain. Although, as noted previously, there is no clear scholarly consensus on what constitutes a "consolidated" democracy, few scholars would disagree with the categorization of Spain as a fully consolidated democracy. Indeed, the comparative literature on democratization generated by the global democratic revolution of the last three decades holds Spain as the "paradigmatic" case of consolidation with some going even further. In the view of Richard Gunther et al., in the context of Spain one can speak not only about democratic consolidation but also about "democratic persistence." This ultimate status of democratic maturity is defined as "the end product of a long democratization process whose attainment is contingent upon the successful negotiation of transition and consolidation by a multitude of actors in a given society."[58]

Several notable features of Spanish democratization help make sense of all the praise that scholars have bestowed upon this case. The first is the peaceful and orderly nature of the change between regimes. The transition to democracy in Spain was orchestrated within the framework of Francoist legality since it was executed from the inside out by state elites employing the very laws and institutional mechanisms of the old regime.[59] Therefore, in Spain there was no formal political or institutional rupture as the nation transitioned from dictatorship to democracy. Following the death of General Francisco Franco on November 22, 1975, his handpicked successor, King Juan Carlos I, designated Adolfo Suárez, head of the almost defunct official state party of the Franco regime (the *Movimiento Nacional*) to put into motion a transition to democracy. This expedient and orderly democratic transition—the first of its kind in world history—provided a blueprint for nonviolent regime transition to democracy, especially in South America and Central and Eastern Europe.

A second feature of democratization in Spain is the dazzling pace with which the tasks of democratic consolidation were accomplished. By almost any measure, the speed and scope of democratization undertaken by Spain since the demise of the Franco regime is nothing short of breath-taking. In the estimation of Linz and Stepan, Spain is a case of "rapid consolidation" since democracy was consolidated by 1982 (and perhaps even earlier!) just a few years following the first democratic elections of 1977.[60] No less impressive is the multiple and diverse range of political and economic transformations experienced by the country. Adam Przeworski offers what is arguably the most exuberant summation of democratic consolidation in Spain. Writing in the early 1990s, he observed: "Spain is a miracle ... in only fifteen years the country has succeeded in irreversibly consolidating demo-cratic institutions; allowing peaceful alternation in power; in modernizing its economy and making it internationally competitive; in imposing civilian control over the military; in solving complicated national questions; in extending citizenship rights; and in inducing cultural changes that made it part of the European community of nations."[61]

The recognition of Spain's new democracy as consolidated is vividly illus-trated in the data provided by Freedom House, whose rankings of civil and political rights are widely recognized as the benchmark for gauging the qual-ity of democracy worldwide. With the death of Franco in 1975 and the initiation of political reforms, Spain moved from the category of "Not Free," to "Partly Free." After the democratic elections of 1977, it moved from the rank of "Partly Free" to "Free," a classification the country has retained ever since. More suggestive is that since 1982, just a few years since shedding its authoritarian regime, the scores for respect for political and civil rights in Spain are virtually indistinguishable from those of older and presumably more mature democracies such as Italy, France and Germany.

In light of these many successes in the realm of democratic consolidation, it is perhaps not surprising to learn of the existence among Spaniards of highly positive public appraisals of democratic government and its institu-tions. The most extensive study of public attitudes in Spain since the demise of the Franco regime concludes that "political legitimacy has deepened in Spain as the new regime took a life of its own, surpassing that of the early days of the transition, when it benefited from the vivid contrast between dic-tatorship and democracy."[62] An important indicator of the study is trust in government, which during the transition to democracy rose from 27 percent in 1978 to 41 percent by 1984.[63] Another key indictor is the regard of the general public for the democratic political process. By 1984, the percentage of Spaniards who thought that elections and the congress were needed was 91 and 81 percent respectively.

These highly positive appraisals of political institutions and the democratic process in Spain mirror the fact that since the democratic transition, Spanish public opinion has been strongly pro-democratic and has overwhelmingly rejected all possible alternatives to democracy, including a military government.[64] By 1978, 77 percent of Spaniards deemed democracy "the best political system for a country like ours" with only 15 percent preferring authoritarianism. By 1985, ten years after Franco's death, 76 percent of the population expressed pride in the transition and only 9 percent said that the transition was not a source of pride. These favorable impressions of democracy have held steady over the years despite the travails faced by the nation's new democracy including widespread terrorism courtesy of Basque separatist groups and Western Europe's highest unemployment rate. By 1981, the percentage of Spaniards deeming democracy the best possible system was 81 percent; 85 percent by 1988; and 79 percent by 1993.

Positive Foundations for Democracy

Many explanations have been offered to account for Spain's stunning democratic success and, not surprisingly, a vibrant and robust Civil Society is not one of them. As demonstrated in this chapter, it is difficult to sustain the argument that Spain entered the democratic era with a strong civil society, as conventionally understood. While clearly not a flattened organizational landscape, the configuration of the post-transition civil society in Spain departs significantly from prevailing scholarly models of civil society strength. Not only is associational life sparse in Spain when contrasted to many other newly democratic nations, it is also organizationally weak and dotted with many organizations whose aims can generally be regarded as "anti-system" and detrimental to the building of a strong civic community.

Perhaps the most obvious factor in aiding democratization in Spain is the relatively high levels of economic and social modernization attained by the country by the time of Franco's death, a point that gives credence to the widespread notion that economic wealth breeds democracy.[65] Between 1960 and 1973, only Japan boasted faster and more sustained economic growth, a development that fully transformed Spain into an industrial society and propelled the country's economy to the ranks of the world's ten largest by the mid-1970s.[66] Economic progress and its corollaries (affluence, consumerism, education and improved standards of living) aided democratization by undermining the influence of traditional institutions such as the Catholic Church (which itself ceased to support Franco by the late 1960s). A growing economy also lessened the tendencies toward political radicalism that have traditionally dominated the country's political culture. This was especially the case of the Spanish working class, which prior to the advent of the Franco regime in 1939 had a lengthy history of radical activism and combative politics.

Democratization in Spain was also aided by an emergent political culture that emphasized consensus, moderation and pragmatism and that stood in stark contrast to the political extremism and polarization of the interwar years that drove the nation into a horrific civil war (1936–1939). Underlying this transformation of Spanish political culture was a process of social learning ensuing from the bloodshed and destruction occasioned by the civil war. While remaining deeply divided over what actually happened during a conflict that claimed the lives of an estimated 1 million people, upon Franco's death Spanish society had reached a fundamental understanding of the human and political costs derived from this chaotic and traumatic experience.[67] It emphasizes collective culpability for the crimes committed during the war and the desire to avert the rise of a similar conflict in the future.

Another often-mentioned factor in explaining the success of democratization in post-Franco Spain is the country's favorable geographic location.[68] The country's proximity to the core of Western Europe facilitated its rapid entry into supra-national organizations such as the European Community (EC) and NATO, thereby helping solidify fledgling democratic institutions and attitudes. Admission into the EC in 1986 incorporated Spain in both symbolic and real ways into the fold of Western Europe and reinforced the nation's claim as a European state and that of its people as European citizens entitled to all the rights accorded to this status including democratic government. As suggested by Gunther, Spanish membership in European institutions such as the EC and NATO represented "a symbolic shift toward a new status as a western, industrialized, and democratic society."[69] Furthermore, joining Europe placed Spain squarely within the Western European context by reversing the country's "long-standing non-aligned status" (ensuing from its absence from World War I and II) as well as its "traditional self-image as a bridge between Europe and Latin America and between Europe and the Arab world."[70]

The Primacy of Politics

However important the factors outlined in the previous section are to our understanding of the success of democratization in Spain, their explanatory value is actually limited. Focusing on socioeconomic development and a favorable geographic location can mislead us into thinking that the Spanish transition was an overdetermined success. These factors, according to Linz and Stepan, "misinterpret the actual process of democratic consolidation and fail to appreciate the serious obstacles that Spain had to surmount in the late

1970s and early 1980s."[71] The years that followed Franco's demise were filled with incertitude, ambivalence and risk, befitting a nation with a long history of fractious politics, a multilingual and multiethnic character and no significant tradition of living under democratic rule. Prior to 1977, Spain's democratic experience in the twentieth century was limited to the Second Republic (1931–1936), a period that illustrates what one scholar refers to as "the long tradition of violence of the Spanish people."[72] This tradition pointed to a change of regimes fraught with mishaps and uncertain outcomes that did not preclude the rise of "a more complex and explosive regime" that which ended with the death of Franco.[73]

More important, perhaps, explaining away democratic consolidation in Spain as a product of economic development and/or external factors ignores the behind the scenes political maneuvering that in Spain made the difference between a successful and a stalled or failed democratic transition. To what outsiders looked like a predictable and even rational process of regime change from dictatorship to democracy was in reality a carefully executed political enterprise requiring tremendous political skill and ingenuity. Therefore, it is to the composition of Spain's domestic political institutions and structures rather than to civil society and the other factors mentioned previously that most scholars have turned to account for the country's democratic success.

The dominant (if not hegemonic) narrative of Spanish democratization stresses the effective and innovative political leadership exhibited by King Juan Carlos I and the democratic governments of the post-transition era.[74] More bluntly put, the conventional wisdom about Spanish democratic democratization holds that its success depended largely upon the astute, responsible and well-timed actions of its political leaders both inside and outside of government.[75] This contention is in keeping with the privileged role granted to political elites and political engineering in the making of a successful democratic transition by scholars such as O'Donnell and Schmitter.[76] This it hardly surprising since the political contours of Spanish democratization, especially its negotiated nature as well as the many positive and unpredictable choices made by the nation's political class, are generally credited with informing the elite-centered approach in the study of contemporary democratization.

The present analysis largely supports the prevailing narrative of Spain's success at democratic consolidation. It does, however, add one important new dimension by suggesting how political actors and institutions made democratic consolidation possible in Spain by developing the foundations of social capital and successfully wedding them to the process of democratization.

As noted next, the absence of a textbook example of a vibrant and robust civil society in Spain should not mislead us into thinking that social capital, especially trust in its many guises, was missing from Spanish democratization. Quite the contrary, no other new democracy has embraced democratic governance with as high a propensity among its citizens and social organizations (political and otherwise) to engage in trust-based collective action for the sake of achieving the mutual goal of democratic consolidation. Indeed, trust, solidarity and networks of reciprocity of the very kind praised by Putnam in *Making Democracy Work*, involving government, parties, managers and workers, define the very nature of post-transition politics in Spain. The facilitating sources of this social capital in Spain was not a thriving and robust civil society, but rather the political system, especially its effectiveness in meeting people's expectations about democracy, credibility and roots in society. Before examining the performance and structural conditions that facilitated the building of social capital in Spain, an overview of the values and behaviors comprising this social capital and how it interacted with the politics of democratic consolidation is in order.

Social Capital and Democratic Consolidation in Spain

The prevalence of social capital in the consolidation of democracy in Spain is best suggested by the successful deployment of the policy of "social concertation" as a means to address the complexity of the transition between regimes. It entailed a series of political, social and economic compromises, which depended for their creation and implementation upon many of the values and behaviors thought to make up social capital, including most notably widespread trust across Spanish society. Broadly speaking, trust permeated the process of social concertation across three different levels of societal relations. The first is among the political elites that negotiated explicit "social pacts" that incorporated representation from both political and civil societies. The second is the civil society organizations such as the trade unions and the employers associations entrusted with the task of sanctioning the social pacts and facilitating their implementation across Spanish society. The third and last is the general public, which by agreeing with the contents of the social pacts guaranteed their success and the legitimacy of the negotiators.

The Moncloa accords, signed on October 27, 1977, and named after the residence of the Spanish prime minister, formally inaugurated the policy of social concertation.[77] These epoch-making agreements were negotiated by

Prime Minister Suárez outside of parliament with representatives from the leading national political parties at a critical juncture in the consolidation of Spanish democracy: right after the general elections of 1977 and just before the drafting of a new democratic constitution a year later. Subsequent to the bargaining process, the Moncloa accords were discussed in the national parliament, where they were rapidly turned into law. The accords committed the nation's political class from a broad ideological spectrum, including Christian democrats, social democrats, communists, socialists, conservatives and regional-nationalists, to a wide-ranging program of political and economic reforms to be implemented expeditiously and in as nonconfrontational a manner as possible.

The best-known aspects of the Moncloa accords are those of relation to the economy, given that their most urgent and controversial purpose was to stabilize and protect the economy from the domestic repercussions of the international energy crisis of the mid-1970s. The biggest economic concern during the transition was inflation, which in 1977 appeared to be skyrocketing. To that end, the most important component of the Moncloa accords was the implementation of a wage band dictating that salary increases could not exceed 20–22 percent in anticipation of an inflation rate of 20 percent. This wage scheme, which clearly relied upon the capacity of employers and workers to abide by the dictates of the accords, aimed at slowing down the growth of inflation by decreasing wage demands, alongside containing labor conflict and encouraging economic activity and business profitability.

Notwithstanding their economic importance, political objectives were the principal drive of the Moncloa accords. The chief architect of the accords, vice president for the Economy Enrique Fuentes Quintana, has noted that Moncloa "was basically a political pact whose chief purpose was to neutralize the political arena as a way to facilitate the acceptance of a democratic constitution by all the relevant political forces."[78] With that end in mind, the pacts incorporated multiple political compromises including an agreement with the political parties from the Left regarding state immunity for human rights violations committed under the old regime and the restoration of the Spanish Monarchy. In exchange for these concessions, the government extended political and civil liberties such as the right to strike and organize independent syndicates, undertook the immediate dismantling of the vertical syndicate and the transfer of its assets to the unions and curtailed military prerogatives.

Although born within the political system, the Moncloa accords enjoyed the explicit support of most sectors of Spanish civil society, including the media, the Catholic Church, the business community and most surprisingly, the labor movement. Indeed, labor was the most important representative of civil society in the process of social concertation, even though the major unions themselves were not signatories of the Moncloa accords, its opening act. Labor's engagement in the process of concertation began with its participation in the meetings held by Prime Minister Suárez at the very onset of the democratic transition to explore the potential scope of a social pact. It was solidified with the support that the pacts enjoyed from Nicolás Redondo, the head of the Socialist UGT, and Marcelino Camacho, the head of the Communist CCOO.[79] Both voted in favor of the accords as delegates of the Socialist and Communist parties (respectively) in the national parliament thereby officially giving the unions' blessing to the accords.[80] The unions also promoted the Moncloa pacts' acceptance among the workers. The CCOO praised the accords as "an historic agreement" and "an important victory for the forces of labor and democracy that served to repay the workers for their sacrifices during the dictatorship."[81] Moreover, the organization agreed to carry out a campaign in favor of the accords among the workers in factories across the land and to participate in the tripartite commission comprising government officials, business and labor leaders organized by the government to supervise their implementation.

Subsequent accords carried over the spirit of societal trust, solidarity and cooperation embodied in the Moncloa accord, making social concertation an important feature of the political economy of democratic consolidation in Spain. This explains widespread characterizations of post-Franco Spain as a neo-corporatist society, for the extent to which bargaining and consensus dominate state–society relations as well as the policy-making arena. Between 1977 and 1986, with the Moncloa accords serving as the template, social pacts became the preferred policy mechanism for solving most of the crises faced by the new democracy: from controlling inflation, to rising unemployment to military threats. A key distinction between Moncloa and subsequent social accords, however, was the prominent role that civil society actors assumed in the bargaining process after 1978. In contrast to the Moncloa accords, where union representation was essentially delegated to the parties of the Left and that of employers' groups fell into the hands of the government, civil society organizations took center stage after 1978 while the government and the political parties remained in the background.

The first set of accords to follow the Moncloa pacts was the 1979 *Acuerdo Básico Inter-confederal* (ABI) and the 1980–1981 *Acuerdo Marco Inter-confederal* (AMI). These accords were signed by the *Confederación Española de Organizaciones Empresariales* (CEOE), Spain's leading employers' association, and the Socialist union UGT. They regulated pay guidelines, working hours and industrial productivity and served as the basis for the drafting of Spain's Workers' Charter, a sort of bill of rights of Spanish workers. It recognizes the right to strike, the legitimacy of trade union representation at the company level and the autonomous role of employers' organizations and trade unions in regulating the process of collective bargaining. The 1981 *Acuerdo Nacional del Empleo* (ANE), signed by the UCD, CEOE, UGT and CCOO, sought to alleviate a growing unemployment problem that by the early 1980s had reached 16 percent. Its real purpose in the eyes of many observers, however, was to present a unified political front to the military after its 1981 attack on the nation's young democracy on the eve of the granting of regional home rule to Catalonia and the Basque country. This explains references to the ANE as "the pact of fear."

The 1983 *Acuerdo Interconfederal* (AI), signed by the CCOO, UGT and the CEOE, accompanied the Socialist victory of 1982 and the rise to power of Felipe González. As was the case of the ANE, this social pact had a political imperative, since it served to calm fears and uncertainty about the first transfer of political power within the new democracy. The 1982 Socialist victory returned the Left to power in Spain since the tumultuous years of the Second Republic. The 1985–1986 *Acuerdo Económico y Social*, AES (Social and Economic Accord), signed by the UGT, the CEOE and the PSOE, is the last of the great social accords of the period of democratic transition and consolidation. Among its central purposes was industrial reform with an eye toward making the Spanish economy more competitive in anticipation of the country's entrance into the EC.

The Legacy of Social Concertation

Although there is a tendency among students of Spanish politics to oversell the importance of the policy of social concertation, its positive effects upon the country's democratization politics are undeniable and far-reaching. The Moncloa accords had immediate, positive results, especially in the economic realm. The annual rate of inflation fell from almost 25 percent in 1977 to 14 percent by 1982 and the rate of wage inflation was reduced from 30 to 15 percent.[82] By 1986, when the last social pact expired, inflation stood at 8 percent. The pacts' success in curbing inflation meant that in striking contrast to many other new democracies in which democratization and economic crisis coincided, in Spain hyperinflation was successfully avoided. In turn, avoiding hyperinflation ensured that the task of consolidating democracy in Spain was not complicated by the loss of government credibility as was the case in numerous new democracies.

The Moncloa pacts and subsequent accords were also successful in containing industrial conflict in a nation long known for its combative labor politics. Although the number of strikes in Spain remained one of the highest in Europe for the period 1977–1986, the number of days lost to strikes dropped from 16,641.7 in 1977 to 2,279.4 by 1986.[83] More revealing, perhaps, is that general strikes, a central feature of Spanish politics during the 1930s and of redemocratization politics in South America during the 1980s, were conspicuous by their absence in Spain. The country's first general strike in the democratic period was staged in 1987, ten years after the transition, and long after the nation was thought to have consolidated democracy. By contrast, 14 general strikes rocked Argentina during its first post-transition government (1983–1989).[84] The social pacts also had a positive impact on business profits. As noted in Sebastián Royo's extensive review of the economic legacies of social concertation in Spain, labor costs have always been an important component of total costs for Spanish business—no less than 60 percent in the 1970s. But by 1982, and as a consequence of the wage moderation schemes built into the social pacts, that figure had been reduced by 6.4 percent, and this coincided with the recovery of profits.[85]

The economic success of the social pacts in Spain mirrors the extraordinary degree of societal compliance that accompanied what was agreed to by the bargaining agents, especially regarding wage policy, itself compelling evidence of widespread trust within the polity at both the elite and mass levels. In 1978, the first year the Spanish economy operated under a social pact, 1,838 collective agreements were signed covering nearly 70 percent of the salaried population. Only in few and isolated cases did these agreements break the wage ceiling imposed by the Moncloa accord. Broad support for the social pacts is also reflected by the popularity that the social pacts themselves enjoyed with the general public. A survey conducted by Spain's *Centro de Investigaciones Sociológicas* found that by the time the last accord expired in 1986, an overwhelming majority of Spaniards had a positive impression of them. It found that 23 percent of the public thought the pacts were "very necessary" to the nation's democratic well-being while 43 percent deemed them "sufficiently necessary."[86]

Politically, the benefits of social concertation in Spain are multifold, albeit not altogether self-evident. First and foremost, social concertation aided in the consolidation of Spanish democracy by assisting in the integration of society around the project of democratization and by creating a new (and to a certain extent radical) way of doing politics in Spain. In Pérez Díaz's eloquent characterization, the policy of social concertation was "a self-administered process of shock treatment to cure the traumata of Spanish history and to create a new democratic political culture."[87] More concretely, the policy of social concertation can be credited with wedding "civil" and "political" societies into a collective body working together on behalf of the consolidation of democracy. They brought together the organizations most centrally concerned with the consolidation of democracy (the government, the state bureaucracy, the party system, organized labor and employers' groups). Simultaneously, they isolated the social forces most likely to disrupt or derail Spain's new democracy: the military, ETA and extreme right-wing groups.

Social concertation also aided in the consolidation of democracy in Spain by assisting with the task of political representation. On the one hand, the bargaining process over wages and other matters served to strengthen the participating organizations from both political and civil society. Pacting helped in the development of party discipline in Spain as party leaders began to deemphasize popular mobilization and instead focus on developing internal party rules and parliamentary procedures to make the pacts work.[88] The unification of business organizations in Spain under the umbrella of the CEOE, one of the most notable developments in the post-Franco era in the area of interest representation, is unthinkable without the emphasis granted to cross-class negotiation by the government during the democratic transition. The same effect on interest centralization can be appreciated within the labor movement. The process of concertation can be credited not only with centralizing representation of the Spanish working class within two major unions (the UGT and CCOO), but also with enhancing internal discipline and organizational skills.

On the other hand, concertation provided a mode of interest representation that allowed for fast and effective recognition of mutual interests to a plurality of actors and for the resolution of many of the tasks confronting them. Almost no task or problem encountered by Spain remained outside of the concertation process: from the dismantling of Francoist institutions, to the making of a new democratic constitution, to the implementation of wage and inflation policy. Most significant, perhaps, is the way in which the social pacts served to advance a wide range of civil society objectives by allowing for direct access to groups such as the unions in the national policy-making process. They include the early liberalization of the trade unions from the trappings of the vertical syndicate (a condition for the Left's support of a negotiated transition) and the numerous socioeconomic gains made by the labor movement through the policy of social concertation until its expiration in 1986. A 1989 assessment of the role of social pacts on labor and industrial relations in Spain best expresses this point. It notes:

> Through these pacts the social partners have been granted a degree of power in the realm of government policy formulation that would generally not evolve from the normal collective bargaining process. With respect to the trade unions, this power has far exceeded what one would expect to accrue to an ideologically and geographically divided and financially suspect trade union movement which has a very low membership base and weak organizational at the workplace.[89]

Paradoxically, the most compelling sign of the success of the policy of social concertation was its formal termination with the expiration of the AES in 1986. The most often-noted explanation for concertation's demise in Spain is the deterioration in relations between the Socialist government and the unions, and especially the antagonistic relationship that developed between Prime Minister Felipe González and the UGT leader Nicolás Redondo.[90] A less evident but arguably more compelling explanation is that by the mid-1980s Spanish democracy was already firmly established and no longer in need of protection by explicit social agreements intended to unify the nation and minimize social conflict. Redondo best articulated this point in 1987 when he asserted: "The grand pacts are no longer possible. They were viable during the transition because the nation was in need of legitimating the democratic system."[91] While some of the demons that haunted the democratization process in Spain (political violence and regional nationalism in particular) have settled into seemingly permanent fixtures of democratic political life, these conditions are no longer regarded as threats to the stability of democracy. In sum, having accomplished its intended objective, the rapid consolidation of democracy, concertation died a victim of its own success.

The collapse of concertation in 1986 raises the intriguing question of what happened to all the trust, cooperation and reciprocity generated by the democratic transition and the concertation process itself. At a general, abstract level the argument can be made that the social capital built during the transition lives on in the social contract implicit in the consolidation of democracy. A more concrete exploration of the question, however, must look at the institutions whose creation reflect the sense of trust and cross-class collaboration embedded in the concertation process.[92] Notable among them is the Spanish Constitution, one of the few in the world that stipulates a role for the trade unions and employers' groups in the policy-making process. More suggestive is the *Consejo Económico y Social*, CES

(Social and Economic Council), a body entrusted with the task of coordinating policy between the government, the unions and the employers. Initially envisioned with the Moncloa accords (but not fully developed until years later) the CES was critical in restarting process of social pacts in 1996 after the departure of the Socialist government for the purpose of preparing the nation for the exigencies of European monetary policy. In this way, institutions such as the CES have served as a depository of social capital in Spain, serving the purpose of "storing" trust and cooperation that the nation can rely on in times of crisis and/or in need of social integration.

CHAPTER 4

Political Institutions and Democratization in Spain

How can the extraordinary stock of social capital that underpinned the consolidation of democracy in Spain be explained? Certainly, it cannot be attributed to a vibrant and robust civil society. Nor can it be explained away as a product of Spanish history. Prior to the transition to democracy in 1977 there was no history in Spain of autonomous cooperation between the state and actors from civil society such as organized labor. Contemporary Spanish history is, after all, a long, tortuous tale of entrenched social conflict, especially class strife, which was at the heart of the Spanish Civil War and the collapse of the Second Republic. Moreover, the history of the labor movement in Spain, one of the pillars of the social concertation process, hardly predisposed it to engage in trust-based interactions with the state and the employers. The successful deployment of social concertation in Spain is more compelling still because attempts to erect analogous policies of negotiation and compromise by other democratizing societies have failed to get off the ground and have had the unintended outcome of exacerbating rather than alleviating social conflict. As shown in chapter 5, a dearth of trust among the social partners explains the failure of social pacts as a means for assisting in consolidating democracy in Brazil.

In the following analysis I attribute the making of the social capital that underwrote the policy of social concertation in Spain, and by extension, the consolidation of democracy, to the performance and institutional configuration of the political system. I emphasize, first, the commitment of democratically elected leaders to the principles and practice of democracy and the manner in which they served to create a sense of national solidarity around the project of democratization. Second, I focus on the role of the state in promoting social and economic welfare prior to the transition to democracy and the manner in which this enhanced trust within Spanish society and endowed the state with credibility and legitimacy. Third, I stress the influence and reach of the party system, especially the Socialist and Communist parties, which served as a bridge in the relations between the state and civil society. I demonstrate how parties conditioned the willingness of key sectors of civil society (especially the labor movement) to assume risks by entering into explicit agreements with previous enemies, namely the government and the employers. They also assisted the policy of social pacts by fostering moderation across civil society, including sacrificing short-term political gains for the more important, long-term goal of consolidating democracy. Parties in Spain could play these roles because of their capacity to incorporate and represent civil society.

Governing Regime Change

Numerous aspects of governance in post-Franco Spain can be credited with promoting trust, solidarity and reciprocity and none is more obvious and suggestive than the role of King Juan Carlos I in shepherding the nation through the transition to and consolidation of democratic government. His courageous and steadfast support for democracy is generally credited with providing a symbol around which all Spaniards could rally around and aiding in legitimizing the institutions of the new democratic system as well as introducing moderation, restrain and civility in a country traditionally known for its zero-sum politics. These contributions of the king to the process of democratization figure prominently in analyses of the cooling of passions and the depolarization of politics evident in Spain in the post-Franco era. McDonough et al. write:

> The King has functioned as a bridging figure, uniting Spaniards of traditional and modern persuasions, if not their regions. Juan Carlos gave the transition an elemental coherence, adding more than just a grace note to the ground bass of depolarization. Moral drama invigorated dull calculation.[1]

Upon gaining control of the nation following Franco's death in 1975, Juan Carlos expertly and judiciously exploited the vast powers granted to him to lead his nation out of four decades of institutionalized authoritarianism and into a Western-style democracy. This role fittingly earned him the title of *El Piloto del Cambio* (the Pilot of the Change).[2] He began by firing the last of the Francoist presidents, Arias Navarro, whose government was "a failure both as an initiative for reform and as an attempt to control the process of change" and announcing a transition to democracy to be headed by Adolfo Suárez.[3] Notwithstanding the popular clamoring for democracy by nascent civil society organizations and the historic opposition of the Franco regime (namely the Socialist and Communist parties) that followed Franco's death, the king's embrace of democracy could have hardly been anticipated.

Many expected the king to assume an apolitical stance during the transition, typical of someone perceived to be something of a figurehead. A more expected role for the king was to seek to preserve the old authoritarian order. In the years preceding the democratic transition, Franco had personally groomed the king to assume political power and with the passage of the 1974 Law of Succession (which returned Spain's monarchy to power) he had received every assurance from the king to uphold the principles of Francoism. Thus, it was the element of bravado and of seizing the moment in the king's actions that so powerfully conveyed the notion of that he was acting on his own sense of what he felt was right for Spain. In the words of the historian Stanley Payne, "Juan Carlos took responsibility for initiating the change, and provided shrewd leadership and determined courage in its implementation and development."[4]

In boldly betraying Franco's plan and siding with the wishes of the people, the king opened the way for political liberalization and eventually democracy. Simultaneously, he legitimized the monarchy in the eyes of the general public and secured a role for this institution and himself in the emerging democratic system. Later on in February 1981, when democracy came under attack by the military, the king once again came down on the side of democracy. The king's behavior during the 1981 coup became "an emblematic narrative" in the building of trust in political institutions in Spain.[5] He stood up to the military coup plotters (who had expected the king to endorse their actions) thus becoming a critical figure in the survival of democracy, the growing confidence of the public in the emerging democratic system and the transformation of the country's politics. Through these actions, the king exerted independent weight of his own in promoting the development of democracy in Spain by shaping new political perceptions, norms and values among the general public at a crucial point in Spanish history. As explained by McDonough et al.: "The commitment of the king to democracy reflected deliberate choice at a tipping-point—one that helped turn the political culture of the country around."[6]

Democratic Commitment and Competence

Just as exemplary (although less known outside of Spain) as the role of the king in the transition was that of Spanish politicians, whose capacity for bringing the nation together and averting social conflict in the midst of profound political change remains peerless among new democracies. Scholars of the Spanish transition converge in praising Adolfo Suárez's stewardship of the transition by successfully negotiating the many perils that have stalled or complicated other democratic transitions. Payne notes that Suárez discharged his functions with "an extraordinary combination of political deftness and audacity that met with the overwhelming approval of the Spanish public."[7]

Undoubtedly, the most compelling evidence of Suárez's political competence is the dazzling speed with which democracy consolidated. This achievement is the more impressive when we account for the complexities of the democratic transition in Spain. Suárez was burdened with the unenviable job of convincing the Francoist parliament to disband and peacefully relinquish its hold on power. This was the equivalent, in Linz and Stepan's analysis, "of Gorbachev convincing the Communist Party and the legislative organs of the complex constitutional structure of the Soviet Union to allow multiparty elections, freely contested elections for a parliament of the union which would then have the duty and power to form the government."[8] Equally challenging for Suárez was the task of convincing the historic democratic opposition to the Franco regime led by the Communist and Socialist parties to give up plans for a revolutionary overthrow and their cherished dream of creating a Third Republic. It is worth recalling that the Spanish Left has traditionally regarded democracy as synonymous with Republican government.

In approaching the awesome challenges resting upon his shoulders, Suárez relied on his negotiating skills, which were essential to the development of the politics of consensus that dominated Spain's return to democracy in 1977. Linz has observed that during the transition Suárez exhibited "a great capacity for personal dialogue and engaging those with whom he had to negotiate, listening to them, and creating a certain sense of trust without necessarily making promises he was uncertain about being unable to satisfy."[9] According to Edward Malefakis, "Suárez proved masterful in domestic diplomacy, inducing the Franquist Cortes to disband and slowly winning over the democratic opposition, which also became infected with his enthusiasm for consensus politics."[10] In discharging his responsibilities as leader of the transition, Suárez also displayed an unflinching commitment to democracy and its values. This was evident early in the transition and well before it had become his own responsibility. In an influential speech to the

Spanish Parliament that is thought to have inspired the king to select him to preside over the transition, Suárez stated: "I think that our historic task is very simple: the government, the legitimate manager of this historic moment, has the responsibility to put into motion the mechanism necessary for the definite consolidation of a modern democracy."[11]

By all accounts Suárez was faithful to his words. Almost from the first day of his appointment, he was a tireless advocate for a swift transition to democratic governance. By October 1976, just three months after his appointment as manager of the political transition, he submitted to the national parliament a program of political reform that aimed to simultaneously put this body out of business and liberalize the country from the grip of Franco's authoritarian rule. When the Francoist parliament balked at the idea of self-liquidation, Suárez went directly to the people to ask for a mandate to dismantle the old regime. On a referendum organized on December 1976, 94.2 percent of Spaniards approved the program of political liberalization. Once translated into law, the 1977 Law of Political Reform legalized political parties and independent trade unions and provided for the organization of free elections for June of 1977.

Just months before the nation's first democratic elections, Suárez took his most audacious step during the transition by legalizing the Spanish Communist party (PCE) on April 9, 1977. This action stunned the Spanish people and political observers alike. As recently as September 1976, Suárez had assured the military that he would not legalize the party "however strong the pressure put on me."[12] In making this promise, Suárez was reflecting decades of virulent anti-Communist propaganda by the Franco regime and unfounded fears among political elites (even among those advocating for the country's return to democracy) of a Communist plan for radicalizing Spanish society. In choosing to break his promise to the military, Suárez was recognizing that the emerging democratic system had more to gain from legalizing the PCE than from keeping it in its illegal and clandestine status. As he argued with respect to the PCE:

> I do not think that our people want to find itself fatally obliged to see our jails full of people for ideological reasons. I think that in a democracy we must all be vigilant of ourselves, we must all be witnesses and judges of our public actions. We have to instore the respect for legal minorities. Among the rights and duties of living together is the acceptance of the opponent. If one has to confront him, one has to do it in civilized competition. Sincerely, is it not preferable to count in the ballot boxes what otherwise we would have to measure on the poor basis of unrest in the streets?[13]

Notwithstanding the tension and hostility that the legalization of the PCE provoked (the secretary of the navy resigned in protest while the Army Supreme Council remarked that it was repulsed by this action) this move proved to be a blessing for Spanish democratization. For starters, Suárez consolidated his democratic credentials in the eyes of the general public by declaring his independence from the old regime, especially the military. Suárez's decision to legalize the PCE also enhanced the legitimacy of the institutions of the emerging democratic regime. For him the question of legalization of the PCE was "an issue affecting the inclusiveness of contestation, an essential element of democracy, and therefore the credibility of the Spanish regime's democratizing effort."[14] Finally, and perhaps most importantly, by legalizing the PCE in a timely and courageous fashion Suárez reinforced the moderating tendencies within this party and brought into the process of political reform and the politics of consensus an organization that otherwise would have certainly posed a powerful challenge to the legitimacy of the emerging democracy. After it was legalized, the PCE abandoned the strategy of regime change based on *ruptura*, an abrupt break with the past, and adopted in its place *reforma*, a model of regime change based on negotiation.

Advancing Consolidation

Suárez's party, *Unión de Centro Democrático*, UCD (Union of the Democratic Center) was the clear winner of the general elections of 1977 with 34 percent of the vote and 47 percent of parliamentary seats, just short of a parliamentary majority. The UCD's electoral triumph came as no surprise to anyone in Spain. After the passage of the 1977 Law of Political Reform, which effectively ended the Franco regime, Suárez was the nation's most popular and respected politician and the one deemed most capable of solving a whole series of problems—including prices, public order, unemployment, strikes and the inauguration of democracy.[15] Most important, Suárez's lead among his cohort was largest on the matter that meant most to the public: democracy. According to a 1976 opinion poll, on the question of which politician could best handle the transition, 38 percent of those polled did not answer, but 45.4 percent named Suárez while his nearest rival, Felipe González of the Socialist party, garnered a paltry 5.9 percent.[16] This political capital afforded Suárez and the UCD the legitimacy to convene the societal bargaining leading to the successful negotiation of the Moncloa accords on October 25, 1977. Due to the tremendous public support Suárez enjoyed during the critical years of democratic crafting, 1977–1980, few politicians would dare attack him. He was, in Eusebio Mujal-León words, "unassailable."[17]

As prime minister, Suárez used his popularity to advance policies that while highly beneficial to the consolidation of democracy, in the short term proved to be politically devastating for himself and his party (the UCD). Between 1977 and 1981, Suárez took on Conservatives, the business community (his core source of electoral support in the 1977 elections) and the military on a wide range of issues for the purpose of fostering consensus, moderation and trust.[18] In 1977 he deeply angered business elites by insisting on negotiation with the labor movement and the Communist and Socialist parties with the purpose of forging the Moncloa accords. As a result of this, the employers' association, the CEOE, was the only major representative from civil society to openly criticize the accords, which it deemed as "evidence that the UCD was executing a socialist economic program" and that the "Marxist parties were in effect the ruling parties."[19] Although the business community certainly favored wage moderation, it feared that that the negotiated aspect of the government's economic policy would grant the unions a disproportionate role in policy-making.[20]

As seen already, the Moncloa accords were key to the rapid consolidation of democracy in Spain. This is due in great measure to the incorporation into the pacts of almost all the politically significant forces active during the transition. But a seldom-noted aspect of the pacts of great importance to the consolidation of democracy (arguably their real genius) is that they incorporated virtually the entire political and economic program of the UCD government. Thus, their approval in parliament, shortly after the pacts themselves were signed by the nation's leading parties, meant that in a single legislative scoop, the nation was placed on a fast track toward resolving many of the issues confronting the new democracy. Although inflation policy attracted the most attention, the Moncloa accords covered a wide economic terrain including tightening tax laws, reforming the welfare state by expanding access to education, housing and unemployment and liberalizing the financial market. To be sure, not all of these policies were implemented at once or even during the rule of the UCD, but they provided a blueprint for economic and political reform for the nation's political leaders to follow.

Bolder yet was Suárez's willingness to confront the military by granting limited self-governance to Catalonia, the Basque country, and Galicia, the first step toward the quasi-federalization of the nation with the construction of a system of 17 so-called *autonomías* (autonomous regions). It ensued from an exquisitely ambiguous compromise embedded in the 1978 Constitution that recognizes both the unitary nature of the Spanish state together with the existence of multiple Spanish "nationalities" and the right of the regions and its peoples to seek home rule. This accounts for characterizations of Spain as "an imperfect and incomplete federation," "a hybrid system of federalism and regionalism," a "covertly federal state," and "a state based on the right of self-government for which time alone will provide the final definition."[21] But by the time the system of autonomous regional governments was instituted, it represented Western Europe's largest process of devolution of administrative powers from the central state to regional governments in the postwar period.

Suárez's propensity toward consensus in policy-making was widely shared within the UCD and his administration, especially those in charge of the nation's economic affairs, thereby ensuring an internal consensus within the government regarding the policy of pact-making.[22] The principal intellectual force behind the UCD's economic program was Enríquez Fuentes Quintana, the vice president for the economy and former director of the Bank of Spain. From the onset of the transition he impressed upon Suárez the overall utility of a political pact with the opposition while discouraging the imposition of an economic adjustment program by decree.[23] In a policy paper entitled "A Program of Recovery and Economic Reform," Fuentes Quintana warned that only a negotiated approach to economic management could prevent a situation of economic collapse with serious consequences for the nascent democracy.[24] Specifically, this paper highlighted a broad agreement with the opposition to simultaneously consolidate democracy and stabilize the economy. Fuentes Quintana argued that the complexity of the economic crisis, its political ramifications and the configuration of political forces that emerged from the elections of 1977 made ordinary adjustment programs either ill-suited or inefficient. In his own words: "it was imperative that the economic program pursued by the government was supportive of the consolidation of democracy and that it possessed a critical quality: it had to be pacted."[25]

Fuentes Quintana's desire to involve participation of societal actors in policy-making seemed misguided to many who at the time thought that the economic crisis demanded a more aggressive response and that inflation could be tamed without the complexity of having to negotiate with actors from outside of the state.[26] A broad political pact, however, was in keeping with the political pragmatism and technocratic orientations prevalent within the state's economic bureaucracy. A product of the bureaucratic revolution of the late Franco period, Fuentes Quintana fully embodied the political pragmatism, technical innovation and economic progressiveness for which the technocracy of the late Franco period had come to be known for by the mid-1970s.[27] Fuentes Quintana saw the transition to democracy as a critical juncture in Spanish history and specifically as a unique opportunity to correct or at least avoid mistakes from the past. The one mistake he was determined to avoid was the dearth of societal compromise among political forces that had doomed the Second Republic, which became his main historical reference in the crafting of the Moncloa accords.[28] The striking parallels between the economic and political conditions prevalent in Spain in 1931 and 1977 triggered much of Fuentes Quintana's thinking about the Second Republic. In both instances, the nation faced the unfortunate and dangerous situation of undertaking to democratize in the midst of an international economic crisis.

Policy as a Source of Social Capital

The government's policy of consensus imparted a weight of its own in deepening and expanding trust, cooperation and reciprocity in Spanish political life. Especially notable is the way in which the Moncloa pacts themselves served to enhance collaboration among political actors. Pact-making in Spain allowed political leaders to think of the opposition in terms of "adversaries" rather than "enemies," which had been the prevailing mode of interaction among political elites in Spain prior to the transition.[29] This shift in political attitudes had important policy implications for the new democracy. Comparative research into the policy outcomes of pacted transitions (such as Spain's) and non-pacted transitions (such as Argentina's) convincingly demonstrates that the social pacts in Spain had a significant impact on intra-party collaboration lasting well past the immediate years of democratic consolidation.[30] This collaboration also went beyond minimum-winning coalitions thus explaining the efficacy and speed with which Spain's first democratic government was able to formulate and implement many of its policies. This finding led to the conclusion that "pacted transitions may produce democracies in which there is a greater degree of political party collaboration than democracies produced by non-pacted transitions."[31]

The role of social pacts in creating and furthering social capital and its various components in Spain extended into civil society. The success of the pacts in advancing multiple political and economic objectives served to change attitudes toward cooperation with government among groups previously leery of such interaction. A noted UGT leader has observed that the Moncloa accords "eliminated labor's rejection of the social pact and opened a new horizon for the trade unions since they demonstrated that an accord could be a profitable one in terms of advancing democracy, reducing inflation and securing reforms and re-distributive claims."[32] This capacity of the Moncloa accords to assuage fears within the labor movement about cooperation with both the business community and the government was critical to the survival and expansion of the policy of social concertation. As noted previously, while the leading political parties had negotiated the Moncloa pacts, subsequent social pacts were anchored on direct negotiations between the trade unions and employers' groups with the encouragement of the government.

Pact-making in Spain also had a positive impact in creating and enhancing social capital values and behaviors within Spanish society at large. Interestingly enough, this may have had more to do with the symbolism the pacts conveyed to the general public than with their actual outcomes. The ritual of pact-making sent the message to the citizenry that both the government and the opposition were taking responsible and concrete actions with respect to the stability of the new regime. And since the social accords almost always promised to do more than their creators knew they were capable of delivering, the impression that consensus could resolve almost any problem was effectively lodged into the body politic. As noted by two close observers of the negotiation process: "by appearing to do more than they actually could, the social partners were able to achieve a certain degree of trust which in the final analysis has proved to be of considerable importance."[33]

Arguably, the most compelling evidence of the deepening of social trust occasioned by the Moncloa accords in Spain across all levels of Spanish society is the making of the 1978 Constitution. As would be expected, the constitution-making process raised all the hot issues that have historically divided Spanish society including the roles of the Monarchy and the Catholic Church in national politics and the demands for autonomy from culturally distinct regions. But the aura of consensus that preceded the drafting of the constitution essentially took the bite out of the anticipated confrontation that this document was expected to generate. The Moncloa accords served as a prelude for Spain's constitution-making process, whose speedy and consensus-driven dynamics are simply inconceivable without the environment of trust, solidarity and compromise generated by the accords.[34] As observed by former prime minister Leopoldo Calvo Sotelo (who replaced Suárez in 1981), "one cannot understand the consensus surrounding the making of the constitution without the trust created by the Moncloa accords."[35]

Spain's new constitution is the first in Spanish history not to be imposed by one group over another one, as was clearly the case during the Second Republic and the Franco regime. In the case of the Second Republic the Liberals imposed their will upon the Conservatives and the opposite prevailed during the Franco regime. Instead, widespread societal consensus marked the enacting of the 1978 constitution, turning Spain into a paradigmatic example of "the consensual style of constitution-making" for the extent to which the drafting of the constitution involved elite negotiation and popular consent.[36] Rare among new democracies, Spain's new constitution was first approved by the national parliament before it was submitted to a national referendum, in which it garnered 88 percent approval from the public.[37] The aim of the referendum was "to gain maximum legitimacy to the new constitution."[38]

State Structures and Institutional Legacies

The constitution of the state in Spain prior to the democratic transition also favorably conditioned the disposition of social actors and the general public to engage in and offer support to a wide range of trust-based collective inter-actions. Among recent cases of democratization, Spain stands out for the degree of state cohesion, credibility and legitimacy inherited from the authoritarian period. These attributes reflected the processes of reform, mod-ernization and internal democratization of state institutions that Spain underwent during the late Franco period. They also reflect the continuing evolution of the Franco regime and its amazing ability to change with the times, a point corroborated by assessments of policy-making in the twilight of the Franco dictatorship. Charles W. Anderson's 1970 review of Spanish policy-making under Franco notes that the Francoist technocratic apparatus "demonstrated a flexibility and openness to change quite as great as that of most Western nations."[39]

Anderson's characterization of the Francoist state during its last decade speaks volumes about the institutional modernization that had taken place within the administrative apparatus of the state in Spain during the long life of the Franco regime. During the Franco regime's first phase, the so-called New State, 1939–1959, Spanish public administration was left "to a coterie of army and naval officers who tried to run the country like a military barracks."[40] Not surprisingly, by the 1950s, the Franco regime had become "a by-word for misery, retardation and almost abject poverty in just about every facet of economic life."[41] Its disregard for market realities and overall economic mismanagement had conspired to create an environment dominated by "favoritism, corruption, the emergence of an important black market, galloping inflation and crucial shortages of basic foodstuffs, raw materials and capital goods."[42]

The most compelling sign of state modernization during the transition is that by the time of the 1977 elections, the country was well on its way toward achieving civilian supremacy over the military, a legacy of the many institutional transformations undertaken during the late Franco period. As reported by Felipe Agüero's comparative study of civilian–military rela-tions in Southern Europe and South America, despite "Franquist nostalgia among the armed forces," around the time of the transition the Spanish military was placed "within well-bounded spheres of competence and did not interfere with political decisions made by civilian officials."[43] This meant that in Spain politicians such as Suárez and technocrats such as Fuentes Quintana could engage in direct negotiations with leaders of the opposition such as the labor movement without having to consult with military officers or fear retaliation from them.

As seen already, Spain's first post-transition government successfully challenged the military on a wide range of policy issues and highly sensitive matters, from the legalization of the Communist party to the partition of the nation into autonomous communities. These challenges, as Agüero points out, generated numerous episodes of military protest and even rebellion until at least 1982, as suggested by the failed coup of February 1981, but none succeeded in derailing democracy or affecting its consolidation. Indeed, an outcome of military discontent was resolution by civilian governments to further curtail military prerogatives, as was the case of the passage of a special organic law in 1984, which ended any ambiguity in the law regarding the status of the military. As a result, today military resistance in Spain consists of "bureaucratic infighting not uncharacteristic of advanced democracies with large military establishments."[44]

The transformation in state administration is generally credited to a new cadre of new technocrats that rose within the Franco regime in the early 1960s, which was affiliated with the Catholic organization *Opus Dei*.[45] Their entry into government was facilitated by the economic crisis of 1959 together with Franco's realization that only a radical reorientation of the regime could extend the life of the dictatorship. A direct outcome of their milieu (higher education, jurisprudence and economics in particular), the *Opus* technocracy reinvented the Franco dictatorship by modernizing its legal structures, creating the foundations of a welfare state and most significantly, by revamping the country's outmoded economic structures.[46] Having wrestled away control of the economic institutions of the state from the military, *Opus* technocrats executed a wholesale restructuring of the economy without altering the basic political constitution of the state. They opened the country to tourism and outside investors (something that Franco had traditionally opposed for fear of contamination from the outside world), collaborated with the World Bank on the implementation of a sweeping program of economic stabilization and undertook to reform the state's bureaucratic apparatus. For instance, *Opus* technocrats centralized the state's decision-making process and implemented a merit-based recruitment program aimed at stamping out cronyism, clientelism and corruption. As a result, around the time of the transition out of Francoism, "there was no groundswell of support for a purge of the state administration on the grounds that it was bloated and inefficient or staffed by incompetent hacks."[47]

A Legacy of Interdependence and Trust

Opus technocrats also modernized the Franco regime's archaic system of industrial and labor relations. While retaining the rigid façade of the vertical syndicate, *Opus* enacted a wide range of reforms that significantly increased the level of workers' representation within the structures of the state, granting the Franco regime a unique profile in the context of modern authoritarian regimes. As noted by Robert Fishman, "Spain stands alone among essentially exclusionary and repressive authoritarian regimes for the extent of democratic worker participation and representation allowed (and even encouraged at times) within the official union structure."[48] Such developments had far-reaching consequences on the lives of the workers under Franco's rule as well as the political proclivities of civil society in the post-transition period.

One of the first reforms adopted by *Opus* technocrats in the realm of labor relations was recognition of independently created workers' organizations such as CCOO.[49] By the mid-1960s, the state was not only tolerating the presence of CCOO in the workplace but also had granted the organization the status of "semi-official" allowing its leadership to receive financial aid from the directors of the vertical syndicate. Officials at the Ministry of Labor also began to tolerate workers' strikes as long as the demands they pressed for were of an "economic" nature.[50] A more important and radical change introduced by *Opus* technocrats was collective bargaining, a rare feature in an authoritarian regime given the degree of influence it granted to the workers within the state's official labor institutions.[51] This development, which stands in striking contrast to the South American experience and its entirely exclusionary corporatist schemes, was implemented through the creation of a vast network of locally organized and democratically elected works councils, found in firms employing more than 50 workers. The works councils are credited with engendering nothing short of a revolution within the old regime's industrial relations system.[52]

With the works councils in place, collective bargaining spread like fire throughout the Spanish economy. The number of contracts jumped from 63,000 in 1963 to 438,000 by 1965.[53] The works councils also served to enhance the state's management capacities even though their creation effectively ended the state's unilateral imposition of wage policy, in place since the inception of authoritarian rule. Above all, the composition of the councils as democratically elected bodies empowered by law to handle collective bargaining forced state officials to learn to manage industrial and labor relations and cope with industrial conflict without having to resort to explicitly repressive measures. It is reported that despite the widespread mobilization of the workers around the democratic transition, when political demands began to replace economic demands as the reason for strikes, labor leaders arrested as a result of union activity were "clearly in the minority."[54]

The works councils also gave the workers a stake in the economic system, as they allowed for direct bargaining between employers and workers on a wide range of issues including wages and working conditions. This, in turn, served to introduce considerable interdependence and trust in capital–labor relations across the national economy. Survey data of working-class attitudes around the time of the transition found little "hostility" toward employers and the state.[55] More revealing, perhaps, is the finding that 52.1 percent viewed their places of work as "a team effort in which the common goal was to produce more and for the benefit of everyone."[56] In light of such developments it is not surprising that the works councils survived the transition out of authoritarian rule virtually intact. Employers, unions and state officials were convinced that the councils "were an institutional element of the Franco regime that was worth including in the new system of industrial relations."[57]

The continuation of the works councils in the new democracy was especially fortunate for the implementation of social pacts negotiated at the peak level by the unions and the employers. The high level of compliance that characterized Spain's experience with social pacts did not have to rely upon the ability of the unions to "deliver" the workers to the state and the employers. This was simply unlikely given the organizational weaknesses of the unions both at the top and especially at the factory level. Rather, it depended upon the high levels of societal cooperation and interdependence embedded in the nation's system of industrial and labor relations and, as noted next, the credibility and legitimacy of the state.

Economic Development and State Legitimacy

Arguably, the most notable contribution made by the new technocracy was the so-called Spanish Miracle, the dramatic expansion of the economy that preceded the transition to democracy. Anchored upon the opening of the country to foreign tourists and investors that, between 1959 and the mid-1970s Spain experienced an economic boom that transformed the country from a primarily agrarian society into an industrial one. GNP rates averaged over 7 percent from 1960 to 1974, the unemployment rate was one of the lowest in Western Europe and averaged 1 percent from 1960–1973, and inflation averaged 7.1 from 1960–1973. Among the many consequences of this expansion of the economy was enhancing the legitimacy of the state, once the traditional sources of Francoist legitimacy had been exhausted. By the mid-1960s, Franco's claims that he saved the country from the chaos and savagery of civil war and that his rule was needed because "Spain was different" due to an inherent propensity toward conflict resonated very poorly with the general public. In their place, economic development began to emerge as the new source of legitimacy for the authoritarian regime and the chief justification for its continuation.

The economic boom of the late Franco period transformed the lives of the vast majority of Spaniards by bringing living standards quite close to those of their European neighbors. Unlike other so-called developmental dictatorships such as Brazil, the Spanish workers benefited tremendously from the economic growth generated by the authoritarian state. Wage earners in Spain were receiving per capita about 12 percent more of the national income in 1975 than they had in 1962.[58] The total flows of revenues into the nation's social security system more than doubled as a share of GDP from 4.2 to 9.3 percent.[59] The share of the budget devoted to education between 1953 and 1973 more than doubled from 8.2 to 17.7 percent of government spending.[60] These social gains were made possible not only by the expansion of the economy but also by scaling down military spending. By the early 1970s, and despite Franco's military background, the Spanish government was spending less (as a percentage of GDP) on defense than any other European country except Luxembourg.[61] Between 1953 and 1973, the share of the national budget devoted to defense spending fell from 30.4 to 13.2 percent.[62] None of these developments made Franco's rule "legitimate" in the eyes of the general public but they reinforced the view of the state as a protector and benefactor of the workers.[63]

A direct result of improved economic conditions for the Spanish working class was the reshaping of workers' attitudes and political proclivities. The economic bonanza generated during the late Franco period helped turn a formerly radicalized working class into a model of political restraint and moderation. In Malafakis's analysis, the economic boom of the late Franco period occasioned a "kind of embourgeoisement of the masses" and a "partial erosion of class barriers."[64] Unsurprisingly, assessments of the Spanish proletariat during the democratic transition make note of the existence of "a crisis of class consciousness" among the workers.[65] Survey data of the time demonstrates that only 37 percent of workers identified themselves as belonging to the working class.[66] This explains why during the democratic transition, the Spanish working class showed little if any enthusiasm to transform the existing socioeconomic order.

Spanish workers also entered democracy very suspicious of radical political change and quite reluctant to follow the lead of union officials seeking to mobilize them against the government and its economic program. This is suggested most compellingly by the dismal failure of the CNT, the powerful anarchist syndicate of the Second Republic, to revive itself in the post-Franco era and rally the workers in opposition to the government and the employers. Instead, during the transition the workers gravitated toward the union perceived to be the most moderate (the CCOO), as suggested by its explicit ringing endorsement of the Moncloa accords. The social pacts were quite popular with the workers as they were with the general public. A survey of workers' attitudes toward the Moncloa accord found that "for one reason or another, the working class saw no other alternative to economic policy than that suggested by the government."[67]

The credibility and legitimacy gained by the state technocratic apparatus in Spain prior to the democratic transition proved to be an important asset for Suárez as he sought to implement an economic program anchored on consensus and compromise. Fishman's study of unions in democratizing Spain reports that about a third of union leaders responsible for enforcing collective bargaining were inclined to break the wage caps imposed by the Moncloa pacts, but they knew that they could not count on the support of the workers to reject the government's plea for cooperation.[69] This willingness of the workers to moderate wages demands was rooted in their conception of the legitimacy of the state. This is another important conclusion of Fishman's study, which states that the single most important variable that explains workers' acceptance of the principle of restraint by negotiated pacts is "the belief in the legitimacy of the state and its ultimate right to regulate society."[69] He found that the majority of union leaders at the inception of democracy acknowledged the legitimacy of the state accepting in principle its rights to use repressive powers to enforce the law even if that should involve the arrest of workers or unionists who have acted illegally.

Political Parties and Democratic Consolidation

Finally, the social capital developed in Spain prior to and during the process of democratic consolidation depended upon the efficacy of the emerging party system, especially its capacity to integrate and represent society. As seen already, in Spain the party system played the leading role in brokering the elite agreements that made possible the transition out of nearly 40 years of institutionalized authoritarian rule. This performance accounts for the fact that notwithstanding the alienation that Spaniards tend to profess toward parties, they are keenly aware of their importance to the functioning of the democratic system. "We know we need parties; but we don't like them," a stance hardly uncommon in mature democracies, including the

United States, is the attitude toward parties adopted by the Spaniards in the last decades.[70] The positive aspect of this attitude (the need for parties in a democracy) is reinforced by the very favorable memory of the performance of the political parties during the transition. Leonardo Morlino and José Montero's analysis of legitimacy and democracy in Spain, Italy, Portugal and Greece finds that "support for parties is most strongly related to democratic legitimacy in Spain."[71] They add that the most plausible explanation of this finding is that "it was in Spain that parties played the most important role in the transition to democracy, a highly successful transition."

The contribution of the party system in Spain to the project of democratization should not be taken to imply that Spain's party system resembles in any meaningful way conventional definitions of a coherent and well-organized party system. Largely owing to poor democratic traditions and historical difficulties in creating and sustaining associations of any type, the party system that consolidated in the post-Franco era hardly fits the model of institutional strength and links to society suggested by the United States and Britain and Latin American democracies such as Argentina, Chile and Uruguay.[72] A history of fragmentation, bitter internal feuds and low membership levels are some of the most pronounced characteristics of the political parties that dominated democratization politics in Spain. Nonetheless, several features about the constitution of the parties that were formed or resuscitated following the demise of the Franco regime proved to be invaluable assets to the new democracy, most notably deep links to the popular sectors, and more generally civil society, among the parties from the Left. The strength of the ties between the parties of the Left and mass and grassroots level organizations ensured that the Socialist and Communist parties would become part of the institutional cartel negotiating the democratic transition. This in turn allowed for the incorporation of important segments of civil society and their political agenda into the process of democratic consolidation. Indeed, it was the reach and influence of the PSOE and the PCE over the masses that explains why having initially opposed a model of democratic transition and consolidation based on compromises and political and social pacts, many civil society organizations eventually agreed to support it.

Strong Ties to Civil Society

The weakest link in Spain's party system at the inception of democracy was the ruling party. Usually described as a center-right party, the UCD lacked any history as a political institution.[73] It was hurriedly put together by progressive-minded Francoist insiders like Suárez in time for the 1977 elections and embraced a diverse political clientele including Liberals, Conservatives,

Christian Democrats and Social Democrats. The ideological heterogeneity of the party made it difficult for the organization to consolidate an institutional leadership and to develop a mass-based constituency, factors that eventually caused the collapse of the party in the early 1980s. At the inception of democracy, however, the UCD possessed important connections to emerging groups within civil society. The most important of these connections was the party's links to employers' organizations. Many within the UCD leadership, such as former prime minister Leopoldo Calvo Sotelo, were among Spain's leading capitalists and played a leading role in the founding of the CEOE in 1978, Spain's leading business association in the democratic period and the principal representative of capitalist interests in the social pacts.[74] This meant that at the time of the democratic transition the UCD enjoyed the capacity to enter into bargains on capital's behalf, much in the same manner in which the parties of the Left represented the interests of the labor movement during the making of the Moncloa accords.[75]

Paradoxically, the strength of the Spanish party system at the inception of democracy resided within the Socialist and Communist parties, which bore the brunt of Franco's repression and explicit ban on political parties. Throughout the transition to and consolidation of democracy both parties played to great effect the role that Linz has termed "the loyal opposition." It includes "commitment to participate in the political process, elections and parliamentary activity without setting up conditions beyond the guarantee of the necessary civil liberties for a reasonably fair democratic political process."[76] The willingness of the PSOE and the PCE to play this critical role throughout the process of democratization reflected the profound ideological transformation that had taken place within the Spanish Left since the volatile days of the Second Republic. During that fateful period in Spanish history, left-wing organizations had taken a leading role in radicalizing the workers and mobilizing them against conservative sectors such as the Church and the business community. In the new democracy, the parties of the Left once again would play a critical role in molding the political proclivities of the masses. But this time around, consensus and pragmatism rather than confrontation and extremism were the values imparted by left-wing parties to their civil society constituencies.

The role of the parties of the Left in Spanish democratization has three distinct phases. The first can be traced from the years preceding Franco's death in 1975 through the democratic elections of 1977. During this period the PSOE and the PCE, while still operating under the cloud of illegality, used their organizational resources and political expertise to organize society against the authoritarian order. At the center of this mobilization effort was the Communist party, which served as the incubator for the rebirth of Spanish civil society during the late Franco period. Indeed, it is virtually impossible to speak about the resurgence of civil society in Spain, as well as its incorporation into the politics of consensus of the democratic transition, without accounting for the actions of the Communist party. It literally created much of what we regard as civil society in Spain during the late Franco period and the early phase of political liberalization. Not surprisingly, by the time of the advent of the transition to democracy the PCE had the best-organized party structure including the most comprehensive network of chapters throughout the country, the largest membership and the deepest and most influential links to civil society.

Unlike the PSOE, whose leadership largely operated from outside of Spain during the long reign of the Franco regime, the PCE operated underground and devoted itself to creating clandestine organizations in an effort to fight the authoritarian regime from within its very structures.[77] In doing so it presented the most effective societal opposition to the Franco regime.[78] So closely associated was the Communist party with the struggle against Francoism that participation in its anti-Franco activities "made membership or collaboration with the Communist party almost a necessary rite of passage for the new generation of Spaniards coming onto the political scene."[79] In 1962, Communist leaders founded the *Unión de Juventudes Comunistas* (Union of Young Communists) to rally students against the Franco regime. A year later in 1963 Communist leaders organized the *Movimiento Democrático de Mujeres* (Women's Democratic Movement), a forerunner of the contemporary Spanish feminist movement, with the purpose of bringing non-working women into the anti-Franco struggle. The PCE was also the key player behind the organization of the grassroots neighborhood movement that sprung up around Madrid around the time of the democratic transition. It is reported that over 68 percent of the delegates attending the fourth congress of the Communist party were members of the neighborhood associations.[80]

Last, but certainly not least, during the final decades of the Franco dictatorship, the PCE employed the nascent labor movement organized around the CCOO, which the party fully controlled by the mid-1960s, as its key instrument in the fight against Francoism. It did so by facilitating the union's penetration of the vertical syndicate and providing an organizational nucleus for the mobilization of the workers. By the late 1960s, illegally formed unions were leading demonstrations in Madrid with workers chanting "Franco no, democracy yes."[81] These mobilizations, as seen previously, increased in the aftermath of Franco's death and were critical in provoking the crisis within the authoritarian state that triggered the democratic transition. But it is important to highlight that they were not spontaneous expressions of civil society activism, but rather part of a broader political strategy orchestrated by the PCE to erode the foundation of authoritarianism in Spain by mobilizing civil society. Their success did not depend on the organizational capacity of the resurgent unions but rather on that of the PCE leadership. As explained by Collier: "The first reason why Spanish labor was well positioned to open space within the authoritarian regime and to lead the pro-democratic protest was the advantage brought by the leadership of the Communists, who could draw on a tradition and experience of unusual organizational capacity and underground strategizing."[82]

Incorporating Civil Society

The second and perhaps most important phase of the role of the parties of the Left in Spanish democratization began with the victory of the UCD in the 1977 elections. At this point the PSOE and especially the PCE dramatically shifted their political strategies. Confrontation came to an end as both parties agreed to cooperate with the newly elected democratic government for the sake of attaining a consolidated democracy. This cooperation was made possible by Suárez's willingness to open negotiations with the opposition as well as the desire of the leadership of both the PSOE and the PCE to put their own troubled political past to rest. After 1977, the Socialist and Communist parties worked diligently to project an image of moderation and of belonging to the political establishment as a way to distance themselves from the politics of extremism that had marked their prior participation in electoral politics. They supported Suárez's politics of consensus as suggested by their strong endorsement of the Moncloa accords, negotiated a consensual constitution, induced labor's cooperation with the government and incorporated civil society at critical points when the new democracy seemed in peril.

The incorporation of civil society carried out by the PSOE and the PCE after 1977 entailed, in essence, deactivating a wide range of social movements soon after many of them had been created or liberalized. In signing the 1977 Moncloa accords, the Socialist and Communist parties agreed to restrain the unions from excessive striking. This is one of the key reasons why Spain's entire process of democratization was spared general strikes, which in other national settings (and in other periods of Spanish history such as the interwar years) proved to be disastrous for political stability. Other segments of civil society were also deactivated by the Left once the process of political pacting got underway. For instance, the end of the vigorous mobilizations organized by grassroots, urban movements came to an abrupt end once the leadership of the Communist party made the decision to support a negotiated transition to democracy. As reported by a study of neighborhood activism in Spain around the time of the democratic transition, "the PCE's strategic changes shaped the strategies of the neighborhood movement by virtue of their close ties."[83] The analysis notes that together with withdrawing its political demands for a democratic rupture, which would have excluded authoritarian elites from the democratization process, the neighborhood movement accepted the negotiated settlement organized by the parties and the government.

Similar dynamics to those dictating the grassroots movements' acceptance of a negotiated regime change shaped the trade unions' acceptance of the Moncloa accords in 1977. Notwithstanding the much-discussed moderation of the Spanish working class during the transition, union leaders did not enter democracy predisposed toward accepting explicit compromises with either the state or the employers. Ideological reasons dictated that at the inception of democracy labor elites were opposed to direct involvement of the unions in policy-making. For many UGT leaders, their objection to pacts stemmed from their historic opposition to cooperation with an authoritarian state that for decades had repressed labor rights. For many CCOO leaders, the participation of the unions in pacts amounted to class betrayal. Emblematic of this perspective was that offered to *El País*, Spain's leading newspaper, by Nicolás Sartorious, a noted labor leader during the transition. Around the time when Suárez began to talk about a social pact, Sartorious warned that the labor movement should oppose such a pact because it "would hurt the process of democratization by diminishing the role of agent of political change for the working class."[84]

Despite their reservations about pacts, neither the UGT nor the CCOO was willing to contradict or even challenge the political decision made by the Socialist and Communist parties to support the Moncloa accords and the larger policy of social concertation. In the end the unions were willing to set organizational and ideological proclivities aside for the sake of complying with the objectives of their parent organizations. Certainly, the deference that the unions paid to the political parties during the transition reflected a significant degree of trust and confidence in the ability of the Socialist and Communist parties to articulate and represent the interest of the workers, a role that these parties played to great effect. At the inception of democracy, the Left's conditions for delivering union support for the policy of pacts were best expressed by Santiago Carrillo, the very pragmatic leader of the PCE, who prior to the transition had severed ties with Moscow and turned the PCE into a prominent exponent of

"Euro-communism." He noted that the Communists' demand for participating in a social pact and inducing the labor movement to comply with its stipulations was simple: that the "sacrifices" and "advantages" of any pact be adequately distributed.[85]

The willingness of the left-wing parties to cooperate with the government, while decried by many a party faithful who had hoped for a radical form of regime change, proved to be a boon for both democracy and civil society. It is difficult, if not impossible, to envision the gains made by civil society in Spain between the years of 1976–1982 without the mentoring and support it enjoyed from the parties from the Left. Throughout the years of democratic transition, the PSOE and the PCE were highly effective vehicles for advancing a wide range of civil society objectives. They include the early liberalization of the trade unions from the trappings of the Francoist vertical syndicate, the extension of a wide range of rights to the workers, as well as the socioeconomic gains made by the labor movement through the policy of social concertation from 1977 through its expiration in 1986. These concessions and provisions were a condition for the Left's support for a negotiated process of regime change.

Clearly, contrary to what civil society theorists would suggest, the demobilization and ensuing decline of civil society in Spain carried out by the Left after 1977 did not hinder progress toward a consolidated democracy. Quite the contrary, the Spanish experience suggests that it was only after civil society was demobilized and incorporated into the pro-democracy work of the political system and after it began to shift its strategies from confrontation toward cooperation that democratic consolidation became a reality. Of course, only political institutions deserving of civil society's confidence and deference could manage this feat.

Democratic Consolidation under a Socialist Party

The third and final phase of the Left's role in the consolidation of Spanish democracy commenced with the PSOE's victory in the 1982 elections. They are generally deemed the most important in the new democracy since the foundation elections of 1977. The 1982 elections represented the first time since the 1930s that a left-wing party ruled Spain, a sign of political maturity in the eyes of many, and by extension of democratic consolidation. As noted in chapter 3, 1982 is generally accepted as the year that democracy consolidated in Spain. The 1982 elections were also important for what they meant for the PSOE as a political organization. On the one hand was the impressive level of support granted by the voters (over 50 percent of parliamentary seats); on the other hand was the symbolism conveyed by the party's stunning electoral success. Entirely absent from politics during the long life of the Franco regime, and partially eclipsed by the Communist party during the democratic transition, the 1982 elections represented the PSOE's political comeback and an amazing story of institutional survival.

The PSOE's deep, historical roots in society largely explain the vigorous renaissance of Socialism in post-Franco Spain. Founded in 1879, the PSOE is Spain's oldest political party. The party grew rapidly during the interwar years reaching over 80,000 members in 1933, making it one of the leading parties of the Second Republic.[86] Its most important investment in civil society prior to the advent of the Franco regime was the founding of UGT in 1888, whose membership by the 1930s had reached 1.4 million. Until the transition to democracy of the late 1970s, the so-called Socialist family comprising of the PSOE and the UGT fought the common struggle for workers' rights, socialism and democracy. This struggle was interrupted with the collapse of the Second Republic and the rise to power of the Franco regime, which either jailed or forced into exile the entire PSOE leadership. But despite the repression of the Franco era, the PSOE did not fade way.

Assisting in the resuscitation of the PSOE after 1977 was the survival of left-wing loyalties across generations in communities and families across Spain, especially in such enclaves of working-class militancy as Asturias, metal and steel workers in the Basque country, Barcelona and Madrid. Maravall reports that as many as 37.3 percent of the delegates to the 28th Congress of the PSOE in 1979 were children of parents who had been affiliated either to the PSOE or to the Socialist trade union (the UGT).[87] This finding, in his view, suggests that the case of Spain would support the theory of intergenerational ideological transmission through processes of socialization within the family. The PSOE's rehabilitation was also aided by the work of the exile community and underground resistance leaders inside of Spain. The party held its post-Civil War party congress in 1944 in France and soon after began to reorganize itself in Spain mostly inside the jails of the Franco regime, which housed thousands of PSOE leaders. Simultaneously, it began to organize the first strikes against Franco and to revive the UGT, which had been banned by Franco following the end of the Civil War in 1939.

Between 1982 through 1996, the PSOE dominated Spanish politics like no other party has in the nation's relatively short history of democratic politics. The PSOE repeatedly won national elections between 1982 and 1996 and retained a parliamentary majority until 1993. The party also became an umbrella for a variety of social movements that saw in the political rise of the PSOE the best venue for advancing their political objectives. Under PSOE rule, the UGT surpassed the CCOO as the nation's leading trade union and consolidated its presence in many Spanish firms and the national policy-making process through its participation in the policy of social concertation. From this position of influence, the UGT secured a wide range of social and economic rights for the Spanish working class (more on this later).

Women's groups, whose growth in Spain has historically been stunted by a highly conservative Catholic Church and the very late entry of females into the workforce, saw their political fortunes rise alongside those of the PSOE. While this alliance has been criticized for corporatizing the feminist agenda in Spain and making women's groups part of the political system rather than an independent movement, the benefits for Spanish women speak for themselves.[88] In 1983, the party created the *Instituto de la Mujer* (Women's Institute), a government agency that funds self-managed groups, develops policy and organizes media and educational campaigns. In 1984, the PSOE took on the Catholic Church and the business community, and legalized abortion and incorporated family planning into universal healthcare. The party also enacted strict quotas intended to improve the representation of females within the PSOE as a means to increase the presence of women in public service. In 1988, the PSOE imposed a quota of 25 percent of women in party-controlled posts and in 1996 it adopted a quota of equal representation of both sexes in party committees and electoral lists. This policy has been emulated by other parties at both the national and regional levels and accounts for the impressive advance in representation by women in the Spanish national Congress. While in 1977 only 6 percent of members of congress were females, at the present time, 28.3 percent of the members of the lower house are females and 24.3 percent in the Senate.

The absolute parliamentary majorities that the PSOE enjoyed for much of its time in office, together with a significant degree of internal discipline and the steadfast leadership of Felipe González, proved ideal conditions for executing politically sensitive tasks such as the negotiation of Spain's entry into NATO, historically opposed by the Spanish Left. The PSOE's strength was even more important for the implementation of industrial restructuring, a task delayed or ignored by the UCD.[89] Privatization of Franco's massive industrial complex (grouped around the *Instituto Nacional de Industria*, INI) was accomplished with dazzling speed. A single legislative stroke, the 1984 Law of Industrial Reconversion and Reindustrialization, targeted eleven sectors for reform. This objective was largely realized. By the end of the PSOE's first term in office in 1986 the party sold or dissolved more than 30 state enterprises and the number of jobs at INI-related enterprises fell from 219,000 in 1982 to 160,000 by 1987.

The political and economic successes of the Socialist period account for much of the acclaim the case of Spain has received from experts of democratic consolidation and economic reform. These successes have encouraged a parade of international visitors to the country eager to learn from the Spanish experience with "a dual transition" and turned Prime Minister Felipe González into an international celebrity, especially in Latin America. The Socialist years in Spain, however, were not without noticeable blemishes including several high-profile corruption scandals, complaints by the unions and other allies of arrogance among the party leadership and a covert, dirty war against ETA. They featured prominently in the defeat of the PSOE in the elections of 1996, which saw the rise of *Partido Popular* (PP), the moderate conservative party that currently rules Spain.

Ironically, the one problem that truly marred Spain's Socialist experiment, the country's rise to the very top of Western Europe's unemployment rankings, appears to have been of very little consequence to both the party's defeat and, more significantly, to the process of democratic consolidation. The crisis of unemployment in Spain peaked in the early 1990s at 24 percent or 3.7 million of the active population, a shocking figure considering that under Franco the nation enjoyed Europe's lowest rate of unemployment, averaging 1.5 percent between 1965 and 1974.[90] This dramatic upheaval in the nation's employment picture has led observers to suggest that with the transition to democracy Spaniards "swapped job security for political freedoms."[91] But as suggested by Maravall, in Spain "high unemployment had only limited political consequences. Not only did it not weaken support for democracy, but neither did it prove politically catastrophic for the government."[92] The PSOE repeatedly won national elections between 1982–1993. Moreover, support of the PSOE among the unemployed remained high even during the party's defeat in 1996.

Key to understanding the apparent lack of adverse impact of economic reform upon Spain's democratic institutions is the fact that by the time the economy was liberalized, the democratic political system was widely deemed to have consolidated. Credit for this political happening is usually given to the Socialist party, who came to power following the military coup of 1981. As noted by Morlino and Montero, the popularity of the PSOE in Spain derived from the perception that it had contributed "decisively" to the consolidation of a new democratic regime.[93] By contrast, they observe that in "Portugal and Italy parties are seen as less associated with democracy and more with conflict, instability and poor performance."

Also relevant in understanding how democratic legitimacy was protected in Spain is the policy-making style adopted by the PSOE to implement market-oriented reforms. Widely referred to in the comparative literature on economic reform as "social democratic," this approach is noted first and foremost by the willingness of the government to consult with societal actors and use representative institutions such as the party system and the unions in the implementation of the reform program. By most accounts, this was the case in Spain. Przeworski notes that: "the Spanish socialist government succeeded in conducting the country through a painful program of industrial reconversion with widespread consultation channeled through representative institutions."[94] In Spain this consultation was facilitated by the support the PSOE enjoyed from the unions in the early 1980s but also by the existing framework for societal bargaining established during the transition in the late 1970s. As noted by Pérez Díaz, the policy of industrial reconversion, although outside of the social contracts, benefited from a climate of "continuous conversation between the government, employers and unions."[95]

A second feature of economic reform in Spain of relevance to the nation's politics of democratic consolidation is that although complains from the unions about economic reform and related matters led to a bitter divorce between the PSOE and its long-time ally the UGT, the PSOE never abandoned its redistributive agenda. By the end of the 1980s, Spain was "one of the rare industrial democracies to have undergone a redistribution of income in favor of the poorer strata."[96] This is reflected in the phenomenal growth of social spending in Spain in the democratic era, especially during the Socialist years. In 1975, social spending in Spain stood at 558.2 billion pesetas and 9.2 percent of GDP; by 1986 these figures had climbed to 4,503.6 billion pesetas or 13.9 of GDP; and by 1991 they had soared to 8,385.4 billion pesetas and 15.3 percent of GDP.[97] These figures suggest that in Spain, democratic stability (and perhaps even more importantly democratic legitimacy) was protected by the government's willingness to compensate and protect those most directly affected by economic change.

In sum, the Spanish experience suggests the critical, leading role played by political institutions in bringing about a highly successful process of democratic consolidation. This role entailed not only the conventional tasks usually assigned to political institutions in organizing and maintaining a democratic system, but also those currently being attributed to a strong civil society, most notably the production of social capital. In Spain, the effective performance of post-transition governments can be credited with fostering national unity and solidarity around the project of democratization. The social and economic well-being engineered by the state prior to the transition provided the foundation for the rise of a mode of doing politics (if not an altogether new political culture) based on trust, reciprocity and cooperation. Finally, political parties proved highly effective instruments for socializing the general public into the ways of democracy and for increasing the political capacity of civil society organizations (from neighborhood associations to the trade unions) to press their demands against the state and deepen the process of democratization.

PART III

Brazil: Strong Civil Society, Weak Democracy

CHAPTER 5

Brazilian Civil Society in Transition Politics

T he case of Brazil, like that of Spain, pointedly contradicts the conventional wisdom about civil society and democratic consolidation. Brazil undertook to democratize with a civil society whose vibrancy and robustness would have made Tocqueville proud. But this particular feature of Brazilian civil society, as suggested in this chapter, has been of questionable relevance to the actual consolidation of democracy. While democracy survives in Brazil—which is more democratic today than at any other time in its history—democratic survival is not consolidation. As noted previously, democratic consolidation supposes a wide range of attitudinal, institutional and procedural requirements that Brazilian democracy simply does not meet, including civilian control of the military, adherence to the rule of law, governmental accountability, widespread respect for civil and human rights and especially mass support for democracy. These are, of course, some of the very tasks that a vibrant and robust civil society is meant to facilitate.

The Civil Society Landscape

Several notable developments characterize the resurgence of civil society in Brazil since the country embraced political liberalization in the mid-1970s. The first and perhaps most obvious is that the expansion of civil society in Brazil got underway well before the onset of the formal transition to democracy. In most scholarly estimates, the awakening of Brazilian society began in the "effervescent 1960s" well before the military had given any indication of a willingness to return the country to civilian rule.[1] A second development worth noting is the diversity of Brazilian civil society. Upon undertaking democratization, Brazil witnessed "an historic awakening of new forms of social creativity and resistance in virtually all components of civil society, such as entrepreneurs, the press, lawyer associations, church organizations, labor unions and women's groups," of unparalleled proportions in Brazilian history and anywhere in Latin America.[2] These developments, in Alfred Stepan's apt description, made Brazilian civil society "the political celebrity of the democratic transition."[3]

A third and final notable aspect in the evolution of civil society in Brazil is that its growth has not been stunted by the democratic transition, as has been the case in many other new democracies. In Brazil, the period of democratic consolidation has proved to be as auspicious for the expansion of civil society as the country's political liberalization. To be sure, many of the social movements that gave Brazilian civil society its strength in the aftermath of authoritarian rule have lost some steam in recent years leading some scholars to write about the "partial" decline of social movement politics in Brazil.[4] However, as shown later in this chapter, in recent years newer and larger social movements, such as the mobilization of landless peasants, have joined older groups born or reborn with the democratic transition such as the labor movement and neighborhood associations further enriching the Brazilian associational landscape. A recent overview of the state of democracy in Brazil notes that "the rapidly increasing density of Brazilian civil society constitute what is arguably the most striking difference between the political landscape in the 1990s and that of the previous democratic experiments in 1946–1964. Today, a vibrant and diverse network of fully autonomous, secondary associations provides a countervailing force against state power."[5]

Associational Density

The explosive growth of civil society organizations in Brazil explains the very healthy rates of civic engagement exhibited by the country's new democracy as well as the organizational strength of many of the new social movements and nongovernmental organizations born with the democratic transition. The *World Values Survey* places Brazil at the top among Iberian-Latin nations in terms of the overall density of associational life (see appendix). Indeed, when contrasted to the Brazilian case, civic life in Spain and Portugal, not to speak of neighboring Argentina and Uruguay, is positively anemic. More revealing, perhaps, is that Brazil's organizational cumulative percentage (85 percent) is quoted as being higher than that of many industrially advanced democracies such as France and Italy and just below that of Britain and Ireland.

A more fine-grained portrait of civil society in Brazil is provided by a study on participation in voluntary associations in new democracies by Peter McDonough, Doh C. Shin and José Álvaro Moisés.[6] The central finding of their study is that only about one-third of citizens in Brazil fail to belong to a voluntary association. This proportion of the citizenry involved in voluntary groups is lower than that of Korea, where nine out of ten citizens claim to belong to some sort of intermediate organization. But it towers over that of Spain, where, as seen already, only about a third of the public belongs to any voluntary association. The picture of voluntary association participation in Brazil becomes more clear and impressive when broken down into specific categories and when contrasted with other countries.

The study reports that 18 percent of Brazilian males and 14 percent of Brazilian females belong to a neighborhood association. The percentages for Korea are 17 for males and 9 for females; and for Spain, 7 for females and 10 for men. The study also reports that 11 percent of females in Brazil belong to a labor syndicate and 23 percent of males. The percentages for Korea are 19 for men and 13 for females; and for Spain, 8 percent for males and 2 for females. The study also notes that 28 percent of males in Brazil belong to an athletic club and 17 for females. The percentages for Korea are 25 for males and 11 for females; and for Spain, 13 for males and 5 for females. As for other voluntary associations, 40 percent of Brazilian women report an affiliation with grassroots religious groups and 31 for males. The percentages for Korea are 39 percent for females and 32 percent for males; and for Spain, 3 for females and 2 for men.

Grassroots Movements

Brazil's active civic life mirrors the expansive growth of all types of voluntary associations created in the democratic period including a variety of advocacy-oriented organizations. Prominent among these groups are grassroots movements and organizations in both urban and rural areas that sought to expand the boundaries of the political sphere in a country traditionally identified with political elitism. They include Church-affiliated groups, landless peasant movements, rural unions and cooperatives and neighborhood associations, especially those organized by shantytown dwellers (so-called *favelados*). It is estimated that by the early 1980s, the number of neighborhood associations had reached 8,000 in Brazil, with an estimated 550 in Rio de Janeiro and 900 in São Paulo.[7] Dominating the agenda of the neighborhood movement at the time of their birth in the early 1960s were material needs such as housing, healthcare and education. But by the late 1970s, the agenda shifted as they began to pursue "issues related with democratization of the society, such as party reform, political amnesty and reform of local government."[8]

Another important grassroots movement born with the democratic transition is the world famous *Comunidades Eclesiais de Base,* CEBs (grassroots church communities), a network of citizens' associations sponsored by the hierarchy of the Brazilian Catholic Church, headed by the National Conference of Brazilian Bishops.[9] Since their appearance in the mid-1960s, the CEBs have spread like wildfire and numbered some 100,000 chapters by the mid-1980s (with each chapter comprising between 50 and 100 people) organized along the length and breadth of the Catholic Church in Brazil. The intellectual roots of this movement were laid out at the Second Conference of Latin American Bishops in Medellín in October of 1968. Its core mission was to secure for the Catholic Church in Latin America a more meaningful role in the lives of ordinary people by injecting the basic principles of social and economic justice pronounced in the Second Vatican Council. At the time of their appearance, the CEBs generated considerable enthusiasm with respect to their potential for transforming Brazilian society. Indeed, some accounts of the CEB's birth and their expected impact on politics and society offer sweeping support for neo-Tocquevillean beliefs about the capacity of voluntary groupings to engender pro-democratic proclivities. Ralph Della Cava writes that the CEBs have become as much an "alternative" forum of cultic organization as they are "schools" for educating the exploited in their inalienable human rights, by articulating the most radical, people's critique of Brazilian capitalism and an equally spirited defense of a new socialist order.[10]

Advocacy Groups and Social Movements

Brazil also scores high with respect to the vibrancy of nongovernmental advocacy groups. According to one study, in the developing world, only India, whose population dwarfs that of Brazil, is believed to have more NGOs.[11] It is estimated that in the city of São Paulo alone, 45,000 NGOs are active in a variety of societal pursuits including human rights, the environment and social welfare. Most of these organizations are small, with budgets of less than US$30,000. Nationally, it is estimated that NGOs in Brazil control over US$1.4 billion in resources of which $400 comes from abroad and employ over 1 million people or about 2 percent of total employment in Brazil. With this phenomenal growth has come significant political clout and popular recognition. The NGO world in Brazil is organized around a single umbrella organization, the Association of Brazilian NGOs (ABONG), which meets regularly to coordinate the activities of its many members. This has allowed individual NGO leaders "to become political figures in their own right" who are "regularly consulted by political leaders who have noticed their influence."[12] Flowing from this position of power, is an extraordinary degree of familiarity among the general public with the existence and functions of NGOs. It is reported that the "the label NGO (ONG in Brazil) has passed into the vernacular for many Brazilians and most newspapers use the initials without spelling out the acronym."[13]

Engendering and sustaining the NGO revolution in Brazil is a vast and complex network of organized social movements whose aim is to assert new or submerged identities as well as to channel political demands from groups traditionally excluded from the public sphere. Since the 1970s, Brazil has developed Latin America's largest, strongest and most diverse women's movement. Sonia A. Alvarez reports that "starting in the mid-1970s, both university-educated, middle class women, poor, and uneducated women organized movements to press their gender-specific political claims on the Brazilian political system."[14] By the late 1980s, Alvarez notes that as many as 400 feminist organizations were active in Brazil promoting a political agenda comprising issues previously kept hidden from public discourses: reproductive rights, day care and violence against women, among others.[15] Also noteworthy is that unlike analogous movements that appeared in Latin America around the same time, women's movements in Brazil "did not fade away."[16] Since the late 1980s, "the arenas of gender struggle have in fact multiplied" with the emergence of a large and highly diverse universe of women's groups.[17] Especially impressive has been the growth of organizations with "overwhelmingly working-class memberships" devoted to serving "women at the bottom of the bottom."[18]

Other social groups traditionally excluded from politics have emulated the example set by Brazil's women's movement.[19] Groups such as São Paulo's SOMOS, Rio de Janeiro's Pink Triangle Group and the Gay Group of Bahia (all founded in the late 1970s) emerged demanding civil rights for gays and lesbians and recognition from the state that "everyone had the right to pleasure and to sexual gratification, regardless of whether the object of his or her desire was a member of the opposite sex."[20] The environmental movement is thought to have "exploded during the run-up to the Earth Summit in Rio in 1992."[21] For its part, the Unified Black movement, founded in 1978, assumed the daunting task of combating the myth of the existence of a "racial democracy" in Brazil.

The Labor Movement

Notwithstanding the vibrancy of other social movements, it is Brazil's "new unionism" that provides the face of Brazil's reinvigorated civil society.[22] This is quite a turnaround for organized labor in Brazil, once regarded a backward giant in Latin American labor politics because its unions have traditionally been small, weak, organizationally anemic and easily co-opted and dominated by the state. A late 1960s review of Latin American labor movements concludes that "in no other Latin American country does the state control unions so completely as in Brazil."[23] This image of Brazilian labor has been effectively shattered in the last two decades. Anthony W. Pereira writes that "the labor movements of Argentina and Chile, once seen as far more class-conscious and militant than their Brazilian counterpart, now seem weaker by comparison."[24] This newly acquired status for Brazilian labor can be traced to the emergence of new workers' organizations during the late 1970s that in both spirit and structure significantly altered the landscape of labor politics in the country.

The vibrancy of Brazilian labor is best reflected in the emergence of the *Central Unica dos Trabalhadores,* CUT (Central Workers' Organization), Brazil's largest and most influential union and the most emblematic of the organizations lumped together under the rubric of the "new unionism."[25] The CUT was formed in fierce and violent confrontation with the state in 1983 by metalworkers in the state of São Paulo who saw little gain in using existing channels to advance the cause of the working class. Prominent among them was Luiz Inácio da Silva, better known as "Lula," the current president of Brazil, who would become the personification of the new unionism. The CUT represents something entirely new in Brazilian labor politics. Since its creation the organization saw shop-floor militancy as the only route to labor autonomy both within and outside the workplace, by most indicators a winning strategy. The organization's success in garnering support from the workers made it "practically a parallel trade unionism" to the state's official unions long before the formal transition to democracy.[26]

Pivotal to the rise of the CUT and its agenda of labor autonomy was the landmark strike of May 1978 within the automobile industry. It involved millions of workers and impacted a wide range of sectors of the economy including education, banking and commerce. The strike was triggered by demands for direct wage negotiations with management without interference from the government or the labor court, an objective that was successfully obtained. A jubilant Lula declared that the workers' victory in 1978 was evidence of "the bankruptcy of the existing official trade union structure and also the current strike law."[27] In attacking the existing labor structures, the CUT stood in stark contrast to the "self-interested labor careerists" (the so-called *pelegos*), who supported the government and the official labor system.[28]

The strength of Brazilian labor is also reflected in the phenomenal growth of independent unions in Brazil (the CUT in particular) since the early

1980s. Bucking a worldwide trend that emerged in the early 1980s that saw union affiliation rates plummet all over the world (especially in newly democratic nations), Brazilian unions have grown by leaps and bounds in the last decades. By 1986, the CUT had 1,000 union affiliates and 1,400 by 1989. Currently, the organization controls over 2,000 unions, representing some 20 million workers or a quarter of the voting population.[29] Such developments reflect a dramatic swelling in union membership rolls nationwide in every sector of the national economy as well as a growing appeal for unions among Brazilian workers. At the present time, Brazil belongs to the top tier of Western Hemisphere nations with more than a quarter of its population belonging to a union. In the Americas, only Canada with 29 percent and Argentina with 30 percent surpass Brazil's rate of union affiliation.

Possessing the largest unionized labor force in the Americas is another notable distinction of the Brazilian labor scene. The combined membership of the CUT, the *Central Geral dos Trabalhadores*, CGT (General Workers' Command), a union affiliated with the Brazilian Communist party, the *União Sindical Independente*, USI (Independent Syndical Union), a union affiliated with conservative actors in Brazilian society, and the *Confederação Nacional de Trabalhadores na Agricultura*, CONTAG (National Confederation of Agrarian Workers), an organization that represents more than 3,000 rural unions with a combined membership of over 10 million, may well exceed 30 million.[30] The unions' global budget is thought to exceed 1 billion dollars, which finances the operations of some 10,000 unions involved in more than 30,000 collective agreements, made possible largely by a compulsory *imposto sindical* (syndical tax), which goes directly from the workers' salaries into the unions' coffers.[31]

Labor's strength in Brazil is also evident in the workers' mobilization since the democratic transition.[32] Between 1983 and 1989, the peak years of political liberalization and democratization, the number of strikes rose from 293 in 1983 to 1,201 in 1987, representing one the most intense periods of labor unrest in contemporary Brazil. Furthermore, it is estimated that due to the intensity and widespread nature of strikes in Brazil, between 1976 and 1987 the country lost more workdays in strikes per 100,000 workers than many other countries with reputations for combative labor movements, including Spain, Italy, the United Kingdom and Germany.[33]

Explaining the Vibrancy of Brazilian Civil Society

The strong resurgence of civil society begun in Brazil in the early 1960s is in and of itself puzzling. As Stepan reminds us, "in historical terms Brazil has long stood out as the major Latin American country where state power has most structured and controlled civil society, especially the popular sectors."[34] Broad comparisons with its neighbors bear this out. Unlike Argentina, Chile and Uruguay, Brazil historically has lacked strong working-class unions or political parties, nor has the country experienced a peasant-based upheaval of the like that took place in Mexico. These comparisons suggest that the expansion of Brazilian civil society is a relatively recent phenomenon of direct connection to the nature of the authoritarian regime established in Brazil in 1964 and the dynamics of the transition to democracy begun ten years later.

Societal Spaces for Organization

In contrast to Franco's Spain and its sister "bureaucratic-authoritarian" regimes in South America, the Brazilian military tolerated a variety of spaces for societal organization without direct interference from the state as long as such spaces did not appear to explicitly threaten the stability or legitimacy of the regime.[35] This led to the creation of an environment in which certain segments of civil society could flourish well before the transition to democracy formally took place. While harshly repressing certain forms of civil society organization and mobilization (such as independently organized trade unions), the military in Brazil chose not to regulate others such as neighborhood associations, poor people's movements, women's groups and religious organizations. Thus unlike other cases of democratization in which the resurgence of civil society was a mere reflection of political liberalization, such as Spain, in Brazil a resurgent civil society had deeper roots and a firmer, autonomous institutional foundation from which to form and expand.

In time, social sites regarded by the military as "non-political" became highly politicized, especially after 1974, when the military formally committed itself to returning the nation to civilian rule. A notable example of this organizational trajectory is that of the CEBs. Funded in 1964 as essentially a nonpolitical religious institution, by the 1970s many of the individual chapters had assumed a "para-political mission, allying themselves with opposition parties and adding to the repertoire of insurgent social movements."[36] It is reported that "departures from religious life grew amid clerical cadres, and this shortfall amplified incentives to lay involvement in church affairs and, by extension, in politics *writ large*."[37]

Further boosting the organizational opportunities for civil society development under military rule in Brazil was the fact that the military government allowed the National Congress and state legislatures to remain open. A related development was the decision not to ban all political parties, thus allowing for a meaningful degree of party competition albeit under the watchful eye of the state since the military felt compelled to sponsor national and local elections. This was the case with the elections of 1974, in which the military-sponsored political party, the *Aliança Renovadora Nacional*, ARENA, later renamed *Partido Democrático Social*, PDS (Democratic Social Party), was successfully challenged by the lone opposition party, the *Movimento Democrático Brasileiro*, MDB (Brazilian Democratic Movement), later renamed PMDB. The military government created the MDB as part of the effort to create a two-party system. To its surprise, the MDB won 16 of 22 contested congressional seats, putting into motion the transition to democracy.

The "liberal" attitude of the military regime toward political parties and elections left a very troubled legacy for Brazil's emerging democracy. On the one hand, the elections of 1974 and the military's regime willingness to accept its defeat officially put the country on the path toward democracy and set the foundation for the emergence of a democratic alternative to the authoritarian order. As noted by Thomas Skidmore, "however distorted or insincere their claim, they (the military) did allow at least a segment of the civilian opposition to remain active, especially in congress. The Congressional opposition was therefore able to maintain a thread of demo-cratic legitimacy, even if their votes were buried or disallowed."[38] On the other hand, as suggested later, the apparent "respect" that the military paid to the electoral process was perversely used to manipulate the transition. Furthermore, the democratic opposition's willingness to cooperate with the military regime (or at the very least to play by its rules) made it harder for political parties to gain the trust and respect of civil society.

The Role of Religious Institutions

A second factor behind Brazil's resurgent civil society was the role played by the Catholic Church in organizing and mobilizing the masses during the transition to democracy.[39] This role can hardly be underestimated. In the multi-case analysis of democratization and political participation conducted by McDonough and his collaborators, the Catholic Church is a central explanatory variable for why Brazil bests Spain in levels of civic engagement, no matter how they are calibrated. Facilitating the Catholic Church's pro-motion of civil society in Brazil was its behavior under authoritarian rule. In contrast to other Iberian-Latin countries, such as Spain and Argentina, where the Catholic Church acted as an accomplice to the authoritarian regime, in Brazil such explicit complicity did not materialize. In Brazil, there was no preexisting relationship between the Catholic Church establishment and the authoritarian state, thereby affording the Church the legitimacy and the autonomy to assume an important role in the country's democratizing process with few parallels in the Iberian-Latin world. Consequently, while the Spanish Catholic Church stayed on the sidelines during the transition even refraining from organizing and mobilizing its followers, the Brazilian Catholic Church adopted the very opposite strategy.

Emboldened by the Medellin bishops' conference of 1968, the Brazilian Catholic Church began to encourage the masses to confront the authoritarian state, to marshal its opposition to military rule and to point out to the state its multiple social and economic failures. It is reported that after Medellin, "the once bipolarized conference of bishops (CNBB) converged into a single centrist defense of civil liberties and human rights."[40] This work began in Brazil's impoverished northeast, whose bishops had pioneered since the mid-1950s "new forms of church organization, consciousness raising campaigns for adult literacy, and the first, albeit ecclesiastically controlled and ideologically anti-Communist, mobilizations of rural workers."[41] Gradually, the Church in the industrialized South began to join the revolution of bishops ignited in the Northeast, denouncing the military regime and siding with the opposition on a wide range of issues including political liberalization.

The chief vehicle in the Church's agenda for popular mobilization in Brazil was the previously mentioned CEBs. Critical to their popularity was a message that offered a pointed critique of the government's economic failures and human rights abuses. From their earliest beginnings as a new form of Church structure, the ecclesiastical architects of the CEBs promoted this message among the poor, the jobless and unionized workers. The Brazilian Catholic Church also played an important role in supporting the expansion of the labor movement and shaping its ideological orientations. During the emblematic strikes of the late 1970s, the Church sided with the striking metalworkers, providing a much-needed source of moral, emotional and financial support. Church leaders were also active in organizing and mobilizing workers in the countryside. The Catholic Church's land pastoral (*Comissão Pastoral da Terra*, CPT) is credited with "promoting a combative leadership in the rural unions."[42] Catholic activists also influenced the development of the Workers' Party (PT). Margaret Keck writes that the party's "emphasis on working class-development and mistrust of State and parliamentary institutions were a direct inheritance from both the *autêntico* (authentic) unions and from grassroots-oriented Catholic activism."[43]

Since the demise of military rule in the mid-1980s, there has been a marked decline in political activism by the Catholic Church in Brazil, but this has not meant a decline in the role of religious institutions in stimulating voluntary associationalism among Brazilians. In the last decades, Brazil has witnessed an explosion in the growth of Protestant churches, with their share of the population expanding from 4 percent in 1960 to 15 percent by the mid-1990s.[44] This growth has posed a significant challenge to Brazilian Catholicism while simultaneously diversifying the country's religious life and thickening civil society. Leading the way is a thriving Pentecostal movement headed by the *Igreja Universal do Reino de Deus* (IURD, Universal Church Kingdom of God). The IURD "embraces an economically oriented, individualistic prosperity theology, relies on the media to propagate its message, and is heavily involved in politics."[45]

By all accounts, the IURD's growth has been nothing short of breathtaking. Started in 1977, by the 1990s the IURD had several million members spread across temples all over Brazil, collected as much as $1 billion per year in tithes, and owned Brazil's third largest television network, 30 radio stations, 2 newspapers, a bank and other interests.[46] Just as impressive is the organization's political reach as evident in the emergence of an evangelical coalition in the Brazilian Congress (the so-called *bancada evangélica*), which after the 1998 elections held 35 seats, 14 of them occupied by IURD members. Less evident is the political work conducted by Pentecostal groups such as the IURD at the grassroots level. Around election time, Pentecostal churches often outdo Brazil's notoriously disorganized political parties in organizing their members and demanding political discipline from them.[47]

A Protracted Democratic Transition

A third factor that explains the exuberance of Brazilian civil society is, paradoxically, the controlled and protracted nature of the process of democratization. In striking contrast to the Spanish case or that of many other Latin American nations, political liberalization in Brazil did not lead to a clear rupture with the authoritarian past and to the unequivocal commencement of democratic practices. At least 17 years in the making (and perhaps longer), Brazil's transition to democracy forced civil society to sustain a longer and more intense period of mobilization and opposition against the retreating authoritarian regime than that carried out by civil society in many other Iberian-Latin countries.

The transition to democracy in Brazil began effectively in 1974, earlier than any other democratic transition in Southern Europe or South America. It was not formally completed until 1985, however, with the inauguration of the nation's first civilian government in over two decades. But even after 1985, Brazilian democracy remained heavily compromised by the looming presence of the military within the administration of José Sarney, the New Republic's first president. The Sarney administration was not the product of the people's vote but rather that of a constituent assembly, which although democratically elected was heavily influenced by the military. Direct election of the president would not arrive until 1990, when the presidency was transferred to Fernando Collor de Mello, the first directly elected leader of the New Republic.[48]

The prolonged transition allowed civil society groups time to coalesce in their struggle against the military regime. This was especially the case of the labor movement, which starting in the late 1970s began to reinvent itself institutionally by stressing autonomy vis-à-vis the state. Indeed, the military's refusal to loosen its grip over the labor movement even as the country began to journey toward democracy became a powerful rationale for the mobilization and organization of the working class.[49] The long struggle against the military regime also allowed civil society to forge important intra-group ties. For instance, the decision by the military that the 1985 elections excluded direct election of the new civilian leader was preceded by *diretas já* (direct elections now), a campaign for direct elections widely recognized as the most impressive act of civil society mobilization and solidarity during the transition period. It involved every important group from civil society including students, business, labor and the Catholic Church. These groups succeeded in organizing rallies throughout Brazil in which 11 million people are believed to have participated. The highlight of the movement for direct elections was a demonstration in São Paulo that drew 2 million participants and that is regarded as the largest public demonstration ever staged in Brazil.[50]

An Unconsolidated Democracy

What has been the impact of the significant expansion of civil society in Brazil on the nation's process of democratic consolidation? More directly related to this research is the question of whether the virtuous contributions to the process of democratization that the academic and the development community have attached to vibrant and robust civil societies are reflected in the Brazilian experience. These questions were very much in the minds of those who chronicled the rise of civil society in Brazil around the time of the democratic transition. And, interestingly enough, many of the contributions to this literature predicted wildly optimistic scenarios for a wholesale transformation of Brazilian society, impacting not only the political sphere but also the economy, justice and social relations.[51] One observer of the social movement scene in Brazil writes that "with the resurgence of civil society in the late 1970s, the nation was "at the threshold of a new era, more just and more humane."[52]

As suggested in the following analysis, nearly 30 years since Brazil began the transition to democracy in 1974, and 20 years since its formal inauguration in 1985, democratic governance in Brazil remains within what Philippe Schmitter terms "the excluded middle," a situation in which neither consolidation nor breakdown takes place.[53] This outcome is hardly surprising since it is in fact the most common of all among post-authoritarian democracies. But what makes the Brazilian situation interesting from a theoretical standpoint is that so little of what is expected about democratic consolidation as a consequence of a dramatic surge in civil society development has been borne out. This is not to say that democratic progress in Brazil has not been forthcoming. Certainly, the democratic regime inaugurated in 1985 is more inclusive, participatory and stable than the one in place between 1946–1964.[54] More relevant, perhaps, is that since 1985 Brazil has met procedural and/or minimalistic definitions of political democracy. Indeed, fewer new democracies in South America have embraced the trappings of democracy with as much gusto as Brazil. Free and competitive elections have become routine, as have peaceful transfers of government, multiparty competition is amongst the most unfettered in South America, and a new democratic constitution passed in 1988 guarantees a wide range of political and civil rights unprecedented in Brazilian history. Also notable is that in the early 1990s, Brazil became the first nation in South America in the twentieth century to impeach a sitting president on corruption charges.

Rather, the point I try to emphasize is the noticeable disconnect that exists between what neo-Tocquevillean theories of democratization predict about vibrant and robust civil societies and what the Brazilian experience reveals. Despite notable advances in democratization, the quality of democracy enjoyed by the vast majority of Brazilians leaves a lot to be desired, leading to many discussions of what has been termed "a crisis of consolidation."[55] And many of the conditions underpinning this consolidation crisis are the very same ones deemed solvable or at the very least ameliorated by the expansion of civil society. The following discussion focuses on what I believe are the most problematic assumptions about civil society and democratic consolidation in light of the Brazilian experience. The first is the capacity of civil society to control or at the very least keep under check the abusive powers of the state. The second is the capacity of civil society to generate support for democratic values among the masses. The third is the capacity of civil society to improve socioeconomic conditions in general, especially for marginalized groups. Brazil's process of democratic change gives us no empirical base to sustain any of these assumptions.

State Power and Democratic Change

A good starting point for challenging the impression that a vibrant civil society had any meaningful impact on curtailing the powers of the state in Brazil is, of course, the manner in which the transition to democracy was conceived, executed and managed. We should expect that the rise of a strong civil society of the like that began to form in Brazil prior and during the democratic transition would not only be successful in triggering a rapid regime change to democracy but also in dictating the dynamics of that process. But this was hardly the case in Brazil, where the transition to democracy demonstrated, above all, the historical capacity of political elites to exclude the general public from politics. From the onset of the transition to its completion, civil society movements were simply unable to affect in a direct and systematic manner the dynamics of the democratic transition, including its timing and scope.

In contrast to the case of Spain, the process of regime change that got underway in Brazil in 1974 was not provoked by an internal crisis in the authoritarian regime brought about by pressures from civil society but rather by state actions seemingly unrelated to civil society's activism. Serious opposition from civil society would not begin until the late 1970s, after the authoritarian state had formally declared the beginning of a process of political opening. This point is widely recognized in the literature on democratization politics in Brazil. According to Hagopian, "the Brazilian military itself began the process of liberalization in advance of a demand from civil society."[56] Mainwaring's account of the role of grassroots organizations in the Brazilian transition concludes that "it would be misleading to attribute significant weight to popular movements at the beginning of the *abertura*."[57] He adds that the military regime's success in "controlling the broadest contours of the *abertura* process" prevented civil society from having much of a direct impact on political change. Instead, civil society remained the "conscience of the society," placing on the agenda issues of socio-economic justice, rights for the popular classes and minority groups and popular participation."[58] Even Collier, whose comparative analysis of transitions to democracy is devoted to demonstrating labor's effects on triggering democratization, writes about Brazil that "the first steps toward political opening were initiated autonomously by the authoritarian incumbents, who came to power in a 1964 military coup."[59]

In place of a civil society–instigated transition to democracy, the case of Brazil offers us one of the most genuinely endogenous processes of state-led democratization. Among the most commonly cited explanations to account for the puzzling question of why the Brazilian military embraced political liberalization in the absence of strong civil society opposition was the desire to broaden the basis of regime support. By the mid-1970s, there existed the impression within military circles that the government was less valued by important economic groups and that its mechanisms of torture and surveillance and various excesses of military rule had alienated the middle class and the Catholic Church.[60] Thus, the expectation from the military in 1974 was that an electoral victory would serve to legitimize its rule. However, in losing to the opposition party, MDB (which, as noted previously, the authoritarian regime itself had organized), the military unintentionally put the country on the path toward democracy.

As suggested in chapter 6, the military in Brazil manipulated every step of the transition to democracy, outmaneuvered civil society and its political allies and blatantly influenced the creation of democratic institutions during the democratic constituent period (1985–1988). These maneuverings planted the seed for the general distrust that Brazilians exhibit toward their governing institutions in the democratic period. More disturbing, perhaps, was the tremendous capacity displayed by the military to absorb and withstand the mobilization of an expanding civil society in the wake of the 1974 elections. The military government generally refused to deal with the demands posed by popular movements for a faster and more meaningful process of democratization and instead chose to defeat them behind closed doors. As explained in Maria Do Carmo Campello de Souza's comparison of transition politics in Spain and Brazil, in striking contrast to Spain, the Brazilian transition "did not involve the presence of left-wing parties or representatives of its allied sectors, nor was it conducted in a manner visible to society. The Brazilian agreement followed the logic of a pact among regional elites supported by military factions; it was not an accord reached by spokesmen of party institutions responsible to their voters and constituencies."[61]

Societal repression was another strategy deployed by the military to reign in civil society's demands for a faster and more meaningful process of democratization and to implement its own vision for democratization. Claiming a desire to prevent a Portuguese style-process of democratization in which left-wing organizations gained control of the state, repression of dissent in Brazil remained virtually unabated after the 1974 elections.[62] Joan Dassin's well-known report on political violence in Brazil between 1964 and 1979 paints a grim picture of the terror imposed by the state purportedly in the very midst of a process of political liberalization.[63] By the end of the Geisel government in 1979, the "brutally efficient machine of the Brazilian repressive apparatus" had produced 10,000 political exiles, removed 4,682 persons from office and 245 students from universities, left almost 300 dead or disappeared and engaged in human rights violations that included the deprivation of civil liberties.[64]

Paradoxically, given the strength of NGOs devoted to human rights in Brazil as well as a much publicized campaign against torture by the Catholic Church, unlike neighboring Argentina and Uruguay, Brazil's amnesty law enacted by the military before leaving office was not overturned by the new civilian government after 1985.[65] Nor did the new government move to organize a truth commission like those of Argentina, Chile and Uruguay to document human rights abuses by the military.[66] More disturbing still is that blatant expression of state power and violence has remained a fixture of political life in Brazil's new democracy.

State Violence under Democracy

One of the great paradoxes of contemporary Brazilian politics is that state violence has actually increased in the post-transition period. Accordingly, discussions of human rights abuses in Brazil have become more common in connection with the advent of democracy than the passing of the military regime. State violence in Brazil in the democratic period, however, has a new, disturbing dimension. In post-1985 Brazil, state violence has not been directed at traditional targets such as political dissidents; but rather at those living at the margins of society: street children, homosexuals, indigenous peoples, landless peasants and the urban poor.[67] This type of violence, as contended by Pereira, is no less "political" than the repression of the Left during the 1960s and 1970s because "both types of violence reduce the broad extension of citizenship rights and the democratic control of the state's means of violence."[68]

The best indicator of the magnitude of the problem of state violence in Brazil is found not in raw statistics but rather in a series of highly publicized events of gruesome human rights violations to have taken place since the 1990.[69] They have captured worldwide attention and have led observers to characterize Brazilian democracy as one possessing "low intensity citizenship," and, worse yet, "without citizenship."[70] They also prompted the reformist government of Fernando Henrique Cardoso to implement a National Human Rights plan in 1996, which so far shows little signs of having had much of an impact in curbing state-sponsored violence. At the heart of this plan was reform of the police—whose official name "Military Police" (MP)—"reflects the tendency to act more like a military than a police force."[71]

One of the most emblematic incidents in the annals of state violence in democratic Brazil took place in October 1992 at the *Carandiru* prison, an infamous episode of state violence in which the military police gunned down 111 unarmed prisoners and not a single policeman died. The violence at *Carandiru*, as described by Amnesty International reports and academic analyses, had "Dantesque overtones as prisoners were not only shot randomly but were also bitten, attacked by dogs especially trained to bite the genitals and stabbed with knifes."[72] In July 1993, in what has come to be known as the *Candelária* massacre, the military policemen opened gun fire on 72 abandoned street children who were sleeping in front of the city's most famous church killing seven of them. Another incident that received considerable attention was the 1996 *Eldorado de Carajás* massacre, in which 19 landless peasants were murdered by the military police, a small portion of the 1,158 rural activists assassinated since 1985.[73]

These egregious incidents of state violence mirror a larger problem of societal crime and fear that permeates everyday life in Brazil, itself an indication of "decreasing social solidarity in Brazil."[74] By 1992, it is estimated that Brazil's murder rate was about twice that of the United States, another democracy notorious for its widespread violence.[75] Much of the violence found in Brazilian society, as suggested already, is contributed to or indirectly endorsed by the state, with police brutality being the most pronounced form of state violence. By most accounts, police violence in contemporary Brazil is extraordinary. Paul Chevigny's 1995 chronicle of police abuse in the Americas reports that while excesses of police violence were prevalent in almost all major urban centers included in the study (Los Angeles, New York, Buenos Aires, Mexico City and Jamaica) none of them approached the situation in São Paulo in the 1980s and 1990s.[76] In 1991, for example, 1,171 people died in São Paulo during confrontations with the police, compared to 27 in New York City.[77] The picture from other cities is just as disturbing. Between 1993 and 1996, the Rio police killed 942 civilians, over half in favelas.[78] Many of these crimes were committed in "visible torture chambers" found in police stations.[79]

The seriousness of state violence in Brazil's new democracy explains Freedom House's ranking of the country as "Partly-free" in its 2000–2001 report.[80] In a scale of 1–7, Brazil received a rating of 3 for its respect for "Political Rights" and a rating of 4 for its respect for "Civil Liberties." By contrast, other new democracies such as Argentina, Chile and Uruguay, whose civil societies are not as vibrant and robust as Brazil's (but whose militaries civilian governments regulate more effectively) are all ranked as "Free" societies. Indeed, among major South American nations, only Peru, whose political trajectory since the 1980s has been marked by political violence, civil strife and the actual suspension of democracy, has a worse record of respect for civil and political liberties than Brazil.

This blemish on the face of Brazil's new democracy stands in striking contrast to the powers of a strengthened civil society and its presumed capacity to restrain abuses of power by the state apparatus, a point that has not been lost on observers of the Brazilian political scene. The apparent paradox of the presence of widespread state brutality in the midst of a thriving and progressive civil society is at the heart of Teresa P. R. Caldeira's masterful study of citizenship and violence in contemporary Brazil.[81] Reflecting on the prison massacre of 1991, she writes: "The incongruence is all the greater when one realizes that these events occurred in São Paulo, the most modern city in the country, where social movements and trade unions are strong and have transformed conceptions of political participation since the 1970s and 1980s, and where the mayor at the time of the prison massacre was a member of the leftist Workers' Party (PT)."[82]

Weak Support for Democracy

The case of Brazil also cast significant doubt on the neo-Tocquevillean assumption that links the art of association with widespread support for democratic values. According to the data from the *World Values Survey* (1995–1997) support for democracy in Brazil is the lowest in Latin America and almost as low as that of Russia, which leads the survey's 43 societies in the category of "anti-democratic attitudes." These findings are faithfully echoed in Linz and Stepan's survey of attitudes about democracy of the mid-1990s, which found that Brazilians' support for their new democracy was the weakest among Southern European and South American nations.[83] Only 42 percent of Brazilians deemed democracy as "preferable to any other form of government," versus 73 for Uruguay and 70 percent for Spain. Asked if "in some cases a non democratic government could be preferable to democracy," 22 percent of Brazilians responded in the affirmative versus 10 for Uruguay and 10 for Spain. Asked if a "democratic regime and a non-democratic regime were the same," 24 percent of Brazilians answered in the affirmative versus 8 percent for Uruguay and 9 percent for Spain.

The lukewarm support for democracy that Linz and Stepan found in Brazil in the mid-1990s appears to have eroded even further in recent years. The 2000 data from the *Latinobarómetro*, which traces public opinion in 17 countries in Latin America, notes that since the mid-1990s there has been "a sharp decline in support for democracy in Brazil."[84] It reports of "a crisis in public attitudes towards democracy" as evidenced in the fact that support for democracy in that country dropped from 50 percent in 1996 to 39 percent in 2000. By contrast, support for democracy in neighboring Argentina and Uruguay has remained stable and strong. In 1996, 71 percent of Argentines agreed that democracy was preferable to any other kind of government. This appraisal went up slightly in 1998 (73 percent) before dropping off to

71 percent in 2000. In Uruguay support for democracy was 80 percent in 1996 and climbed to 84 percent for 2000, the highest among Latin American countries.

Brazilians' tepid support for democracy is also mirrored in the low disregard (if not outright disdain) with which the general public regards political institutions. A 1995 *Latinobarómetro* survey found that while 70 percent of Argentines and Uruguayans agreed that parties are necessary for democracy, only 47 percent of Brazilians thought so.[85] Regarding the electoral system, a 1998 poll showed that if given the choice (voting is mandatory in Brazil) 49 percent of Brazilians would not bother to vote.[86] Another survey conducted a year later on which institutions contributed most and least to the good of the country found that the congress and its members scored dead last and far behind bankers, businessmen and even the armed forces.[87] Another poll of the same year found that 60 percent of residents in the state of São Paulo did not trust the National Congress and another 49 percent said they could not trust the president.[88]

In light of Brazilians' ambivalent feelings about democracy and its institutions it is not surprising to learn of the rise during the early 1990s of speculations of a democratic breakdown and for calls from Conservative politicians for the "suspension of congress and a return to military rule."[89] Calls for the return to authoritarianism were encouraged by the perception that the citizenry would actually endorse such a move, as revealed by a number of polls that persistently suggested that military rule might be a desired future alternative for the nation. In a December 1988 comparative survey of new democracies in Brazil, Argentina and Uruguay, only 6 percent of the Montevideo residents polled felt a return of the military would make things better, only 15 percent in Argentina felt so, but 40 percent of the inhabitants of São Paulo felt so.[90] In a national poll a year later, 38 percent of Brazilians concurred with the statement that "the country would be better off if the military returned to power."[91] This troubling openness to authoritarian rule in Brazil remains quite high. The data from the 2000 *Latinobarómetro* notes that support for authoritarianism in Brazil has remained stable at 24 percent (the same as in 1996).

Unmet Societal Expectations

Finally, the case of Brazil shows ambiguous support for the contention that a thriving civil society can have a significant impact on socioeconomic development. In the democratic period Brazil has consolidated its status as "the world champion of inequality," as suggested by the fact that the nation's income distribution is currently the most unfair of any democratic society.[92]

According to the World Bank, in Brazil the top 20 percent earns 26 times what the bottom 20 percent earn. By contrast, in the United States the ration is 9 to 1 and in India, 5 to 1.[93] Such a dramatic disparity in wealth distribution translates into a variety of social ills and pathologies including widespread poverty, illiteracy and crime, all of which are palpably visible in contemporary Brazil.[94]

The picture of society's most disfranchised and oppressed also challenges the positive side effects believed to ensue from a thriving associational life. To be sure, many of the social movements, organizations and institutions created by union leaders, women, Afro-Brazilians, homosexuals and others during and after the democratic transition have certainly changed the political landscape of the country if only by creating voices for change where none existed before. Moreover, there have been some impressive victories such as the repeal of the classification of homosexuality as a sexual deviation from the state's code of diseases. But most studies of traditionally marginal groups in Brazil stress their continuing struggle not only to survive (a point underscored by the increasing violence against the poor, gays and indigenous peoples) but also to escape discrimination ensuing from the country's extremely weak sense of citizenship.[95]

The mobilization and organization of the poor in Brazil appears to have had very little impact on their socioeconomic well-being. In 1990, close to 12 percent of Brazilian population, or about 16.5 million people, lived under miserable conditions. In 1997 the proportion had risen to 15 percent, while the total number of those living below the poverty line constituted 24 percent of the population.[96] Despite its strength, during the transition to democracy the women's movement lost its most important and emblematic battle: the effort to write into the constitution a wide range of reproductive rights. Ironically, assisting in the defeat of the feminist agenda was another sector of civil society: religious groups affiliated with the Catholic Church. Other repressed groups in Brazilian society have fared no better in the new democracy. Despite their energetic mobilization, Brazilian gay and lesbian groups failed to have sexual orientation discrimination banned by the constitution.[97] They have also failed to make inroads into the violence perpetrated against the homosexual community, which by all accounts is extraordinarily high. A recent study names Brazil "the world champion in murders of homosexuals," having registered between the years 1980 and 2001 a total of 2,092 such murders—an average of 104 deaths per year.[98] Notwithstanding the vibrancy of NGOs in Brazil, UNICEF notes that 53 percent of the 17.5 million children and young people forced to work in Latin America are in Brazil and of these 1 million are under the age of 10.[99]

As for Afro-Brazilians, it is reported that between 1960 and 1980 racial discrimination in the labor market increased in Brazil and that the years after 1980 have not altered the situation.[100]

Also instructive is the case of the labor movement, whose political fortunes during the period of democratic change are not commensurate with their membership resources, institutional strength and organizational skills. Brazilian trade unions remained under the strict trappings of the state's corporatist labor code (the *Consolidaçao das Leis do Trabalho, CLT*) until the passing of the new constitution in 1988. Indeed, remarkably little change took place in Brazilian industrial and labor relations from the time the transition was initiated in 1974 until the passing of the new constitution in 1988.[101] As late as 1985, when democratic rule was inaugurated, Brazilian workers were banned from creating nationwide workers' syndicates, and as late as 1988, unions were officially prohibited in the public sector. After 1985 labor remained one of the central subjects of investigation for the state's security apparatus, union leaders were a matter for discussion in meetings of the army high command, and the War College continued to include labor issues in courses concerning national security and economic development.[102] Most suggestive of the government's treatment of the labor movement was the response to the unions' mobilization that accompanied the inauguration of democracy in 1985. It is reported that on numerous occasions the military "unilaterally decided whether or not to send military units to quell strikes."[103]

Alternative Explanations

What explains the glaring discrepancy between what neo-Tocquevillean theories of democratic consolidation presume and what the case of Brazil reveals? A number of aspects about the constitution and evolution of Brazilian civil society in the post-transition period can be enlisted to shed some light on this question. For a start, a convincing argument can be made that Brazilian civil society for all of its exuberance and expansion during and after the military dictatorship needs further boosting. Despite its fantastic growth in the last decades, the union movement in Brazil is only able to reach workers in the formal sector, leaving those in the informal sector (a vast percentage of the population) devoid of affiliation. Another compelling argument is that the presumed pro-democratic benefits of a strong civil society, most notably the production of social capital, take a long time to bear fruit, especially in a country like Brazil with a long history of authoritarian rule. After all, Putnam's analysis of how civil society promotes democratization emphasizes the point that Northern Italy's civil society and impressive social capital endowment was built over the course of centuries. By contrast, from a historical standpoint, we have to conclude that an expansive civil society is a relatively recent phenomenon in Brazil.

It could also be contended that the vibrancy and robustness of Brazilian civil society depicted here is something of a mirage. Studies of civil society in Brazil demonstrate that while the national picture of associational density is high, it is also decidedly uneven with a great concentration of voluntary associations in the urban, heavily populated and prosperous regions of the South and relatively sparse in the impoverished, rural areas of the North.[104] Other studies have suggested that at least since the mid-1980s, social movements in Brazil have experienced a partial decline (thereby depressing levels of associational life), especially among those born with the initiation of political liberalization in the late 1970s. The expansive literature on the fate of social movements in Brazil since 1985 does indeed paint a decidedly bleak picture. A recent summary of this literature by Kathryn Hochstetler notes that "one by one urban popular movements have succumbed to drug dealers, bureaucratization, opportunities to participate in government, the new strength of Pentecostals in the *favelas*, the influence Catholics and leftists, and a host of other pitfalls."[105]

Most of these contentions can be successfully refuted. For starters, the notion that democratic consolidation in Brazil depends upon greater civil society density or a longer period of gestation buys into Putnam's highly deterministic view of democratization that contends that only countries with rich legacies of associationalism are capable of engendering viable democracies. As noted previously, a key finding we can surmise from the *World Values Survey* is that in countries like Spain, France and Japan low levels of civil society density have not prevented the consolidation of democracy (see appendix).

The notion that civil society has been weakened in Brazil in recent years can be successfully rebutted. Although some movements born with the democratic transition (such as the CEBs) have in fact experienced a significant decline, others have flourished (e.g. the labor movement). The post-transition period has also seen the rise of a second generation of social movements leading observers of the social movement scene in Brazil to argue that popular forces remain robust.[106] A case in point is the *Movimento dos Trabalhadores Rurais Sem Terra* (MST), a landless-peasant organization presently regarded as the largest and most vibrant social movement in Latin America. The so-called partial decline of social movements in Brazil also provides a myopic view of the development of Brazilian civil society by focusing principally on national groups (mostly NGOs) and ignoring the vast expansion of new associations at the state and local levels. For example, a recent study of "the development of civil society" in the city of Porto Alegre notes that between 1986 and 1998, neighborhood associations grew from 180 to 540.[107]

Also noteworthy is that civil society in Brazil, in contrast to many other new democracies, remains highly mobilized as suggested by the recent revival of general strikes and popular demonstrations reminiscent of the transition period.[108] These events compellingly demonstrate the continuing capacities of Brazilian civil society to mobilize itself and to coordinate collective action across a myraid of interest groups, social movements and countless ordinary citizens. In late 1999, the country was rocked by a wave of strikes involving multiple sectors of the economy that raised industrial conflict to levels not seen since the late 1980s. More significant, perhaps, are the many popular demonstrations against the Cardozo government organized by civil society groups in recent years. Notable for their size and the broad range of partici-pating groups they are a testament to civil society's organizational capacities. A general strike in 1996, coordinated by all the major unions, succeeded in shutting down all major economic operations: petroleum, metal, chemical and finance. In March 1999, the CUT, the MST, student groups, progres-sive political parties and a plethora of NGOs observed a "National Day in Defense of Brazil," which included marches in every major state capital protesting unemployment, privatization and IMF policies. In August 26, 1999, another huge demonstration was organized in Brasilia, the so-called March of the 100,000, organized by the CUT, the MST and the Catholic Church to protest corruption and the government's neoliberal policies.

Social Capital and Democratic Consolidation in Brazil

Finally, neo-Tocquevillean arguments about the relevance of civil society to democratic consolidation in Brazil are refuted by the fact that there is little evidence to suggest that the dramatic swelling of associationalism experi-enced by Brazil in the last decades has had any discernable impact in build-ing up many of the values and behaviors associated with the concept of social capital, most notably social trust. Quite the contrary, all available indicators point to a dearth of social capital in Brazil's new democracy. Perhaps the most compelling indicator of this is Brazil's ranking in the *World Values Survey* (1990–1993) as the country where citizens are least likely to trust each other (see appendix). Only 7 percent of Brazilians agree that most people can be trusted versus 65 percent of Norwegians, the leaders in the "trust" category. The data from the *Latinobarómetro* (1996) shows a strikingly similar find-ing.[109] When it posed the question of whether most people can be trusted to the populations of 11 Latin American countries, Brazil tied with Venezuela for the last place, both with 11 percent, versus 33 percent for Uruguay and 23 percent for Argentina, the leaders in the survey. In light of these findings it is not surprising that relations between the state and society in democratic Brazil show none of the trust, reciprocity and collaboration that a thriving civil society is meant to engender.

The Failure of Social Concertation

The dearth of social capital in Brazilian democratization is best illustrated in the failure of the policy of social concertation to gain any significant degree of acceptance in the country's policy-making process. This has not been for lack of trying, however. During the life of the New Republic, Brazil has periodically sought to erect a process of national consultation and pacting with very disappointing results. This effort got underway in 1985 under the Sarney administration, with the organization of the *entendimento nacional* (national understanding), a forum that brought together representatives from the unions and the employers to forge a series of compromises on wages and prices aimed at lowering inflation. Another intense period of attempts at concertation took place in the early 1990s, under the Collor administration, which organized the *Forum Nacional de Negociação* (Forum of National Negotiation), a tripartite council comprising representation from the state, the unions and the employers. This effort continued under Itamar Franco, who replaced Collor in 1991. During the mid-1990s, attempts at concertation took a backseat in Brazilian policy-making, given the Cardoso administration's success in bringing down inflation without the help of any explicit social pact. Lula's new administration, inaugurated on January 2003, has indicated a willingness to renew efforts on behalf of a national social pact.[110]

The reasons for the failure of social concertation to take root in Brazil are numerous. For a start, organizational factors have complicated the bargaining process. As I explain in chapter 6, the weakness of the Brazilian party system makes it difficult to aggregate economic interests at the national level. It is worth recalling that in Spain it was the party system rather than civil society groups that initiated concertation politics. Another key factor is, ironically, the very vibrancy of civil society given the multiplicity of actors that in principle could play a role in the bargaining process. As noted already, no less than four central labor federations compete for the representation of tens of thousand of Brazilian unions. The picture among business associations is just as diverse. Befitting its status as Latin America's largest and most vibrant economy, Brazil possesses a plethora of business organizations but none brings together commerce, finance and industry, as is the case in Spain and other Latin American countries.[111] This leaves regional or sectoral groups such as the *Federação das Indústrias do Estado de São Paulo,* FIESP (Federation of Industries of the State of São Paulo), arguably the most influential business association in Brazil, as national mouthpieces for the business community. But such groups, as Ben Schneider has shown, lack the authority to negotiate and enforce agreements for the nation's employers as a whole.[112]

None of these factors, however, prevented the relevant actors from periodically coming together for the purpose of charting a common economic program that could also boost the political stability of the new democracy. More relevant obstacles to concertation in Brazil (as in the rest of Latin America) were the incapacity of the social partners to trust one another and their unwillingness to recognize the legitimate role that each plays in a modern, democratic society. These conditions, in turn, made for an especially difficult bargaining process dominated by free-riding behavior, grandstanding and unreasonable positions, and a blatant absence of civility and solidarity, even when it seemed clear that the economic crisis and lack of integration within the political class were eroding people's faith in democracy.

Employers have been especially lukewarm about social accords, given their opposition to freezes or caps on prices and their awareness that other modes of interaction with the state provide more effective means of influencing policy than a social pact. Indeed, one of the chief reasons for the lack of authoritative collective voices among Brazilian capitalists (and by extension the absence of a tradition of business lobbying) is the clientelistic and personalistic access to the state they have historically enjoyed.[113] Such practices, as seen in chapter 6, are thought to have expanded in the new democracy. For their part, in the democratic period the unions have hardly been predisposed to compromises. During the Sarney and Collor administrations, the CUT operated under an ironclad commitment against any type of formal accord with either the state or the employers. On the day of Neves's election in 1984, Lula repudiated the idea of a social pact in a tour of several factories in the São Bernando area, which he deemed a trick of the state and capital to subjugate the unions.[114]

Despite their official anti-pact discourse, the unions have participated in all the attempts at a social pact, although their behavior (at least through the early 1990s) suggested that they were not especially interested in reaching any pact. Prior to the actual bargaining, the CUT imposed conditions for accepting a pact that even the most agreeable of governments would certainly find hard to meet such as defaulting on the country's external debt, limiting the influence of the IMF over domestic policy and revamping land ownership rights.[115] At the bargaining table, labor representatives would go out of their way to make it clear that the point of the meetings was to consult and not to pact. As put by one CUT leader to the national media: "The CUT accepts dialogue and negotiation but it cannot make any gesture that indicates moderation or retreat."[116] Consequently, the CUT Secretary General Gilmar Carneiro continually pulled out of the talks with the Collor government aimed at reaching an understanding over inflation policy because the meetings possessed "the aura of a pact."[117] This led the government to denounce the CUT as "inopportune" and "anti-patriotic" for its unwillingness to cooperate with the government while the media baptized the organization as the union that "could only say no."[118]

It is the government, however, that is most responsible for the failure of concertation in Brazil. As explained in chapter 6, the lack of cohesion within the state apparatus meant that the state never developed an internal consensus on the merits and desirability of a social pact. Moreover, the entire state apparatus, especially its economic components, suffers from lack of credibility with civil society. Consequently, throughout the process of democratization every important segment of civil society (including most notably the labor movement) was deeply suspicious of the political system including the state and the party system. Finally, the state's bureaucratic culture has been on the whole incompatible with the notion of concertation. State actors tend to regard outside actors, especially labor, as rent-seeking, opportunistic actors, as reflected in the traditional propensity of Brazilian presidents and the technocrats that advise them to rely upon decrees rather than consultation in the implementation of economic policy.

The unions' account of the negotiation process under Sarney and Collor suggests how the state's behavior undermined the prospects for a social pact. For the CUT, the government wanted labor's acceptance of an economic agenda constructed *a priori* by government officials, a position supported by independent accounts of the bargaining process.[119] One study notes that during the consultations for a pact, "the government portrayed the workers' struggles for a living wage as threats to democracy and that it was the trade unions that were asked to do most of the compromising."[120] Another study notes that "a true doctrine of consultation and social dialogue has been impeded by the government's attempt to impose consultation and dialogue by decree."[121] It is further noted that government officials have pursued consultation "only when they wanted something, but had nothing to offer" and that "the general attitude of the trade unions is one of distrust."

In sum, the case of Brazil provides little if any support to the many assumptions linking a vibrant and robust civil society to a successful process of democratic consolidation. In Brazil, a thriving civil society coexists with widespread state abuses, weak support by the masses for democratic values and institutions and multiple social and economic inequities. This would appear to suggest a failure on the part of civil society in Brazil to bring about democratic consolidation by not performing its democratizing tasks. But this, of course, is the wrong conclusion since the country would probably not even live under democracy today were it not for the courageous endeavors of many civil society organizations. Rather, the Brazilian predicament suggests the folly of trying to understand the dynamics of the process of democratic consolidation exclusively through the prism of the configuration of civil society and divorced entirely from the constitution and performance of the political system.

CHAPTER 6

Political Institutions and Democratization in Brazil

Neither the building of social capital nor especially the consolidation of democracy in Brazil is likely to depend on the further enrichment of the country's civil society. Instead, these tasks hinge upon the emergence of a well-functioning political system whose performance and institutional capacities meet the aspirations of the citizenry. This point is implicitly or explicitly accepted by the expansive literature spawned by the creation of Brazil's New Republic in 1985. If there is one dominant theme in this literature it is the failure of formal political institutions—from the presidency to the congress to the party system—to provide much of a reason for Brazilians to care about democracy and its institutions.[1]

Interestingly enough, the contention that political institutions matter to the long-term success of democracy in Brazil is also a dominant theme in the politics of the New Republic. This is suggested, most pointedly, by all the political capital spent in the last two decades by the nation's political class contemplating what kind of political system is best suited for the country. Indeed, more than any other new democracy in either Iberian Europe or South America, Brazil has been consumed with matters of political-institutional design. Much of the debate has focused on whether the country should take the dramatic and unprecedented step for a Latin American country of adopting a European-style parliamentary system or instead retain its American-style presidential system created in the late nineteenth century. This matter was eventually settled by a public referendum in 1993 with the majority of Brazilians voting in favor of the old system. Unfortunately, not much effort has been spent on reforming or improving the performance of the existing presidential system.

In this analysis I focus on the connection between the political system and the production of social capital in Brazil, and by extension the process of democratic consolidation, as dictated by the performance and constitution of political institutions, especially the government, the state apparatus and the party system. This analysis first notes how the military's manipulation of the democratic transition and the democratic ambiguity of the nation's first democratically elected government fostered a political culture that, as detailed in chapter 5, is marked by widespread cynicism and disinterest in all things political. It then suggests how the state's institutional make up—especially its bureaucratic weakness—can be blamed for multiple social ills (including clientelism, crime, corruption and poverty). In turn, these developments have hindered or undermined the rise of trust, reciprocity and civility within Brazilian society and especially toward governing institutions. Finally, the analysis reveals how a poorly institutionalized party system complicated the policy-making process (thereby retarding democratic consolidation) and undermined the capacity of Brazilian civil society for ameliorating the many ills affecting the country including its low-quality democracy.

Governing Regime Change

Much about the lack of social capital evident in the politics of democratization in Brazil (as well as the rise of many values and behaviors antithetical to this concept) can be traced to the manner in which democracy was introduced into the country. Given that democratization in Brazil was initiated in the absence of civil society opposition and managed by a military government in full control of its powers, the case of Brazil provides the most naked expression of state control and manipulation of the political process throughout the various phases of regime change to democracy. At almost every turn in the road toward democracy, the military succeeded in delaying or distorting the process of democratization in an effort to control the transition process and impose its own program of political reform. This reflected the military's considerable ambivalence about its commitment to ending authoritarian rule as suggested by the fact that a plan for executing the transition to democracy was never fully articulated by the government. General Ernesto Geisel's 1975 pronouncement that political liberalization would be "slow and sure" provided the only road map toward democratization in Brazil.[2] This statement turned out to be only partly true, for although democratization in Brazil was a gradual affair it was not without interruptions, if not effective setbacks.[3]

After the 1974 elections the military began to systematically manipulate the electoral process, an important factor behind the delegitimization of political institutions that characterized Brazil's return to democracy. In 1975 the Geisel government enacted a set of laws aimed at curtailing the growth and influence of the MDB, the opposition party created by the military in the hope of making the parties of the Left redundant. This initiative started with the "Falcão law" (named after the Minister of Justice), which greatly restricted the use of the media (radio and television in particular) for political purposes. The effort to weaken the democratic opposition continued with the *pacôte de abril* (April Package) of 1977, a set of reforms designed to prevent further MDB victories and strengthen the hand of the military-backed ARENA party in future elections. Constitutional amendments would need only majority approval in congress, all state governors and a third of the senate would be elected by electoral colleges and federal deputies would be allocated on the basis of population rather than registered voters as had been the case in 1970 and 1974.[4] The April package was characterized in the media as "Geisel's apparent betrayal of his commitment to liberalization," and understandably caused considerable opposition within the MDB.[5] But even many ARENA leaders, who supported the military government, complained about the "damage done to the integrity of the country's representative institutions."[6]

In 1979, the military officially dissolved both ARENA and the MDB with the intention of creating a multiparty system. In reality, however, the new legislation aimed at maintaining ARENA largely intact while dividing the MDB into several parties.[7] The new legislation also forced all parties to incorporate the word "party" into their name. The aim of this odd measure was "to disrupt the growing pro-MDB sentiment by forcing it to change its name (to PMDB) in the hope that doing so would erode the linkages it had created to society."[8] Further manipulation of the electoral process also marked the 1982 elections. The military government succeeded in excepting the office of the presidency from the election. And fears that the government party would not win a large majority to control the electoral college that would choose the next president in the next elections, led the government to push through a "November Package" in 1981 that prohibited electoral coalitions and required that voters vote a straight ticket. Just prior to the elections, the government introduced yet another measure intended to favor the government party by instituting a ballot on which the names of candidates had to be written in instead of being checked off on a printed list. This measure also aimed at hurting the opposition party (the PMDB) since only the government-backed party ARENA "had sufficient local organization to ensure that its voters would learn to fill out their ballots correctly."[9]

More damaging still in fueling mistrust and cynicism within society toward the political system and propelling civil society into an anti-cooperation mood vis-à-vis the incoming civilian government was the military's defeat of the *diretas já* campaign in 1984. Undoubtedly, this was the most blatant act of political manipulation (if not outright betrayal of democracy) of the transition period. And coming at the tail end of the transition, this repression of democracy did not provide an auspicious beginning for democratic values to take root in Brazil. The campaign for direct elections crystallized the desire of the Brazilian people not only for the end of the military dictatorship but also for an expanded universe of political and citizenship rights. Described as "the most sustained and massive political movement in Brazil's history," the petition for the direct election of the country's first civilian government since 1962 was supported by virtually every sector of Brazilian society including the business community.[10] The military, however, insisted on indirect elections and went about accomplishing this by relying upon familiar, old-style politics of exclusion. As reported by Mainwaring: "Vast segments of the society, including many organized social movements, mobilized on behalf of direct elections. However, it was only through traditional elite negotiations behind closed doors that the transition to democracy was secured."[11]

An Ambiguous Transition

The civilian government inaugurated in Brazil in 1985 ushered in a string of failed presidencies that did little to promote the kind of political culture associated with effective democratic governance and/or the virtues of social capital. The first was headed by José Sarney, who stepped into the office of the presidency at the last minute after the untimely death of president-elect Neves just days prior to his inauguration. Unfortunately for Brazil, Sarney lacked many if not most of the attributes that had inspired considerable public confidence in Neves, especially his conciliatory political style.[12] Just a few years into his administration, three out of four Brazilians wanted Sarney out of office.[13] The public's dissatisfaction with Sarney stemmed, first, from the non-electoral route through which he had ascended to the office of the presidency. In the wake of the massive mobilization in favor of direct elections by virtually every sector of civil society that accompanied the last months of military government, many Brazilians found it difficult to accept Sarney as the legitimate leader of the new democracy.[14]

In the eyes of many civil society leaders, the Sarney administration was the outcome of a transition process that had egregiously violated the wishes of the vast majority of Brazilians. This action, they contended, made the new civilian government antidemocratic and therefore illegitimate. The sentiment of illegitimacy surrounding the Sarney administration was articulated most cogently by the leaders of the new unionism, which in many regards emerged as the conscience and voice of civil society during the transition and the principal opposition to the new civilian government. The CUT leadership argued that "without the legitimization of a direct popular vote a new government could not be truly democratic and would not have the legitimacy to implement a real program of transformation capable of creating economic and social rights as well as formal political democracy."[15]

Sarney's acceptance as the democratic leader of Brazil's New Republic was made the more difficult by his close association with the military and the country's most conservative political factions. Only nine months prior to his election as president of the New Republic, Sarney had been the leader of the PDS, the military-backed party previously known as ARENA. He had switched parties from the PDS to the democratic opposition party (PMDB) in an act of naked political opportunism. In a sense, then, with Sarney's rise to power, "the old PDS did win the presidency of Brazil yet again and the historic opposition to authoritarian rule could not savor Neves' victory."[16] This unexpected turn of events accounts for the much-noted lack of a sharp break in Brazil between the old authoritarian regime and the new democracy. Indeed, as suggested by Mainwaring, "Sarney's victory was the most obvious indicator of the continuity between 1964–1985 and the new democracy."[17]

Once in office, Sarney's stayed firmly within the comfort zone provided by the remaining structures of the old military regime thereby exacerbating the strong sense of regime continuity with the old authoritarian order that his selection as president had signaled. He staffed his government with right-wing hacks from the old ARENA party, which in the view of many Brazilians made his "Democratic Alliance" democratic in name only. More worrisome yet lacking a well-defined base of political support, "Sarney increasingly relied on the military, thereby augmenting their real, if somewhat hidden power."[18] He remained totally beholden to the military as suggested by the fact that he showed little if any disposition to challenge the wide range of military prerogatives inherited from the transition years, thereby seriously compromising progress toward democratic consolidation. Consequently, during the Sarney administration the military remained "a privileged and prominent political player."[19] Six military officers sat in Sarney's first cabinet, from which they directly affected the affairs of the new government including the work of the democratically elected constituent assembly responsible for drafting the nation's new democratic constitution.

The prominence of the military in the Sarney administration did not predispose Sarney to seek dialogue with the opposition. Nor was the Sarney government especially interested in incorporating civil society into the policy-making process. In striking contrast to the situation in Spain, at the inception of democracy in Brazil there was neither direct support for a social pact from the executive branch nor internal consensus within the state's bureaucratic apparatus about the merits and desirability of such a pact. Plans for a social pact under the Sarney administration were delegated to Almir Pazzianotto, the labor minister, who had neither the authority nor the resources to entice the social partners from within and outside the state to the bargaining table. Pazzianotto's plan to cultivate cooperation from the unions with the government immediately ran into trouble with the military's hard-line labor policies. The ministry of industry and commerce also grew impatient with Pazzianotto's unwillingness to intervene in the wave of strikes that hit the new government in 1985. Even less enthused with the idea of a social pact were officials at the ministry of finance. They controlled economic policy and as such had the final say on incentives for labor cooperation with the government.

Constraining Consolidation

Sarney's unwillingness to reign in the powers of antidemocratic forces exacted a high price on Brazil's prospects for a deeper and faster process of democratic consolidation. During the constituent assembly period the military was hugely successful in carving for itself a position of influence in Brazilian society and politics that is believed to be superior to that enjoyed by its counterparts in other South American democracies.[20] As a consequence of this action, future democratic governments in Brazil would have to contend with a political inheritance that has undermined democratization and proved difficult to overcome. Under Sarney, military officers secured for themselves immunity for human rights violations committed during the long period of military rule, and, more importantly, they proved quite adept at influencing the architecture and policies of the new democracy.[21] This was most certainly the case of the drafting of the nation's new constitution of 1988. So pervasive was military interference in this process that, according to Linz and Stepan, Brazil's constitution belongs in the category of a "constitution created under highly constraining circumstances reflecting the de facto power of non-democratic institutions and forces."[22]

In an effort to influence the debate over the new constitution that would replace the authoritarian document of 1967 the military spared no expense. As the nation prepared to draft the new constitution the military organized "the country's largest and most efficient lobbying team, with officers assigned full-time to the congress."[23] This helps explain the many successful military interventions in the constitution-drafting process aimed at eliminating or at least softening many of the measures designed to curb the political influence of the military. The most notable military intervention regarding the constitution was the defeat of the plan to create a ministry of defense that would integrate the various branches of the military, oversee military spending and therefore curtail military autonomy.[24] This meant that under the new constitution "the military remained largely autonomous."[25]

Another high-profile intervention by the military was the defeat of the constitutional amendment that would have created a parliamentary system of government in Brazil along the lines of France's Fifth Republic. The passage of an amendment designed to introduce a parliamentary system in Brazil was thought to be guaranteed, as suggested by the fact that the 77 articles of the constitution already passed by the congress presumed that the basic format of the government would be parliamentary rather than presidential.[26] A parliamentary system, however, aimed to curtail presidential powers and potentially cut Sarney's own term in office by one year, prompting him, his military advisors and conservative members of congress into action. Just before a crucial vote on article 78 that would have created Latin America's first parliamentary form of government, the military with the help of its allies in congress and the executive branch launched a powerful counterattack of payoffs and threats to defeat this plan.[27]

During the deliberations surrounding the new constitution the military also managed to retain its historic mandate to keep the nation's internal order. This constitutional right to protect "law and order" was accorded to the Brazilian military in previous constitutions (1881, 1934 and 1967) and has been used by the military repeatedly to overthrow democratically elected governments. In the mid-1980s, civilian politicians attempted with little success to rid the country of this prerogative by limiting military involvement in politics to the external defense of the country. It is reported that "even before the new constituent assembly began its deliberations in 1987, the question of whether the military should retain the constitutional right, however vague, to intervene in domestic affairs was removed from the debate."[28] A result of this failure to circumscribe the powers of the military was the virtually intact survival of the military's intelligence apparatus (the National Information Service, SNI), the primary instrument for spying on society during the military dictatorship. This institutional legacy is a key factor in accounting for the coexistence of democratic governance in Brazil alongside rampant and seemingly unrestrained state violence.

The Sarney government's poor performance in advancing democratic consolidation is matched by its dismal management of the economy. This situation perhaps more than any other during the Sarney years accounts for the deep disillusionment with democracy that Brazilians experienced during the late 1980s and early 1990s. The impact of the economic crisis on people's confidence in democracy and the general mood of the nation were aptly captured in the title of a *New York Times* article: "Economic Ills Sap Brazilians' Faith in Democracy."[29] At the heart of the economic crisis was skyrocketing inflation, which between 1985 and 1994 reached an annual rate of over 4,000 percent. This bout of hyperinflation had immense repercussions in people's everyday lives extending well beyond their perceptions of the political system. By the early 1990s, Brazil was in possession of the world's highest cumulative inflation rate, causing personal incomes to plummet, and sending social conflict (especially strikes and street protests) and crime soaring.[30] Unsurprisingly, by the late 1980s, Brazil's new democracy was in the midst of a crisis of governability with the approval of Sarney's performance by the general public hovering at 20 percent.[31]

Undermining Democratic Legitimacy

Also serving to undermine the building of the foundations of social capital and democratic consolidation in Brazil is the general disregard for democratic institutions that has characterized many of the governments of the post-transition era. This is best suggested by the rise to power in 1990 of Fernando Collor de Mello, Sarney's successor and the first directly elected president of the New Republic. His autocratic and divisive governing style, disdain for representative institutions and poor political judgment placed Brazil's new democracy in great peril.[32] This disastrous administration ended with Collor being deposed from office via impeachment in 1992 on corruption charges, quite the irony since he rode into office on an anticorruption platform.[33] As the first South American nation in the last century to remove a sitting president, this was surely a sign of the strength of Brazil's civil society, which exposed Collor's misdeeds and actively campaigned for his removal from office. But it was not a sign of democratic consolidation. The ambivalence that Brazilians feel about democracy and its institutions reached its highest point during Collor's scandal-prone and corruption-ridden administration.[34]

Collor was the "classic example of the anti-politics and antiparty politician" and his election to presidency represented "the triumph of antipolitics in Brazil."[35] He ran as an outsider and, in open disdain for the political establishment, he did not bother to create a formal political organization until after his election.[36] Instead, Collor promised to solve national problems virtually singlehandedly and without political parties, a point that resonated powerfully with the masses greatly disillusioned with the performance of political institutions.[37] During the campaign and then as president, Collor sought to appeal directly to the masses and the myriad of popular organizations created with the democratic transition and that often presented themselves as alternatives to the political parties. He did this most often via television, which he skillfully used to announce his policies, which usually came in the form of solemn presidential decrees of dubious constitutionality. In his dealing with the congress, Collor employed the same antiparty and anti-system rhetoric adopted by civil society organizations. In 1990, for example, when the congress refused to approve an economic stabilization plan it had no role in conceiving, Collor threatened to mobilize the public with the warning that "there is no doubt that I have an intimate, deep relationship with the poor masses."[38]

By 1993, when civil society had perhaps reached its most visible level of vigor, Brazil's new democracy had fallen into something of a political abyss, with many influential commentators openly discussing the possibility of the breakdown of democracy and conservative politicians calling for the return to military rule. For their part, the general public, deeply disillusioned with the government and the political system, was entertaining the escapist plan of restoring the Monarchy the country abandoned nearly a century ago.[39] That democratic government did not collapse in Brazil during this trying period had little to do with people's positive attitudes toward democracy. As suggested by Linz and Stepan, the survival of democracy in Brazil in the early 1990s is owed not to its support by the public but rather to the fact that no nondemocratic alternatives were attractive or credible and no important groups devoted significant resources to mobilizing support for a coup.[40]

Beset by scandals, hyperinflation and economic recession, Brazilians got a new president in Itamar Franco (Collor's vice president, who assumed power after Collor's removal from office). Franco was a mercurial, inward-looking politician whose tenure in office was notable for the many problems his administration encountered in getting his policies approved by the congress, powerful state governors and a highly mobilized civil society. His dismal performance created a power vacuum within an already seriously weakened political regime that triggered persistent rumors of a Fujimori-style self-coup, in which the president would invite the military into government to restore political order.[41] A turning point in the life of the New Republic came with the 1994 electoral triumph of Fernando Henrique Cardoso (Itamar Franco's former finance minister and a well-known Brazilian social scientist). A subsequent victory in 1998 made him the first Brazilian leader ever to be reelected.

Under the Cardoso presidency (1994–2002), Brazilian democracy gained a new lease on life. Cardoso's most noticeable and impressive achievement was curbing inflation. When his economic stabilization program (the *Plano Real*) was introduced in 1994, inflation was running at an annual rate of 10,445 percent but soon fell to single figures and stayed there.[42] Cardoso's scorecard also shows that during his tenure in government extreme poverty was reduced from 20 to 15 percent, infant mortality fell from 40 per 1,000 births to 28 per 1,000 while the number of children attending school jumped from 83 to 93 percent.[43] These improvements in the quality of governance and life, rather than an expanding civil society, explain whatever degree of optimism Brazilian democracy enjoys today, at least as suggested by the fact that talks of a democratic breakdown, so common in the early 1990s, have dissipated in recent years. Yet the Cardoso administration is revealing of why democratic consolidation in Brazil is likely to remain a work in progress in the years to come.

Timothy Power's analysis of the Cardoso years gets to the point of the matter when he notes that despite Cardoso's successes and lack of talk of a democratic breakdown during his administration, it is a mistake to presume that stable patterns of democratic governance have been established in Brazil. He writes that although in recent years the "G-word" (governability) has virtually disappeared from the political lexicon, "the underlying political structures are no different than they were in 1993, when Brazil had apparently reached the end of its rope and rumors of a coup abounded."[44] On the one hand is the overall weakness of the state—driven by entrenched traditions of patronage and clientelism, bureaucratic complexity and incoherence and poor credibility with the general public. These conditions preclude the forging of the kind of societal support and consensus that is needed to secure political stability and promote social development.

On the other hand is the glaring under-institutionalization of the party system. The Cardoso years were notable for the constant battling between the government and a vast constellation of opposition parties and powerful organized interests as well as within Cardoso's own heterogeneous and fractious four-party coalition. It stretched from his own social democratic party to the right-wing Liberal Front. This meant that during much of his tenure in office Cardoso's program beyond economic stabilization was stalled in congress, crippling progress in such critical areas as land reform, human rights, and restructuring of Brazil's notoriously corrupt judicial system. These failures, in turn, explain much about the dismal standing of political institutions in Brazil in the minds of the citizenry.

State Structures and Institutional Legacies

One of the harshest indictments of the conditions of the central state in Brazil around the time of the democratic transition is that offered by

Alfred Stepan. In the late 1980s he noted: "The Brazilian state apparatus was in such a state of de-composition that the attempt to utilize it, without making serious changes in its structure, values and responsiveness, served only to deepen developmental crises."[45] He adds that the problematic conditions of the Brazilian state account for why in Brazil there has been more "system blame" against the new democracy and more worries about "governability" than found in comparable periods in Spain, Uruguay or Argentina. These remarks, while reflective of a specific historical juncture, fit well within broad patterns of state development in contemporary Brazil.

The general weakness of the central state in Brazil is deep-rooted and can be traced to the founding of Republican government in the wake of the demise of the Brazilian Monarchy in 1889. Oligarchic elites in control of powerful regional states deliberately avoided creating powerful federal structures for fears that they would undermine regional autonomy.[46] Such sentiments found institutional expression in the creation of the Old Republic (1898–1930), whose weak and underdeveloped institutions were both a cover and a catalyst for the clientelism, patronage and patrimonialism that has traditionally characterized Brazilian politics.[47] A centralized state in Brazil did not emerge until the 1940s, under Getulio Vargas' *Estado Novo* (New State), which endowed the state with a wide range of administrative bureaucracies. The Brazilian state was further developed by successive populist/democratic regimes through the 1950s and the military after 1964. During these periods, the state grew exponentially; but unlike Spain's developmental dictatorship of the late Franco period, state institutions in Brazil did not develop the technocratic capacity and institutional autonomy to effectively perform their developmental duties.

Frances Hagopian has argued that for all of the strength that bureaucratic authoritarianism is thought to have brought to the Brazilian state during the 1960s and 1970s, clientelistic networks survived the military dictatorship and in many ways actually expanded.[48] This traditional culture of clientelistism is deeply entrenched in Brazilian politics since it was nurtured by regional elites during the days of the Old Republic as a means to gain privileges and access to the various branches of the state. Its impact upon Brazilian politics is at least twofold. On the one hand, it deprives the federal state of coherence and autonomy making it vulnerable to powerful interest groups and limiting its capacity to enforce federal law. For instance, given the tremendous powers that the individual states exercise over such matters as finance and public security, the democratic governments of the post-1985 period have found it very hard to implement their reformist agenda to the detriment of the consolidation of democracy. According to Human Rights Watch, the tension between the generally pro-human rights position of the Cardoso government and the entrenched, often violent policies of many states constituted the greatest obstacle to the 1996 National Human Rights Plan.[49] On the other hand, the weakness of the federal government has allowed regional political bosses to turn their states into patronage machines for the dispensing of favors to preferred "clients." This is generally blamed for the country's infamous corruption, which according to some studies has increased with the advent of democratic government.[50]

The Legacy of Clientelism

The impact of clientelism upon the politics of Brazil's New Republic goes well beyond the constitution of the state. As contended by Mainwaring, rampant clientelism and the oft-associated progeny—corruption and nepotism—is a principal culprit behind Brazil's travails with democratic legitimacy. He notes that while democratic legitimacy is created on the basis of perceptions that the government furthers "the public interest," clientelism responds to "particularistic interests."[51] This individualistic approach to politics and the delivery of social services, even when employed to serve the poor, hardly benefits the common good for, in Mainwaring's view, "it reinforces dependency rather than empowerment." Since resources are doled out for private and political benefit rather than for social programs that ameliorate poverty or create new opportunities for the disenfranchised, party programs and class issues are undermined to the detriment of the popular sectors. This in turn "demoralizes democratic practices" by contributing to cynicism and depoliticization among the population: why participate in politics when it is a private, corrupt exchange of goods and favors?[52]

As would be expected, the thick clientelistic culture that envelops the political system in Brazil is reflected in the structure and behavior of civil society groups, including those created in the democratic period. The vigorous revival of clientelistic networks and power brokers and their capacity to hand out financial favors and political access outside of the formal political process triggered by the democratic transition has proved irresistible to resurgent civil society groups. Consequently, many of them currently operate "in ways closer to traditional Brazilian clientelism or corporatism than to the ideal of internal democracy."[53] This can be presumed to inhibit their capacity to act as democratizing forces by serving as antidotes to antidemocratic practices such as clientelism and corruption—as civil society theorists expect them to do. Most vulnerable to the culture and practices of clientelism and corporatism are the NGOs, especially those that benefit from contracts from the state, which in Brazil is a significant number. In 1996, 70 percent of all

NGOs reported some kind of partnership with government agencies.[54] Such links have opened the way for charges of corruption, lack of accountability, and inefficiency; in other words the same failings as Brazilian political actors.[55]

Popular associations, presumably more virtuous than the NGOs, have not been immune to charges of antidemocratic behavior. Virtually all the leading social movements of the democratic transition have fought charges of fostering a culture of clientelism and patronage within their internal structures, together with paternalistic leadership, exclusionary practices, self-interested behavior and a host of other social ills including racism and sexism.[56] The behavior of many of the individuals that populate grassroots organizations (especially those comprising the poor) remains deeply embedded in traditional modes of interaction with the elites that does little to advance a democratic political culture. Kurt Wayland reports that "many poor living in the country side or the urban sector continue to rely on clientelistic connections to higher-status patrons in order to guarantee minimal protection and particularistic benefits. While slowing eroding, these vertical linkages hinder horizontal collective action and make it easier for elites to divide and rule thus forestalling potential challenges from below."[57] Also revealing is the case of religious groupings, often credited with granting Brazil its associational exuberance. The fast-growing Pentecostal movement is thought to reinforce "traditional patron-client relations" by engaging in what is termed "participatory authoritarianism," a behavior in which the pastor-president extends patronage and positions to loyal followers but retains the power to make political decisions and name candidates."[58] The Pentecostals' behavior within the political system also shows a similarly disturbing pattern. It is reported that the *bancada evangélica* has gained a reputation "for practicing the sort of crass deal-making for which the Brazilian Congress is famous."[59]

Developmental Failures

State inefficiency flowing from a severe case of bureaucratic weakness and underdevelopment is another key factor contributing to the dearth of social capital in Brazil. Although so-called pockets of efficiency can be found throughout several state-owned enterprises, they swim in a vast and complex bureaucratic environment notable for its incoherence and under-institutionalization.[60] Indeed, when contrasted to the size and complexity of the country and the sophistication of its economy, it is clear that many parts of the Brazilian central state remain underdeveloped. This is especially the case of the state's regulatory apparatus. The finance ministry is poorly equipped to combat tax evasion (something of a national sport in Brazil), especially among the entrepreneurial class, which in Brazil benefits from virtually unencumbered access to the state. The inability of the state to extract revenue from society aggravates fiscal crises and inhibits the government's capacity to shoulder its social responsibilities.

More telling yet (and of greater consequence for democratic consolidation) is the state of the judiciary system in Brazil, which is notorious for its inefficiency. Discussions of Brazil's system of justice and the subject of state-sponsored violence in Brazil often make note of the country's extensive legal apparatus authorizing the police the use of force. This is a legacy of the colonial period, and more specifically of the institution of slavery, which in Brazil remained in place until 1888. It was reinforced by the military regime, and passed on to the new democracy, whose governments have had little success in their attempts to overcome it. Less emphasized, however, is a deficit of institutional manpower to curb the routine physical abuse of citizens. Brazil's judicial system operates with only 7,000 judges for a population of more than 150 million.[61] This situation allows crimes to go unpunished, permits the violation of human rights of socially marginalized groups on a massive scale and harbors chronic corruption.

Despite all the publicity and societal outrage that each event generated, almost no one went to jail for the "Collorgate" scandals and the prison massacre of the early 1990s. This fits well within a broad pattern of incapacity by the state in Brazil to deal effectively with matters of crime, violence and justice. White-collar crime is rarely prosecuted in Brazil and a good deal of the violence generated by the state goes unpunished as well. In 1997, 300 police officers were indicted for torture but none punished.[62] This widespread violation of citizenship concludes Caldeira's study of crime in democratic Brazil, "constitutes the main challenge to the consolidation of democracy in Brazil."[63]

We should expect the state's incapacity to enforce law and order to impinge significantly on the nation's ability to develop its social capital, especially "inter-personal trust." This is starkly reflected in the dearth of trust among Brazilians registered in the *World Values Survey* data for Brazil. It is also evident in aspects of everyday life in Brazil. The cycle of violence that has risen in Brazil since the end of military rule goes hand in hand with mistrust by the general public in the judicial system, but also with mistrust within the population at large. As compellingly illustrated by Guillermo O'Donnell, the failures of political institutions in Brazil not only undermine social trust but also give rise to multiple incivilities such as rampant individualism and free riding and anti-civic behavior, which in turn creates "a massive prisoners' dilemma" that inhibits social and economic development.[64] These scenarios have vividly come to life in the segregation of urban spaces and the privatization of security typical of cities such as São Paulo. Writing about that city, Caldeira notes: "for many people everyday life in the city is becoming a daily management of barriers and suspicion, marked by a succession of little rituals of identification and humiliation."[65]

The wave of crime and fear that afflicts the country has also exacerbated interclass relations (which in recent years have become noticeably nastier) together with the stigmatization of the poor, widely believed by the upper classes and the police to be the main culprits in the spread of violence. A report on relations between rich and poor in Rio de Janeiro notes that the *favelados* are seen by Rio's upper class "as invaders, not residents, of the city and the favelas are seen as evil, crime-breeding places."[66] Widespread violence also accounts for the almost total breakdown of civility in the country, as seen most prominently in the spread of vigilantism and extra-legal police groups (so-called *justiceiros*). Their growth is fueled by the people's decision to bypass legal means of protection and instead take justice in their own hands, either by solving conflicts personally or by private arrangement. It is estimated that by 1998, private security guards in Brazil "greatly outnumbered the 400,000 military police in the country."[67] These security forces are composed of current and former policemen who moved to the private sector for more money.[68]

The lawlessness that envelops Brazilian society has also inhibited the capacity of civil society organizations to perform many of the functions that are thought to make them sources of social capital and by extension a foundation for democratization. A case in point is the neighborhood associations, the largest form of civil society organization in contemporary Brazil. It is reported that by the late 1990s drug dealers controlled one-third of the neighborhood associations in the favelas of Rio de Janeiro. This was facilitated by the failure of the police to protect the *favelados* and has had a chilling impact on the ability of the neighborhood associations to advance their goals and have much of an impact on the political sphere. One study notes that since the advent of drug traffickers, "the activities of the neighborhood associations have been reduced. Their former role of defending the interests of the residents has been undermined, and their mediation efforts with the government, once a key element of their activities, has also been curtailed."[69] Conditioning these developments is not only the "law of silence" imposed by the drug dealers but also the manner in which the drug traffickers have successfully cast themselves in a role that the *favelados* can relate to. As noted by a former president of a neighborhood association, the drug traffickers "act on immediate concerns of the neighborhood such as financing the samba school or building a road."[70]

A Legacy of Mistrust and Exclusion

Social capital formation in Brazil, especially in the relations between the state and organized interest groups such as the labor movement, has also been hindered by the technocratic legacy embedded in state institutions. The military regime endowed the Brazilian state with a technocratic culture that effectively prevented the emergence in the new democracy of modes of policy-making based on consensus and compromise or that would encourage incorporation of civil society into the state's decision-making process. Such interaction between state and society could have hardly been expected in Brazil given, first, the exclusionary and repressive practices that characterized policy-making under military rule between the years 1964 and 1985. This is evident most notably in the realm of industrial and labor relations.

In striking contrast to the Spanish case, where democratization of the political system was anticipated by the liberalization of industrial and labor relations and the advent of collective bargaining and democratically elected works councils, in Brazil the military chose to reinforce existing corporatist controls of the labor movement. Nowhere is this more suggestive than in the area of wage policy. The military government eliminated collective bargaining in 1964 and in its place put a rigid wage structure that was grossly unfair to the workers. Wages were adjusted every 12 months and the adjusted wage was based, among other factors, on the average real wage paid over the previous 24 months. The negative distributive effects of these policies are quite obvious. A result of the belt-tightening wage laws was a significant decline in the workers' earning power. In 1976 the minimum salary in Brazil had only 31 percent of the purchasing power it had in 1959.[71] More revealing were the shifts in patterns of wealth distribution, which by the time the military took over the country were already among the world's most unfair, and remained that way despite the advent of an economic boom.

During military rule Brazil experienced an economic miracle that saw double-digit growth rates during the early 1970s and that propelled the country's economy to the ranks of the world's largest (currently the Brazilian economy ranks ninth in the world in terms of GDP), but income distribution in Brazil actually deteriorated. The poorest 20 percent of the population of Brazil saw their percentage control of total income decline from 3.9 percent in 1960 to 2.8 percent by 1980. By contrast, the richest 10 percent saw their share of total income rise from 39.6 percent in 1960 to 50.9 percent in 1990. As would be expected, this economic upheaval in the lives of the Brazilian working class had a significant impact on the kinds of relationships that developed between workers and employers as well as the general political proclivities of the labor movement. At the elite level, it propelled the rise of a new unionism noted for its militancy, emphasis on class-consciousness, and unflinching stance against cooperation with the employers and especially the state.

At the societal level, the military's economic program made for a particularly contentious climate of relations between workers and employers since the basic model of industrial relations that consolidated during the military period was one that emphasized adversarial relationships between capital and labor under the aegis of a despotic state.[72] Clearly, this environment was not auspicious for generating trust neither within the population at large nor especially toward governing institutions. Nor was this environment conducive to the construction of autonomous networks and arrangements of cross-class cooperation (like Spain's system of works councils) designed to promote bargaining, negotiation and cooperation in the workplace. Consequently, Brazilian workers (unlike their counterparts in Spain) entered the democratic period with little if any significant experience of "positive" interaction with either government or the state.

Also aiding in undermining the values and behaviors of social capital was the technocratic insulation of the state's economic institutions from popular pressures, another defining characteristic of military rule in Brazil.[73] This stemmed from the military's perception that the weakness of the state resided in the kinds of populist alliances made by democratic governments and the labor movement prior to the 1964 coup. Thus, keeping the state's technocracy protected from "special" interests (mostly from the popular sectors) became a central preoccupation of military officers and a key explanation for the secrecy and exclusionary practices that came to dominate state technocratic culture in authoritarian Brazil. In light of this, it is hardly surprising that during the negotiations for a social pact in Brazil in the mid-1980s, state elites flatly refused to share policy decision-making with actors from outside the state, especially organized labor.

Accustomed to operating in a culture of insulation from society that developed during the military regime, the state's technocratic elites entered the new democracy exhibiting "a distaste for and distrust of the political process and a predisposition for solutions that appear to be entirely under government control."[74] The Sarney administration's economics team made no secret of its lack of interest in a pact with the unions. It is reported that during the consultations for a social pact convened by the minister of labor the government's economic ministers were "conspicuously absent."[75] This action suggested that "they did not wish to give up any fraction of their power over economic policy and this obstinacy effectively undermined any attempt to negotiate strategic prices."[76] Accordingly, the first stabilization program in the new democracy (the *Cruzado* plan) stood in striking contrast to the notion of a social pact. It was "prepared secretly within the executive bureaucracy, announced without legislative approval, and implemented over the vigorous criticisms of the heads of the major unions."[77]

Mistrust in the state was another legacy of the bureaucratic authoritarian period in Brazil, a development intimately linked to the onerous record of the military regime regarding such sensitive subjects as wages and inflation. These were central aspects of the negotiation for social pacts between the government and the unions during the 1980s and 1990s. Especially damaging to the credibility of the state on matters of wage policy as the country approached democratization was a history of manipulation and outright deceit of economic information by technocrats hell-bent on raising growth levels at the expense of the workers. This was most clearly the case during the mid-1970s (the peak years of economic growth in Brazil) when the unions' own technical services discovered blatant abuses in the calculation of the cost-of-living index that resulted in a wage loss estimated at 31.1 percent. This finding was later corroborated by the World Bank and launched "the Campaign of 31.1 percent" (also known as the campaign for *reposição*), a search for compensation for the loss of purchasing power occasioned by the government's manipulation of statistical data on inflation. The impact of this campaign went beyond whatever economic demands it raised. The state's manipulation of wages sent the message that state representatives "were not to be trusted."[78]

Lula's words best articulate the coherence of the mistrust toward state institutions that formed within the labor movement as democratization began to play out in Brazil. In a 1979 interview he noted:

> The workers have ceased to believe in the many things that deceived them for a long time. They had believed, for example, that the government could do many things for the working class, because the pseudo-benevolences of Getulio Vargas were still firmly implanted in the workers' mind. The workers believed that the political leadership was elected to do something for their benefit, even though it was not composed of workers but of managerial people and other members of the elite. Today, the worker does not believe in that anymore. Today he believes more in his own strength.[79]

Political Parties and Democratic Consolidation

In the post-transition period Brazil has operated with one of the weakest, most fragmented, and poorly organized political party systems in Latin

America. Mainwaring writes that "many of the cliches about parties in Latin America—clientelistic, dependent upon the state, little impact in formulating public policy—are partially misleading when applied to the other more developed countries of the region, but they are generally true in the Brazilian case."[80] This characterization of Brazilian parties explains why comparative studies of Latin American parties hold Brazil to be a prototype of an "inchoate" party system, a condition in which parties are weakly rooted in society, suffer precipitous declines while others experience electoral upsurges, citizens switch party preferences with regularity and many question their legitimacy.[81]

Much has been made of the consequences of Brazil's party weaknesses on the process of democratic consolidation, especially an extraordinarily high rate of electoral volatility as parties come and go with disturbing frequency. The Pedersen Index of Electoral Volatility, which measures the percentage of seats (votes) that change party hands from one election to another, notes that the average electoral volatility for stable democracies is below 9 percent (in votes).[82] The average rate for Brazil between the years 1982 and 1990, however, was 40 percent, the highest among Southern Cone countries and one of the highest percentages ever recorded. The impact of high electoral volatility in retarding democratic consolidation is best seen in the general inefficiency of the Brazilian Congress. Assessments of its performance during the democratic period make note of its "slow and unproductive nature," as reflected in the finding that most (approximately 75 percent) of the laws that it eventually approves originate in the executive branch.[83]

Weak Roots in Society

Less explored about the consequences of Brazil's party deficit is the impact on social integration, and more specifically on the capacity of the nation to generate consensus and cross-class collaboration. In democratic Brazil, the party system has been generally unable to play the roles of mentor, institutional conduit and power broker for civil society. One of the more striking developments about the dazzling resurgence of civil society that began in the late 1960s and that touched the lives of millions of Brazilians is that it was hardly reflected on the constitution of the party system, at least at the inception of democracy. As seen shortly, representation of civil society in the dominant parties of the democratic transition was scant and this is largely responsible for the apparent inability of civil society to reign in the authoritarian powers of the state and accelerate the pace of democratization after 1974. While able to press for democratization by mobilizing huge numbers of citizens, the actual impact of civil society on the speed and scope of the democratic transition in Brazil was limited. In the end the decision of how to execute the transition remained in the hands of state institutions (the military in particular) and a party apparatus over which civil society had very little influence. At no point in the transition in Brazil could civil society rely upon credible segments of the party system to advance its struggles against the authoritarian state and to leave a strong imprint on the kind of democracy it desired.

Nor could civil society organize its own political agenda and reconcile the often-contradictory objectives pursued by its many different groups. As observed by Wayland, "Brazil's vibrant civil society speaks in innumerable voices and has great difficulty advancing over-arching goals such as redistributive reforms or other types of structural transformation."[84] He adds that the "inchoate nature of the Brazil's political system disables the main institutional mechanism that could in principle advance broad-based bottom-up pressure for a systematic transformation."[85] This prevents the translation of severe structural problems—especially mass poverty and egregious social inequality—into open political contention and ideological polarization.

These developments stem directly from the lack of deep, historical roots of the party system within Brazilian society, a point underscored by how young the individual parties in Brazil actually are. It is astonishing that all the electorally significant parties in Brazil since the transition to democracy date back only to the 1970s. By contrast, party systems in other Latin American countries incorporate parties that trace their origins to the nineteenth century and the founding of Republican government. For example, the two largest parties in Uruguay have existed for 150 years and Argentina's two leading parties have existed for 100 and 40 years, respectively.[86] Implied in the youth of the Brazilian party system is the extraordinary fact that none of the major pre-coup parties survived the military dictatorship. By contrast, in many other cases of democratization in Southern Europe and South America (such as Spain, Chile, Argentina and Uruguay) pre-authoritarian parties were important forces in resurrecting civil society and mobilizing it against the authoritarian regime. They were also key contenders in the first transition elections and many of them remain vital political organizations to this day.

As seen already, the leading political parties of the Brazilian transition were products of the military regime's attempt to create a two-party system in Brazil in the late 1970s. The PDS, which represented the military government during the transition, had no real interest in nurturing or mobilizing civil society given its overwhelming conservative nature and highly profitable association with the authoritarian regime. Its actions in the congress between the years 1974 and 1985 suggested that its commitment to democracy was highly suspect if not nonexistent altogether. As seen already, the PDS and its predecessor (ARENA) did everything within their power to delay and undermine democratization after 1974. Party bosses from the PDS had much to lose from liberalizing the political system. A summary of the behavior of these parties during the transition is apt:

> Between 1966–1984, ARENA and the PDS reaped the benefits of their junior partnership with the military dictatorship. They consistently supported military rule and until 1982, they rarely questioned the generals' edicts. Thus, the conservative parties' pre-1984 record was hardly auspicious for their acceptance of democracy.[87]

The second major party of the transition, the PDMB, was one of five parties that emerged from the split of the MDB enforced by the military in 1979 as well as its most direct heir. It represented the democratic opposition to the military and therefore was the "official" representative of civil society during the transition. But the heterogeneous ideological orientation and the association of many of its leaders with the military seriously compromised this role. Due to its origins as a puppet opposition party under the military regime, the PDMB was essentially an elite-driven organization with few formal ties to the popular sector and largely dominated by conservatives. Just before the 1985 elections and in anticipation of its victory, the PDMB had become a vehicle for former members of the military party (the PDS) to advance their careers in the new democratic regime. This was the case of Sarney, whose ascent to the presidency of Brazil in 1984–1985 and head of the victorious PDMB, immediately disqualified the party as a representative of civil society in the new democracy.

The political constitution of the leading parties dictated that during the democratic transition many civil society groups would remain on the sidelines regarding partisan politics. Indeed, a common strategy of many social movements during the transition was to remain free of party identification and/or affiliation. This was the choice of some of the largest social movements of the transition such as the CEB's and to a lesser degree the neighborhood associations. A corresponding outcome of these decisions is the fact that representation of civil organizations in the Brazilian Congress in the democratic period has been exceptionally weak. It is reported that two-thirds (68.5 percent) of the 700 state deputies across Brazil in the period 1987–1990 had no links with either unions or professional/employer, neighborhood, sport, religious or other associations. Most surprising about this data is the finding that of the major party representatives, 71.5 percent of the deputies of the PMDB had no links with civic associations and 51.5 percent of the workers' Party (a party reputed to have more links with social movements than any other) had none.[88]

A Missing Link: Left-Wing Parties and Civil Society

The dearth of connections between the party system and society in Brazil reflects the absence in Brazilian political history of what Alessandro Pizzorno has referred to as "integration" parties.[89] These parties are most likely to endure repression and institutional crises since they are highly centralized, disciplined and draw a significant membership from the masses. Traditionally, such parties in both South America and Western Europe have taken the form of working-class parties along the lines of the Socialist and Communist parties of Spain and Chile or the Peronist party in Argentina. In all of these cases, integration parties galvanized the working masses and incorporated into the political arena mass-based social movements and popular interest groups such as organized labor; in other words, significant representation from civil society. This was especially the case during the transition to democracy.

Among the reasons for Brazil's failure to develop a classic integration party is the comparatively small size of its urban working class, at least when contrasted to that of Spain, Chile, Argentina and Uruguay. Also relevant is the highly interventionist role of the state in making and remaking the nation's party system. As chronicled by Mainwaring, the state in Brazil has repeatedly shaped party-system formation from above, and it has dissolved party systems in Brazil in 1889, 1930, 1937 and 1979, with disruptive consequences in each case.[90] Additionally, there is the historic failure of the orthodox Left in Brazil to connect to important civil society constituencies, especially the labor movement. This is suggested most pointedly by the fact that neither the Brazilian Socialist party (PSB), nor the Brazilian Communist party (PCB), which was legalized in 1985, emerged as viable political institutions in the new democracy. Surely, this cannot be explained away as a result of military repression, for the treatment of the Left under authoritarian rule was considerably harsher in Spain, Chile and Uruguay than in Brazil.

The lackluster performance of left-wing parties during the democratic transition in Brazil can be attributed to developments within the Brazilian Left that took place long before the initiation of political liberalization. The Brazilian Left is notorious for having flirted in the past with supporting either implicitly or explicitly nondemocratic regimes. For instance, during the 1940s the PCB closely collaborated with the Vargas regime. During the military dictatorship the parties from the Left lent some legitimacy to the authoritarian state by agreeing to participate in military-sponsored elections and by endorsing the military's restructuring of the party system that began in the early 1970s with the creation of the PMDB and PDS. Such cooperation from the Left would have been unfathomable in countries such as Spain, Chile or even Argentina.

During the 1968–1973 period, a "vanguardist" conception of politics permeated the Brazilian Left and there were almost no linkages between clandestine organizations and the masses.[91] This period saw the Left come to regard political democracy and its institutions as a "bourgeois façade," a happening that coincided with the embrace of guerilla warfare against the state, which in Brazil had dismal results. Mainwaring notes that by 1973 "the naivete and tragic consequences of this approach were well all too apparent and the left began to seek new linkages with the popular sectors" in the hope of constructing a democratic regime.[92] The newfound appreciation for political democracy and the popular sectors exhibited by the Left after 1974, however, came too late for its parties to gain a foothold on the resurgent civil society. During the transition many groups in civil society essentially wrote them off in their struggles against the military regime and in favor of democracy.

As an alternative to reaching power, many Communist and Socialist leaders began to run for office under the banner of the MDB, and later the PMDB, which, as noted already, came to be known as the official democratic opposition to the authoritarian regime. This was pursuant to the strategy of the PCB and other left-wing parties during the democratic transition of working together with other forces opposing the military grouped around the PMDB, in the hope of occupying the state after the demise of the military regime. This strategy, however sound from a political standpoint, did little to bring the Left closer to the social movements that dominated civil society during the transition. The PMDB's history of collaboration with the military troubled many civil society organizations, especially the unions, which prized their autonomy and were committed to the struggle for democracy from below.

This brief historical background helps explain why civil society entered the New Republic in 1985 "deeply suspicious" of political intermediaries such as parties. More specifically, this background sheds light on why in the democratic period the prevailing discourse of civil society activists and the public at large has tended to "belittle the role of parties, Congress, and elections."[93] "The parties only want the vote of the people, not their opinion," was the sentiment of 72.4 percent of the Brazilian people in a 1988 survey.[94] Another survey of 1991 found that 52 percent of Brazilians agreed with the statement: "Parties don't do any good, they only hurt more than they help the country."[95] A more striking finding was reported by a 1995 *Latinobarómetro* survey that revealed that 47 percent of Brazilians agreed that "democracy can function without parties."[96] Perhaps the most revealing finding of all, however, was reported in a 1989 survey that found that 52.3 percent of Brazilians thought that social movements such as the unions and others should control candidate selection for public office.[97]

Interestingly enough, disdain for parties by civil society organizations has been aimed most directly at the Marxist Left. A common complaint among neighborhood associations and other popular sector organizations during the transition was that "the Marxist left manipulates the movement for its own ends."[98] Fears of co-optation and manipulation by the parties of the Left also ran deep (perhaps deepest) with the most important civil society constituency of them all: organized labor. At the onset of democratization, "the very term party aroused suspicion among the workers," given the premium that the resurgent labor movement placed on autonomy from the political system.[99] The new unionists that created the CUT were especially critical of the Left's pro-democracy political discourse, which they deemed opportunistic and irrelevant to the workers' lives. They also opposed the strategy of cooperation with the government pursued by the PCB during the transition and especially the party's open support for social pacts. This was anathema to the members of CUT and other organizations comprising the new unionism for whom reaching political office or even defending the institutions of political democracy was secondary to improving socioeconomic conditions on the ground. As argued by Margaret Keck: "the focus of the new unionism on shop floor issues and on winning new rights from employers involved a separation of industrial action from the political role of representing and advocating the rights of labor in the political sphere."[100]

A Ray of Hope?

By far the most successful left-wing party since the transition to democracy in Brazil is the Workers' Party (PT). Formed by CUT leaders, intellectuals and parts of the Socialist Left in 1980, the birth of this party is regarded as the most important development in party politics in Brazil in the postwar era.[101] Indeed, in many regards, the PT is today Brazil's best hope for developing the country's first integration party and for improving society's representation within the political system. The party's debut in the 1982 elections was less than impressive (it received less than 5 percent of the vote), but the PT would make an impressive comeback in local elections in 1985 and reach stunning victories in the late 1980s largely aided by its growing ties to civil society. The PT survived its poor electoral showing in the 1980s because of its ties to civil society, especially an expanding labor movement. In October 2002, the PT reached the pinnacle of political success with the election of Lula to the office of the presidency, the first time in Brazil's history that a left-wing leader has led the country.

For much of the period of democratization reviewed in this study, however, the PT was not able to play the role of transmission belt with respect to civil society that the Communist and Socialist parties played in the Spanish transition. It was not until the late 1980s that the PT gained a sig-nificant national following and began to play a role at the national level. More importantly, for many years after its creation, the party wanted nothing to do with the government, the established party system or pact-making during the democratic transition. As Keck noted about the PT in the late 1980s, "In spite of its legalization and participation in elections, the PT has remained essentially society-centered in its orientation "ensuing from its emphasis on working class-development and mistrust of State and parliamentary institutions."[102]

These positions reflected the PT's ties to a highly repressed labor move-ment and its sense that the Brazilian labor had gained little from its previous affiliations with the state or the party system. Moreover, the philosophy of the party mirrored the significant discomfort that had led many social move-ments, including labor, to disassociate themselves from the parties. At the inception of democracy in Brazil, the PT was the best representative in Latin America of so-called non-party parties, a characterization that speaks to a general disdain for the political establishment. Consequently, during this period the party functioned more as a social movement than an institution-alized component of the nation's party system.[103] As such, for much of its short history the PT has relished its role of outsider in the party system and consequently refused to perform the role of institutional conduit between workers' organizations and the political system. Mainwaring writes that the creators of the PT "eschewed the PMDB's broad-front strategy, arguing that it subordinated popular interests and that it was important to create a partisan vehicle that would support such struggles."[104]

Since the late 1980s the PT has undergone a significant institutional transition from a "non-party party" to a "loyal opposition party."[105] This is evident not only in the many electoral contests that the party has won but also in the alliances the party has made with "established" parties in many electoral contests including the second round of the 1989 presidential elections. More relevant to the purposes of our study, however, is the PT's growing role as a democratizing, socializing force in Brazilian society. In the last decade, the PT has embraced participatory democracy with the dual purpose of mobilizing the masses and changing Brazil's clientelistic political culture. In cities such as Porto Alegre and Belo Horizonte, where the PT has achieved significant electoral successes, the party has opened policy-making arenas such as setting budgetary priorities to citizens' groups. These activities have served to educate the citizenry, restore the people's faith in representative government and promote the actual growth of civil society. It is reported that in Porto Alegre "innumerable new neighborhood organizations have appeared in response to this policy, often in areas that were previously dominated by closed, ineffective associations that served little more than tools of clientelist party politics."[106]

The Legacy of Negative Social Capital

A central challenge of the new Lula administration is overcoming the cynicism and mistrust deeply engrained in Brazilian political culture. This negative form of social capital thrives in Brazilian society because it represents a defense and a mode of coping with the failures of the political system. To be sure, Brazil is not alone in this regard. As insightfully noted by Marta Lagos of the *Latinobarómetro*, in Brazil, as in the rest of Latin America, "distrust" has historically been a crucial tool for survival.[107] What is worrisome about Brazil, however, is the manner in which distrust (especially toward the political system) has been internalized into a wholesale rejection of the political system, a project largely driven by several components of civil society.

The execution of this project is clearly understood from the standpoint of political and even human survival, but it does little to advance the process of democratic consolidation. Many of the civil society groups that have emerged in Brazil since the late 1970s have cultivated what is essentially an antipolitics and antiparty institutional identity. Indeed, many have built their appeal to the masses by repudiating the political system and exploiting its failures. The much-praised CEBs, for example, did much to create cleavages between the social movement sphere and the political system. Thomas Skidmore notes that attempts by left-wing parties to court the CEBs yielded little success given that the "radical Christian doctrines" based on the theology of liberation that they espoused reinforced "mistrust in political institutions."[108] Consequently, the CEBs "strongly opposed any party identification."[109]

More revealing perhaps is the trajectory of the CUT, the nation's leading union. During the early days of the New Republic the CUT leadership was explicitly disdainful of the party system and its political rhetoric did not shy away from flirting with radicalism. As recently as 1985, Lula was advocating "armed struggle as the only way to bring profound change to Brazil."[110] Such thinking found its way into the platform endorsed by the CUT in its second national congress of 1986, which called for the invasion of idle property, prompting President Sarney to remark that "the CUT did not have the right to encourage the radicalization of the country."[111] With the gradual incorporation of the PT into the political establishment, the strategies of confrontation of the CUT and other labor organizations born with the transition have undergone a process of moderation, and this bodes well for democratic consolidation in Brazil. But the Brazilian public sphere remains far from being fully integrated into the democratic political system. Largely fueled by the very failures and shortcomings of the new democracy, a second generation of post-transition social movement activism has been born in Brazil, which perhaps more intensely than the first exhibits a significant detachment from political society and an ambiguous democratic hue. Many of these movements operate under a rigid civil society versus state dichotomy in which confrontation is the sole currency for interaction.

This behavior is the case of an uncomfortably high number of civic organizations in Brazil that in recent years have contributed to the radicalization of domestic politics. Their behavior if not anti-system is decidedly uncivil, violent and even radical. The crisis of crime and fear, for instance, has generated a right-wing opposition movement to human rights that opposes humanizing prisons, police reform and other innovations. With the aid of important allies in congress, the so-called *bancada da segurança* (security bloc), a staunch defender of a violent police, this movement has succeeded in distorting much of the universal discourse on human rights and thwarting progress in curbing police violence. In their view, those that support reform of the judicial system advocate "privileges for bandits." As remarked by Caldeira, for the anti–human rights forces, "the defenders of human rights are transformed into people working against the rights of honest citizens and in favor of criminals."[112] Such arguments, which have gained significant resonance within the public, explain the serious difficulties the Cardoso administration had implementing his 1996 National Plan for Human Rights.

The rise of negative forms of social capital in Brazil is most prominent in remote parts of the country, where the presence of political institutions (both the state and the party system) is often insignificant and where their failures are most patently evident. Groups active in these areas have refurbished the rhetoric and repertoire of collective action espoused by their predecessors with a more radical approach to making demands against the state. While the promotion of democracy occupied the time and energies of the first cycle of post-transition social movements in Brazil, the second cycle is devoted to exposing the failures of democracy and finding alternatives to the venues for political participation that it provides. Notable among them is *Sem Terra* (MST), whose motto for land reform, "by law or disorder," sums up its political agenda.[113]

Capitalizing upon the failure of the state to correct a situation in which 3 percent of the population owns two-thirds of the country's arable land, MST-instigated conflicts over land ownership have spread like wildfire in Brazil in the last decades. Created in 1985 and lacking affiliation with any political party, the MST is credited with organizing 151,427 landless families in the illegal occupation of 21 million hectares between the years 1990 and 1996. This success has inspired other social movements to adopt similar tactics thereby radicalizing the making of social demands. Directly inspired by the MST, since the mid-1990s, a movement of small farmers (MPA) has been blocking roads and occupying government offices and private estates to press its case against the state. This activism by the MPA has spilled onto older and more established organizations such as the CONTAG, the country's leading rural union, which since the late 1990s has joined the MPA in facilitating land occupations. In 1997 *Sem Terra*'s "combativeness" also spawned an urban version of itself, the *Movimento dos Trabalhadores Sem Teto Urbano* (Homeless Urban Workers' Movement), active in Rio Grande do Sul.[114]

Much of the preceding analysis suggests that overcoming negative forms of social capital in Brazil will require nothing short of a political miracle. Yet there are reasons for optimism, all linked to political developments ensuing from the 2002 presidential elections. The elections themselves gave a much-needed boost to Brazil's beleaguered political system. Most of the attention has been focused on Lula's rags-to-riches political saga. Less noticed, however, was the execution of the election itself, a model of civility, efficiency and transparency that is currently being praised as a model for other large and complex democracies including the United States. Lula also became the first president in the new democracy to enjoy the backing of a well-developed party infrastructure with internal discipline and significant connections to civil society constituencies. As such, his government holds the promise for the transformation not only of the political system but also of civil society itself. While obviously vibrant and robust as far as its associative capacity is concerned, Brazilian civil society remains a reluctant partner of the political system, a situation that limits its role in facilitating the consolidation of democracy.

PART IV

Comparative Perspectives

CHAPTER 7

Civil Society Reconsidered

At the heart of the present study is a critique of the much heralded and widespread association that has been made in the last decade between strong civil societies and sustainable democracies. In particular, I have relied upon the experiences of Spain and Brazil to challenge the assumption that a vibrant and robust landscape of voluntary associations is a precondition or a must-have for nations seeking to consolidate democratic governance. The case of Spain convincingly illustrates the point that a deficit in civil society development is not a handicap to the successful consolidation of democracy while the case of Brazil suggests that democratic consolidation is not guaranteed when it faces a vigorous civil society. The cases of Spain and Brazil have also been enlisted to reconsider some of the central theoretical assumptions underlying the presumed importance of a strong civil society to democratic consolidation. Above all, I have sought to locate the formation of social capital, that subjective phenomenon comprising a range of values, attitudes and behaviors believed to lubricate democracy, within the constitution and performance of political institutions rather than the configuration of civil society. Although provocative, the view of civil society as the exclusive domain of the production of social capital neglects to take into account the role of the political system in engendering and undermining the principal components of social capital.

This final chapter has two central goals. The first is to explore the validity of my arguments outside of the Spanish and Brazilian experiences. The second is to gather the study's implications for the comparative study of political institutions, theories of social capital and the role of civil society in the consolidation of democratic regimes.

Beyond Spain and Brazil

Given the prominent place that postwar Italy occupies in much of the theorizing about civil society and social capital it is fitting to commence with this case to prove the validity of my arguments beyond the empirical terrain of Spain and Brazil. Putnam's critics provide the primary evidence. Sidney Tarrow's thoughtful critique of Putnam's analysis of Italian politics in *Making Democracy Work* pointedly challenges Putnam's faith in the powers of a thriving civil society to preserve a democratic community by highlighting the decay of Italian democracy (especially in the North) in the last decade.[1] Tarrow wonders what Putnam would have made of the successive explosions in northern Italian public life that were erupting as his book was going to press and that have significantly tarnished the North's fabled civic community.[2] They include the rise of the separatist and xenophobic Northern League, corruption scandals, political kidnappings, terrorism and Mafia infestation of politics. These developments have risen hand-in-hand with the deterioration of the Italian political system in the last decades.

Tarrow's more substantive criticism of Putnam's work, however, deals with Putnam's dearth of attention to political institutions and processes in the building of the North's widely heralded social capital endowment. Tarrow contends that the operative cause for the superior performance of regional institutions in Italy is neither cultural nor associational (as Putnam's analysis implies) but rather political. He argues that some of the areas in which Putnam finds the greatest levels of social capital and positive institutional performance are also the same areas in which progressive and Catholic political parties made a deliberate attempt to aid in the development of civil society by creating and promoting civic institutions.

In the areas in which civil competence appears high, Tarrow notes, "electorates were deliberately mobilized on the basis of networks, mass organizations and social and recreational associations."[3] He concludes that in the North, civic competence was deliberately developed after World War II as a symbol of the left-wing parties' governing capacity and skills to connect to the masses. By contrast, Tarrow notes that both progressive politics and civic capacity were correspondingly weak in the South. Tarrow also focuses on divergent processes of state building and their effects on indigenous civic capacity. He observes that "every regime that governed southern Italy from the Norman establishment of a centralized monarchy in the 12th century to unification in 1861 was foreign and governed with a logic of colonial exploitation."[4] Their purpose was not to establish effective democratic government but rather political control.

The post-Communist world, where theorizing about the virtues of civil society has also been intense, provides another fruitful setting for exploring our arguments, especially the impact of the performance of political institutions and their legacies in effecting the production of social trust among nascent civil society organizations. As noted earlier, most attention to civil society in Eastern Europe and the former Soviet Union has focused on building up the flattened landscape of these regions' associational life.[5] In this setting, as in Spain and Brazil, the faith in the capacity of a dense civil society to engender democracy appears to have been misplaced. Certainly, in comparing the civil societies of the post-Communist world with those of South America and Southern Europe it is important to highlight notable developmental differences. In nations such as Spain and Argentina (where the density of civil society appears to be lower than in some post-Communist societies) strong traditions of independent workers' organization, party politics and the legacy of what Juan Linz has termed "limited pluralism" have provided useful foundations for the resurgence of relatively autonomous civil societies in the post-transition period.

These comments point to the importance of building up civil society as part of the overall project of democratization in the post-Communist world. But this project of civil society construction will have a real impact on the consolidation of democracy only if situated within the appropriate political, institutional environment. In other words, a political system endowed with capable and legitimate institutions. As illustrated in the appendix, a decade after the collapse of Communism, the density of civil society remains a poor indicator of the fate of the democratization project and the democratic constitution of civil society. A more convincing variable is the performance of the political system. Russia's democratic development in the last decade is a case in point.

The failure of successive governments to secure political stability and socioeconomic well-being in Russia and other post-Communist states accounts for the rise of what Laurence Whitehead refers to as civil society "incivilities." This refers to such phenomena as the "impersonal irresponsibility of modern commercialized mass media, the impulsiveness of an uprooted and disoriented electorate, the short-termism of speculative financial markets and the insecurity generated by well-organized crime, typically lodged on such strategic sectors as arms trafficking, money laundering, and the narcotics trade."[6] These pathologies of civil society serve to contribute to the general impoverishment of the public sphere and to contaminate other forms of civil society organization that can be expected to serve the cause of democratization such as unions, recreational associations, students' organizations and the like.

Further complicating the picture for civil society in Russia is the almost complete lack of trust that permeates relations between political and civil society, a consequence of the legacies of suspicion and mistrust embedded in state structures. Peter Reddaway notes that the political culture left behind by the Communist state is not conducive to the emergence of a civil society at least not as classically defined; therefore, expectations that the development of civil society will somehow transform the post-Communist polity are largely misguided. He writes that due to the Communist experience Russia "lacks any political tradition of democratic compromise, honest debate, and coalition-building, and the prevalence in the Soviet political culture of intrigue and diktat have made the emerging pluralistic culture anything but tolerant and civilized."[7] This political culture explains why some "radical" democratic politicians have been as bad as the "politically threatened conservatives," as well as why civil associations have been unsure about the desirability of association with a discredited regime. Consequently, Reddaway concludes, civil associations and the government have built no bridges to each other.

Analogous developments can be found in other former Soviet Republics. A study on Kazakhstan finds that social trust is in scarce supply due to the legacies of the state.[8] It notes that part of the Soviet legacy was widespread mistrust among the members of society, a situation promoted by the general unresponsiveness of government to the needs of its citizenry. This is exemplified in the manner in which the government overlooked the environmental and health consequences of nuclear energy for decades. As a result, it is noted that civil society organizations in Kazakhstan are "suspicious of most of the information they receive even if it comes from the international community." It is also noted that not only do individuals not trust their representatives in government, but these representatives do not seek to establish ties with constituencies who want to participate in the legislative process.

In light of the political culture left in its wake by Communism, we find arguments suggesting that even if post-Communist nations were to succeed in filling their "missing middle," by creating dense civil societies, this may not mean much to the consolidation of democracy. Given the political context in which civil society organizations are being born into, the kind of social capital that such organizations are likely to produce is that which has been termed "non-communitarian" social capital. In sharp contrast to conventional views of social capital, "non-communitarian" social capital is defined as "a legacy of and a reaction to inadequate and inefficient state socialist institutional arrangements, particularly networks and informal connections and related phenomena such as clientelism and corruption."[9] This negative form of social capital permeates the daily life of Russians and other post-Communist societies not only because of what the ancient regime may have left behind, but also because of what it represents in the everyday life of the citizenry. As in Brazil, non-communitarian social capital thrives in the post-Communist world because it represents an efficient means of coping in the face of the difficulties connected with transition and governmental failure.[10]

The Primacy of Political Institutions

The central lesson of the present study is the primacy of political institutions over nonpolitical ones in facilitating democratic consolidation. This lesson, in turn, suggests that it is the political system rather than civil society that is in greatest need of boosting across the democratizing world. These findings lead to the unavoidable conclusion that the most important challenge facing new democracies at the present time is not building vibrant and robust civil societies but rather developing viable political institutions whose performance can inspire trust and confidence within civil society and the general public. Blinding advocates and scholars of civil society to this reality is the popularity of the concept of civil society itself and its intense antipolitics orientations. As noted in chapter 2, characteristic of the revival of civil society is an open disregard for the importance of political institutions to the consolidation of democracy and the constitution of civil society itself.

The celebratory tone of much of the civil society revival of the last decade from both the Left and the Right belittles the importance of political institutions, occasioning widespread skepticism about their importance in contemporary democratic politics. The rhetoric of many of the social movements that animate the so-called New Left (environmentalists, feminists, human rights activists, among others) has led to widespread skepticism about the value of political institutions (parties in particular). For their part, ardent civil society advocates from the Right regard political institutions (especially the government and the state bureaucracy) as colonizing pariahs whose penetration of civil society leads to the demise of democracy. The expectation of both camps is that flourishing civil societies will either fix whatever ails political institutions, including the state, or else render them obsolete. As noted by Carothers' critique of civil society global assistance programs, "the rise of civil society induces some to see a nearly state-free future in which tentative, minimalist states hang back while powerful non-governmental groups impose a new, virtuous order."[11] The political and social logic underpinning this assumption is deeply flawed.

At a practical level, it is inconceivable to envision a well-functioning modern polity without stable and efficient political institutions. Thus, it would be unwise (if not tragic) for any society to neglect political institutions in favor of civil society at the inception of democracy. Even under the best of circumstances, the capacity of civil society to organize society, ensure that all players abide by the rules of democracy and serve as conduits for channeling popular demands is tenuous at best. Most civil society organizations are organized around a specific issue and do not usually enjoy regular interaction with policy-makers. Moreover, the resources that make civil society a powerful actor in society are not necessarily those that are best suited to the actual promotion of democratic consolidation.

Civil organizations are certainly capable of mobilizing the general public, but this much-vaunted commodity is of limited relevance to the politics of democratic consolidation. Mobilizations (whether in the form of convocations, demonstrations and strikes) can certainly bring about a transition to democracy, but in a post-transition environment, these activities lose much of their currency as elections, social and political pacts and other practices of the democratic game gain ascendancy. Its key players are not civil society organizations but rather political institutions, parties in particular, whose rise during the transition is triggered by the restoration of electoral politics and the demands of crafting new democratic institutions, such as a democratic constitution. Successful accomplishment of these tasks in a manner that is timely and does not provoke an authoritarian reversal often requires political parties to demobilize civil society and encourage institutionalized forms of political participation such as elections and parliamentary deliberations. Unsurprisingly, it is in countries with a strong tradition of political parties with significant internal connections to civil society (such as Spain) that the link between political institutionalization and civil society demobilization is most compellingly demonstrated. It is also in these countries that the process of democratic consolidation has proceeded furthest.

Beyond ensuring the workings of the democratic system, political institutions also ensure its stability. Samuel Huntington's classic work on political development, *Political Order in Changing Societies*, reminds us that a well-ordered polity requires a recognizable and stable pattern of institutional authority and political institutions that are sufficiently strong to provide the basis for legitimate political order and a working political community. He wrote: "Without strong political institutions society lacks the means to define and realize its common interests. The capacity to create political institutions is the capacity to create public interests."[12] In the absence of strong political institutions, Huntington warned, society, especially those with highly organized and mobilized publics, can degenerate into instability, disorder and even violence. He appropriately aimed this cautionary statement at developing societies whose underdevelopment he argued rested on "a shortage of political community and of effective, authoritative, legitimate government."[13]

Huntington's ominous scenarios are being recreated in numerous countries in which political decay is the order of the day and in which civil society, both literally and figuratively, has emerged as the only opposition to a beleaguered and discredited government. A case in point is Venezuela, whose recent political experience provides vivid lessons of the devastating consequences for democracy ensuing from the convergence of a mobilized civil society and failing political institutions. Venezuela's current crisis can be traced to the ossification and complete collapse in 1998 of what was once Latin America's most stable party system, a consequence of corruption, incompetence and neglect of the electorate's basic needs.[14] This allowed for the rise of Hugo Chávez, an antiparty, anti-establishment leader whose appeal to the masses is rooted in the failures of the political system and whose commitment to democracy is at best suspect. Chávez's ascent made Venezuelan civil society rather than formally organized political forces the principal opposition to the government and one of the few defenders of democracy against encroaching state authoritarianism (itself the consequence of the lack of formal political opposition to the government). On April 2002, civil society led by the nation's leading unions and business associations moved to solve the governing crisis created by Chávez's erratic rule, but in the absence of credible political institutions the streets rather than the courts, the legislature and the electoral system became the principal setting for the confrontation between civil society and the government. Chaos, bloodshed and the brief ouster of a democratically elected leader were the ensuing results of this confrontation.

Darker still is the picture emerging from the Islamic world, where the recent expansion and radicalization of civil society is seen by some analysts as "a reflection and a cause of local states' declining effectiveness and legitimacy."[15] The failure of state development in much of the Arab world, especially the troublesome legacies of Arab socialism with its nationalizations and heavy-handedness as well as recent policies of economic liberalization, have left people deeply dissatisfied with the political status quo. These state failures have in turn enticed the masses to embrace alternatives to political institutions, which more often than not have come from civil society.

Across the Arab world civil society organizations have moved in to fill the void left behind by failing governments by offering a wide range of social services from education to transportation to healthcare. But this development hardly bodes well for democracy since it has come at a high price: the general "Islamization" of society ensuing from the rigid religious and often intolerant character of the civil society organizations now performing functions previously in the hands of state authorities. In countries such as Egypt, the rise in influence of organizations such as the Muslin Brotherhood is helping to transform Egyptian society by "Islamizing Egypt from below" by, among other things, attacking secularism and promoting Islamic Shari'a as the law of the land.[16]

By raising the profile of political institutions in the consolidation of democracy my intention is not to suggest that political institutions are infallible social structures or incapable of harming society. Poorly developed or employed, political institutions can introduce many vices into civil society and imperil democracy. The work of Linz and Stepan on the breakdown of democratic regimes reminds us that many democratic failures are rooted in the loss of efficacy and legitimacy of political institutions.[17] Spain's Second Republic, and Allende's Chile, to name just a few, are all shinning examples of governments whose erratic policies served to undermine democracy by polarizing society.[18] More recently, the experiences of Italy and Venezuela suggest how party decay and misbehavior can have important consequences on regime stability and people's confidence in democracy. These cautionary examples of political failure, however, do not detract from the fact that when functioning well and properly configured, political institutions provide the best foundation for the sustainability of democracy.

Implications for Social Capital Theories

The present study also affords fresh insights into the concept of social capital and its relevance to the politics of democratization. Its main contribution is the consideration of the virtues of social capital as the result of the performance and constitution of political institutions rather than participation by citizens in the activities of civil society associations. Largely ignored by the current civil society revival, this contention possesses an important scholarly pedigree, though presently mostly forgotten. Indeed, in making the argument that political instructions matter to the production of social capital I am essentially borrowing and recycling social science history, especially that concerned with political development. One of the reasons for Huntington's instance on strong political institutions over economic or societal variables to explain conditions of underdevelopment across the Third World is the capacity of political institutions to instill and build trust and solidarity within the polity, in other words, social capital. He wrote: "Those societies deficient in stable and effective government are also deficient in mutual trust among their citizens, in national and public loyalties, and in organizational skills and capacity."[19]

Such insights about political development, as Berman's revisionist reading of Huntington's work reveals, found considerable resistance at the time they were issued and this may account for their relative obscurity.[20] They cut against the grain of the prevailing conventional political wisdom of the time (the late 1960s) that premised democratic development upon political pluralism and socioeconomic development. Huntington's arguments also ran contrary to the empirical evidence emerging from the political development of the United States, which served as the foundation for pluralist and modernization accounts of democratization. But, as Berman points out, in the late 1960s, as in the contemporary period, scholars prone to extrapolate from the American experience have failed to appreciate the uniqueness of the American political experience and its limitations when exported outside of its borders. She writes: "Blessed in the century after its founding with a high level of social harmony and equality, economic abundance, and a lack of external threats, the United States was able to modernize without the assistance of a strong centralizing government or political institutions. Unfortunately, history offers few examples of such harmony."[21]

More surprising still is the reluctance of contemporary admirers of Tocqueville's work to appreciate the role that he himself granted to political institutions in fostering social capital. Contrary to neo-Tocquevillean scholars, the original Tocqueville regarded political institutions (parties in particular) as a critical training ground for the creation of other forms of associationalism. Political associations were, in his words: "the large free schools, where all the members of the community go to learn the general theory of association."[22] Thus, he reasoned that the more people got used to participating in political institutions the more likely that they would become engaged in nonpolitical ones. He wrote that it is through political associations that Americans "acquire a general taste for association and grow accustomed to the use of it."[23]

Tocqueville also endowed political institutions with an important role in socializing the citizenry into the habits of democracy. For Tocqueville, well-designed political institutions were just as important (if not more so) for the creation and maintenance of democracy as nonpolitical ones. As noted in Keith E. Whittington's analysis of Tocqueville's journey through

Jacksonian America, for Tocqueville laws and political institutions did not simply establish a neutral arena for competing social interests but were themselves purposive and sought to shape the polity.[24] Whittington writes: "In Tocqueville's analysis the appropriate habits of the heart for a democratic citizenry did not depend on a re-invigorated civil society. Rather, democracy required the direct intervention of political institutions into the development of individual character to instill citizens with a proper sense of social purpose and to serve as a corrective to defects in democratic society."[25]

Our analysis also yields more discreet lessons about social capital that emerge from placing political institutions at the center of its production. The first is the need to exercise greater specificity in the application of this concept to the study of how democratic institutions and practices consolidate. This especially is the case in regard to "trust," generally thought to constitute the primary indicator of social capital. The Spanish experience suggests that what proved most important in this particular case with respect to the consolidation of democracy was not mass-level "inter-personal trust" but rather trust amongst rival political elites as well as trust by society at large in the political system. This type of "political trust," underwritten by political institutions themselves, underpinned the capacity of elites to institutionalize pacts and other agreements and the societal acceptance of these negotiations and settlements. That noted, the Spanish experience also suggests that democratic culture, even after the consolidation of democracy is presumed to have been attained, need not be blind trusting, a point often ignored by social capital theorists. In the democratic era, Spaniards have managed to place significant trust in political institutions while simultaneously showing a healthy skepticism toward them, much like citizens of older democracies. This skepticism prevalent in Spanish political culture, however, does not veer into political cynicism, a wholesale rejection of all things political as it appears to be the case in Brazil. Preventing this from happening in Spain is the basic legitimacy of political institutions.

A second insight concerns how social capital is diffused throughout society. Ensuing from the assumption that social capital originates in the socializing functions provided by voluntary associations, boosters of civil society lead us to think that its virtues circulate within society along the lines of a rigid bottom-up model. Produced at the grassroots level through the face-to-face interaction that voluntary groups afford the citizenry, social capital is thought to rise up through the walls of civil society before migrating out onto the general public, where it can be put to use for the common good. By contrast, the present study suggests a more complex model of social capital diffusion in which social capital is manufactured and channeled by political institutions either resting atop of society (such as the government and state agencies) or embedded within society such as the party system.

Third, our study suggests a more dynamic understanding of the building of social capital than that which currently informs debates about civil society and its importance to democracy. Given the presumption that patterns of associationalism fixed in time and across space dictate the availability of social capital, the prevailing view of how this commodity develops is quite static to say the least. The recent experience of Spain, however, suggests that this is not always the case. It suggests that trust-based collective behavior leading to the construction of new societal relations and institutions can in fact be accomplished in the absence of the requisite associational landscape, and more importantly, with the aid of purposeful state intervention. In this light, the availability of social capital as a means to facilitate democratic consolidation becomes less of a historically constrained possibility than scholars such as Putnam have us believe. This, for a change, is good news for struggling democracies.

Implications for the Study of Civil Society

The present study also offers various lessons about civil society and the consolidation of democratic regimes. The most obvious is that a vibrant and robust civil society is a poor indicator for predicting the consolidation of a democratic public life. Although the existence of many organizations thought to constitute civil society can be deemed crucial to democratization by providing links between the political system and society, there is little evidence that aggregate measures of associational membership have any bearing on the health of democracy or the prospect for democratic consolidation. The importance of this lesson rests not only in suggesting how we might have erred in overestimating the democratizing capacities of civil society but also in cautioning about issuing indictments about any country's democracy based on the composition of its civil society. Democratic states around the world have different institutional configurations, and a key variant among them is the density of their civil societies. To base assumptions about the quality and performance of democracy based on the shape and size of civil society can lead to inaccurate conclusions and serious misrepresentations.

Another lesson flowing from our analysis is that a vibrant and robust civil society is not always a sign of a healthy polity, as it appears to be the belief of neo-Tocquevillean scholars. Quite the contrary, such a state for civil society, especially in a newly democratic nation, may be a sign of serious problems in the political system or at the very least societal discontent with its performance. The logic of this statement resides in the notion that when political institutions are relatively coherent and perform well, we should expect less of a need from the part of the citizenry to mobilize and organize itself against the nascent democratic regime. By contrast, in the context of weak and failing political institutions, civil society expansion and mobilization is likely to become the preferred venue for citizens' activism and mobilization. There is little doubt that in Brazil the expansion of civil society and its continued state of mobilization has been fueled by the failure of political institutions and the belief by citizens that voluntary organizations can best meet their social and political aspirations.

The present study also questions the kind of civil society that many scholars and the democracy aid industry deem best suited for the consolidation of democracy. On the one hand, is the issue of associational density as the primary means to gauge the strength of civil society and by extension its importance to democratic consolidation. Arguably, a more meaningful criterion is the organization and institutionalization of civil society. Our comparison of Spain and Brazil suggests that while weaker in associational terms, Spanish civil society was organizationally better suited for becoming an effective partner in the consolidation of democracy than Brazilian civil society. Fewer and more centralized actors among labor and capitalist groups proved an advantage for Spain in organizing arrangements of cooperation such as social pacts.

On the other hand is the issue of civil society autonomy. In the eyes of many scholars and policy-makers only a civil society that is fully autonomous from the political sphere is regarded as effective in advancing the consolidation of democracy. This belief is anchored in the notion that civil society can best advance democracy by acting outside of the political system and mostly in a confrontational, watchdog mode rather than working in tandem with political institutions. It is also sustained by the sense that collaboration of civil society with political society will inevitably lead to the co-optation and/or contamination of civil society. This message is implicit in Diamond's critique of social pacts. He warns that "corporatist-style pacts" between the state and peak interest associations "pose a serious threat to democracy in transitional or newly emerging constitutional regimes."[26] He adds "that the risk appears greatest in countries with a history of authoritarian state corporatism where the state has created, organized, licensed, funded subordinated and controlled 'interest' groups."[27]

Diamond may well be writing about Spain, a prototype of state corporatism until the very last days of the authoritarian regime. But he was mistaken in assuming that corporatist pacts could not be effectively put to use as vehicles for the rapid consolidation of democracy. The dismissive and even contemptuous attitude toward social pacts that incorporate participation of civil society can also be found in the work of the democracy aid industry. Carothers notes that "a critical element of the transitology literature is the concept of national pacts; yet one would look in vain in the many US documents from the second half of the 1980s dealing with democratic assistance in Latin America for any reference to the concept of pacts. And neither would one find the concepts of pact formation or promoting pact formation in the actual programs."[28]

Finally, the present study calls for the demystification of civil society in our understanding of how democracies are consolidated. Notwithstanding the heroic images of civil society emerging from the many recent episodes of democratization, there is nothing intrinsically democratic about civil society as a political actor. Whatever good it is likely to bring to the process of democratic consolidation is largely dependent upon the constitution and performance of the political system. Moreover, this study suggests that civil society is not an unmitigated blessing for democratic politics, especially when its expansion is fueled by the failures of the political system. This is another point emphasized by Tocqueville but largely overlooked by his contemporary admirers. In his writings, voluntary groupings were not merely a foundation for democratic governance but also a potentially disruptive force since their activities fell outside of the control of the state. He cautioned about unrestrained associationalism and warned that private associations could "form something like a separate nation within the nation with all the moral prestige derived from the representation of their members."[29]

Tocqueville's warnings should give pause to democratic promotion programs anchored upon the creation of a flourishing civil society in failing and/or illegitimate states. Such programs, as noted previously, aim at thickening civil society and are the international aid community's self-proclaimed best hope for improving the quality of democracy in post-authoritarian societies the world over. In this political context, however, civil society promotion may well serve the unintended purpose of strengthening antidemocratic forces rather than supporting the deepening of democracy.[30] This concern should not be taken lightly. Paradoxically, the quality of governance in many newly democratic societies has deteriorated with the progression of the institutionalization of democratic practices such as free elections, leading to widespread repudiation of political institutions. Indeed, in many new democracies the political system is less legitimate and possibly even less consolidated today than when democratic government was first inaugurated. Largely a consequence of the many traumas presently associated with democratic transitions (hyperinflation, unemployment and corruption, to name just a few), life in many new democracies is filled with profound cynicism and mistrust of political institutions. This in turn is causing people to retreat to the organizations within civil society, in desperation over the failures of the political system. Under these conditions, the prospect for democratic consolidation appears decidedly inauspicious, as does the viability of a democratic civil society.

APPENDIX

Democracy, Civil Society and Social Capital

A richer overview of the problematic relationship between the associational density of civil society and democratic consolidation can be established by comparing data sets that provide a reasonably accurate indication of the dimensions of each of these variables in a wide range of cases. To measure the level of democratic consolidation, I rely on the surveys from Freedom House. This organization rates each country on a freedom scale according to the extent to which political and civil rights are respected. The first category, political rights, is equated with such things as a significant range of voters' choice and the extent to which political leaders can openly compete and be elected to positions of power in government. The second, civil rights, refers to the protection of religious, ethnic, economic and personal freedoms, as well as freedom of the press, belief and association. Freedom House rates each country on a seven-point scale, for both political and civil rights, with 1 representing the most free and 7 the least. It then divides countries into three broad categories: "Free" (countries whose ratings average 1–3), "Partly Free" (countries whose ratings average 3–5.5), and "Not Free" (countries whose ratings average 5.5–7). It is fair to presume that only "free" countries approximate the status of consolidated democracies.[1]

The indicator of the density of civil society is provided by the *World Values Survey* (*WVS*), the most comprehensive data for establishing an empirical baseline with which to compare civil society (both in terms of the overall size and scope of individual sectors) across national boundaries.[2] It does so by providing a national organizational cumulative percentage of participation by the citizenry in voluntary organizations.[3] The *WVS* covers the following category of organizations: labor unions, religious organizations, sports/recreational organizations, educational/cultural organizations, political parties, professional associations, social welfare organizations, youth groups, environmental organizations, health volunteer groups, community action groups, women's organizations, Third World development groups, animal rights groups and peace movements.

It is important to note that the *WVS* does not make particular judgments with respect to the strength or weakness of civil society. Instead, the survey provides raw data about patterns of participation in voluntary associations in each of the nations studied. But the organizational cumulative percentages speak for themselves. They range from a high of 242 (for the Netherlands) to a low of 3 (for Argentina). A fair characterization of the density of civil society based on the findings of the *WVS* would place all countries with an organizational cumulative average above 150 as "exceptionally strong," those between 75 and 150 as "strong," those between 25 and 50 as "weak," and those below 50 as "very weak."

As suggested in Figure A.1, the general impression that emerges from cross-pollinating data about democracy and civil society is that the link between a vibrant civil society and a successful democracy is indeed quite strong. The nations with the

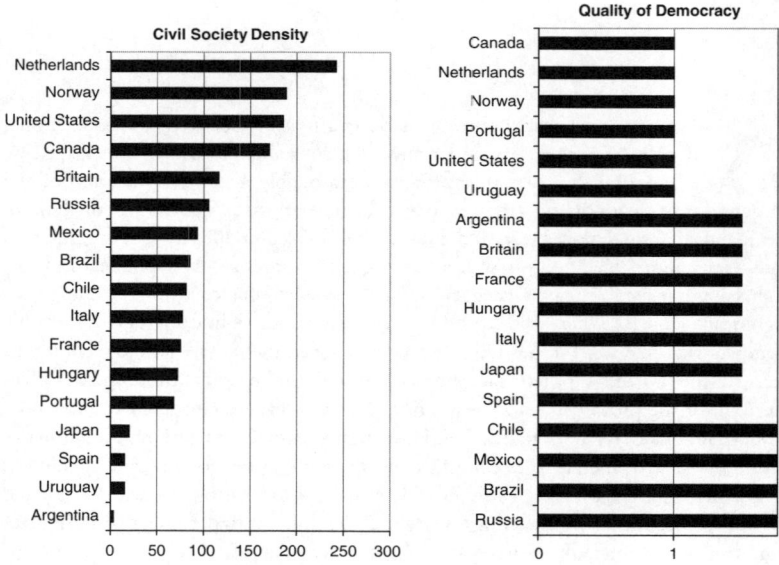

Figure A.1   Civil Society and Quality of Democracy Around the World
Note: A civil society density index above 150 denotes an exceptionally strong civil society, between 75–150 a strong civil society and below 50 a very weak civil society. Regarding the quality of democracy, 1–3 denotes a free society (or the highest level of democratic maturity), 3–5.5 denotes a partly free country and 5.5–7 denotes not free, or the absolute lack of democracy.
Source: "The 2000 Freedom House Survey," *Journal of Democracy* 12 (January 2001) and *World Values Survey*, as reported in Ronald Inglehart, *Modernization and Post-Modernization: Cultural, Economic and Political Change in 43 Societies* (Princeton: Princeton University Press, 1997).

densest civil societies possess the healthiest democracies. A case in point is the United States, whose democracy and civil society are regarded by many to be ideal prototypes. The U.S. Freedom House average is 1, the highest level of respect for civil and political rights. Its organizational cumulative percentage is 185, amongst the highest in the *WVS* (exceeded only by Iceland and the Netherlands). This provides compelling evidence of the long-suspected assumption that the United States is, in the famous words of the historian Arthur Schlesinger, "a nation of joiners."[4] It also suggests that, not withstanding the much-hyped crisis of civic life in America observed by Putnam and others, Americans possess a highly participatory civic culture.

Also suggestive are the findings illustrated in Figure A.2, which contrasts levels of civil society density with the length of democratic experience. The nations with the densest civil societies are also those with the longest records as democracies. By contrast, the nations with the thinnest civil societies are the ones with the shortest experience as democratic societies. Indeed, dictatorship (whether from the Left or the Right) rather than democracy has been the norm rather than the rule for many of these nations. This section of the *WVS* is populated by nations that in recent years have undergone a transition to democracy, especially in Southern and Eastern Europe and Latin America. Their experience with democracy, together with that of countries like the United States and other advanced industrial democracies, led Ronald Inglehart, the director of the *WVS*, to conclude that "our findings support the Tocquevillean-Putnam hypothesis: membership in voluntary associations is strongly linked with stable democracy."[5]

But is there a causal connection between the density of civil society and the actual progression of the process of democratization, as implied in the neo-Tocquevillean hypothesis? In other words, does the density of civil society has any real effect on the creation, development and maintenance of democratic institutions? To explore this question, it is imperative to look at the composition of civil society in recently democratic countries and contrast it to specific advances in the realm of democratic consolidation. Of course, we cannot presume that the composition of civil society alone will determine the project of democratic consolidation. Nonetheless, if civil society does in fact have the kinds of causal effects on democratization attributed to civil society, we should find a strong correspondence between the density of civil society and the quality of the emerging democracy. This causality, however, is not borne out by the empirical evidence.

As suggested by Table A.1, among post-authoritarian societies in Southern Europe and South America, the ones at the bottom of the civil society density index (Spain, Portugal and Uruguay) are, paradoxically, the only ones around which there is a strong scholarly consensus about their status as consolidated democracies.[6] This point is also broadly corroborated by the Freedom House data. Clearly, the most interesting case in this group is Spain, given its standing as the paradigm of democratic success among Third Wave democracies, whose organizational cumulative percentage (15) is astonishingly low. Indeed, among the 43 countries included in the 1990–1993 *WVS* data, only Argentina beats Spain in this category of the survey. But just as

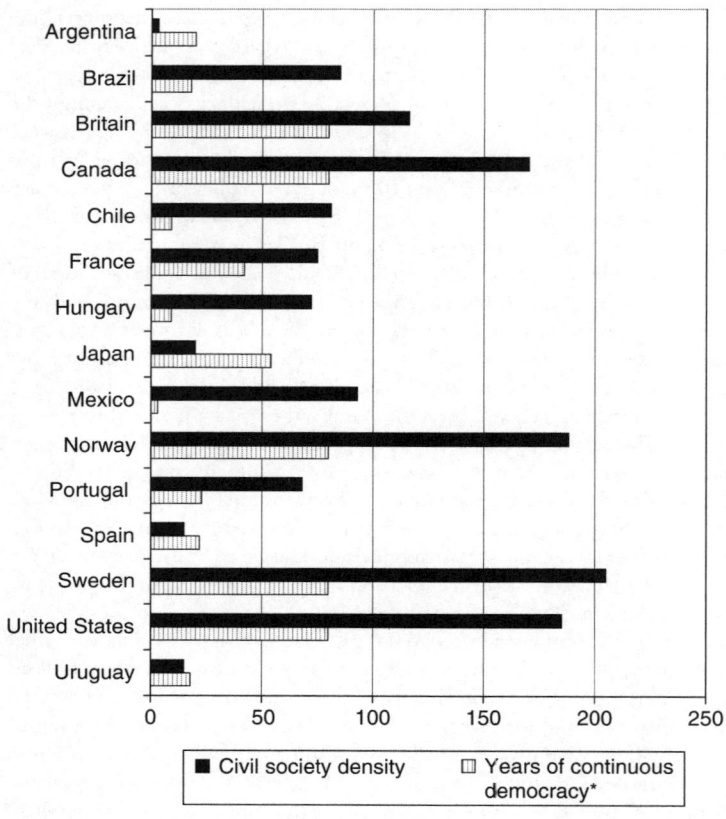

Figure A.2 Civil Society and Democratic Stability Around the World
Source: World Values Survey as reported in Ronald Inglehart, *Modernization and Post-Modernization: Cultural, Economic and Political Change in 43 Societies* (Princeton: Princeton University Press, 1997).
*This category has been updated to the year 2002.

interesting is the case of Uruguay, historically one of the most democratic societies in Latin America and at the present time the only South American democracy deemed fully consolidated, as determined by the criteria established by Linz and Stepan. Uruguay's 2001 Freedom House average is a perfect 1 (higher than Spain's), yet its civil society density is the same as Spain's.[7]

The case of Argentina is in and of itself revealing. Despite its standing as the "thinnest" civil society in the *WVS*, recent assessments of Argentine democracy place the country near the very top in connection to democratic consolidation. This is suggested not only by the country's healthy Freedom House ratings but also by its

Table A.1 Quality of Democracy and Civil Society in New
Democracies

Country	Quality of Democracy			Civil Society Density
	Political Rights	Civil Rights	Average	
Argentina	1	2	1.5	3
Brazil	3	3	3	85
Bulgaria	2	2	2.5	70
Chile	2	2	2	81
Hungary	1	2	1.5	72
Lithuania	1	2	1.5	87
Mexico	2	3	2.5	93
Portugal	1	1	1	68
Romania	2	2	2	45
Russia	5	5	5	105
Slovenia	1	2	1.5	62
South Korea	2	2	2	145
Spain	1	2	1.5	15
Uruguay	1	1	1	15

Source: "The 2000 Freedom House Survey," *Journal of Democracy* 12 (January 2001) and *World Values Survey* as reported in Ronald Inglehart, *Modernization and Post-Modernization: Cultural, Economic and Political Change in 43 Societies* (Princeton: Princeton University Press, 1997). The data for Uruguay's civil society index comes from the 1995–97 *WVS*.

success among South American nations in demilitarizing its politics, investigating human rights violations and in popular support for democracy. As suggested by the data on support for democratic and authoritarian rule in Latin America (see Figure A.3) mass support for democracy in Argentina is surpassed only by Uruguay, whose levels of support for democracy and authoritarianism are comparable to those of the most democratic European nations.

By contrast, Mexico, Brazil and Chile, the leaders in associational density category among Iberian-Latin countries, are all problematic cases of democratization. Mexico has the region's longest history of authoritarian rule (and consequently the weakest democratic traditions) and was the very last of the major Latin American countries to enter the democratic age. In fact, when the *WVS* data used in this study was collected (1993–1995) Mexico had yet to undergo a formal transition to democracy. In Chile, despite a long history as a democracy prior to the Pinochet coup of the mid-1970s, the process of democratic consolidation has been compromised by the lingering power of the military. A case in point is Pinochet's *Leyes de amarre*, the legislation designed by the old regime to restrict the freedom of successor democratic governments. Brazil's new democracy, as seen already, is a case study of a seriously flawed or

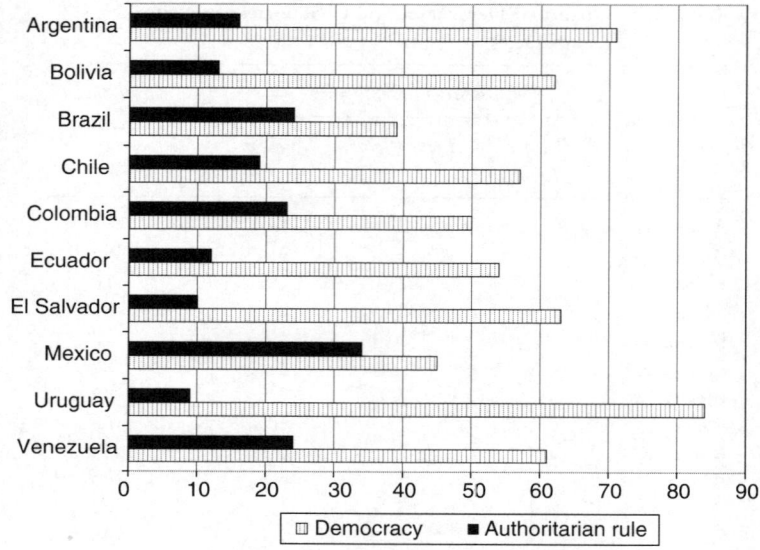

Figure A.3   Support for Democracy and Authoritarian Rule in Latin America
Source: Latinobarómetro (2000).

frozen process of democratic consolidation. Since abandoning military rule in 1985, Brazil has operated as a partly free country, a reflection of the poor quality of its democracy.

The evidence from the post-Communist world is just as revealing as that emerging from the Iberian-Latin world. Among the leaders in this group with respect to associational density is Russia, whose democratic travails have come to define the struggle for democratic consolidation in the post-Communist world. By contrast, associational life in Slovenia and Hungary, both pictures of democratic health, is decidedly weaker than in Russia.

The *WVS* data are also especially useful for what they reveal about civil society, democracy and "inter-personal trust," as measured by the percentage of people who profess to trust other people. This is critical for gauging national levels of social capital for it forms the basis of social trust. As seen in Figure A.4, the *WVS* data suggest a strong correlation between democracy and trust, a point made decades earlier by Gabriel Almond and Sidney Verba in *The Civic Culture*. The regions with the most stable democracies are also those with the highest percentages of people that profess to trust other people. Levels of interpersonal trust range from 58 to 66 percent for the Scandinavian nations; 52 to 50 for the United States and Canada, 37 to 34 percent for Italy and Spain and below 33 percent for Latin America. But is this link between democracy and trust dependent upon the composition of civil society, as implied in

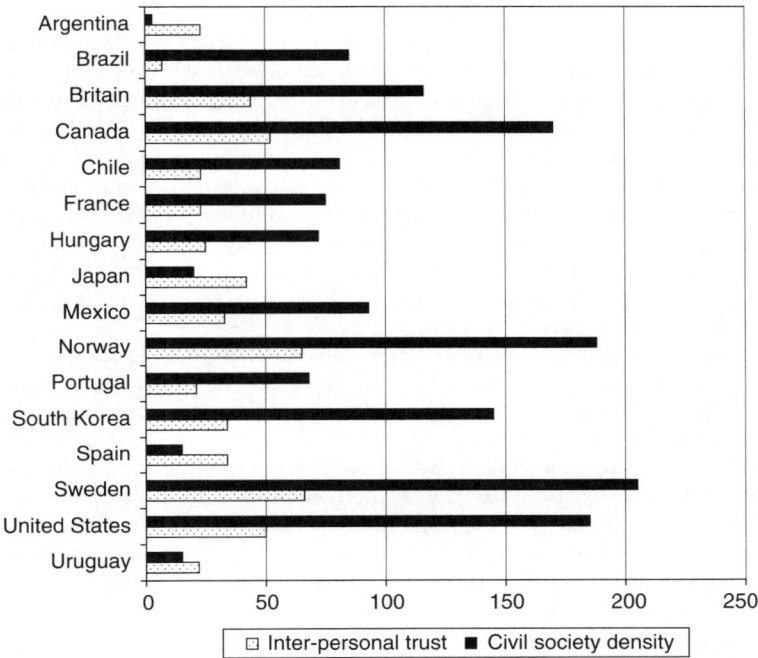

Figure A.4 Civil Society and Trust Around the World
Source: *World Values Survey* as reported in Ronald Inglehart, *Modernization and Post-Modernization: Cultural, Economic and Political Change in 43 Societies* (Princeton: Princeton University Press, 1997).

the work of neo-Tocquevillean scholars such as Putnam? As explained next, the link between the density of civil society and levels of interpersonal trust is at best tenuous.

In Japan, despite possessing one of the lowest civil society density indexes among industrialized countries, an impressive 42 percent of the population professes to trust others. Spain, as noted previously, a notorious case of civil society anemia, scores a respectable 34 percent regarding interpersonal trust, amongst the highest in newly democratic nations. By contrast, Brazil, whose civil society is among the densest among new democracies, possesses the lowest percentage of interpersonal trust of any country in the *WVS*. Only 7 percent of Brazilians claim to trust other people. South Korea, whose associational density towers over that of most newly democratic nations, shares the same percentage of inter-personal trust with Spain.

These and other national experiences explain why many scholars have suggested that while the link between democracy and trust is indeed strong, the sources of trust may rest away from the nature of civil society including, most notably, democracy itself. This has given rise to a vigorous debate centered on the question of whether democracy begets social trust or the other way around? A study by Edward Muller and Mitchell Selington makes the case for sustained democracy being the source of social trust.[8] It finds that in 27 European and Central American societies, democratic experience causes interpersonal trust. Inglehart, however, is decidedly less certain. In presenting the *WVS* data he notes: "The available evidence cannot determine the causal direction but it does indicate that culture and political institutions have a strong tendency to go together."[9] Elsewhere, he has tied trust to socioeconomic well-being, a point that explains the relatively high levels of interpersonal trust not only in mature democracies but also in relatively affluent new democracies such as Spain. He writes: "The people of rich countries show higher levels of inter-personal trust than the publics of poorer ones."[10]

In sum, the most reliable available data available on civil society density does not lend much support to the presumed critical importance of a robust and vibrant civil society to the creation or maintenance of a democratic public life. Among the conclusions (tentative, to be sure) that we can reach from this analysis is that as democracy strengthens so does civil society.[11] It is interesting to note that the oldest democracies appear to have the densest civil societies (the United States and Western Europe) and the newest ones have the thinnest (Russia and post-Communist Europe), with Southern Europe and Latin America falling somewhere in between. This suggests that a strong civil society may well be a product rather than a prerequisite for democracy.

Notes

1 Introduction

1. Scholarly works that posit civil society as a prerequisite or must-have for democratic consolidation include Robert Putnam, *Making Democracy Work: Civic Traditions in Modern Italy* (Princeton: Princeton University Press, 1993); Ernest Gellner, *Conditions of Liberty: Civil Society and Its Rivals* (New York: Penguin, 1994); Larry Diamond, *Developing Democracy: Toward Consolidation* (Baltimore: Johns Hopkins University Press, 1999); and Francis Fukuyama, *Trust: The Social Virtues and the Creation of Prosperity* (New York: Free Press, 1996).

2. For an overview of these debates see: Gary Hansen, *Constituencies for Reform: Strategic Approaches to Donor-Supported Civil Advocacy Programs* (Washington, D.C.: USAID, 1996), Amanda Bernard, Henry Helmrich and Percy B. Lehning, eds., *Civil Society and International Development* (Paris: North-South Centre of the Organization for Economic Cooperation and Development, 1998) and Thomas Carothers and Marina Ottaway, eds., *Funding Virtue: Civil Society Aid and Democracy Promotion* (Washington, D.C.: Carnegie Endowment for International Peace, 2000). For scholarly assessments of civil society–based democratic assistance programs see: Alison Van Rooy, ed., *Civil Society and the Aid Industry* (London: Earthscan, 1998); Thomas Carothers, *Aiding Democracy Abroad: The Learning Curve* (Washington: Carnegie Endowment for International Peace, 1999); and Omar G. Encarnación, "Tocqueville's Missionaries: Civil Society Advocacy and the Promotion of Democracy," *World Policy Journal* 17 (Spring 2000).

3. Putnam, *Making Democracy Work*, p. 173.

4. The rise and fall of modernization theory comes to mind here. Like civil society, modernization created quite a sensation when it debuted in the 1950s and engendered multiple synergetic links between academics and the policy community before falling into disregard. Modernization scholars had drawn a causal and linear connection between economic development and political democracy. Critical to this sequencing of events was the perceived positive impact upon society of corollaries of development such as literacy, mass media, industrialization and most importantly, the emergence of a middle stratum in society, which came to be

regarded as the linchpin for democratization. Yet the felicitous association that modernization theory had presumed between economic development and political democracy proved to be highly problematic. Modernization theory could not explain why during the 1960s and 1970s, the most economically and socially advanced nations in Latin America (Argentina, Brazil, Chile and Uruguay) descended into military dictatorship, which institutionalized political regimes that brought about unprecedented levels of state violence, terror and repression. For a broader presentation of modernization theory and its assumptions about democracy see: Seymour Martin Lipset, "Some Requisites of Democracy: Economic Development and Political Legitimacy," *American Political Science Review* 53 (1959).

5. Nancy Bermeo, "Civil Society After Democracy: Some Conclusions," in Nancy Bermeo and Philip Nord, eds., *Civil Society Before Democracy: Lessons from Nineteenth Century Europe* (Lanham, Md.: Rowman and Littlefield, 2000), p. 239.

6. For broad empirical overviews of democratization around the world since the mid-1970s see: Guillermo O'Donnell, Philippe Schmitter and Laurence Whitehead, eds., *Transitions from Authoritarian Rule* (Baltimore: Johns Hopkins University Press, 1986); Samuel Huntington, *The Third Wave: Democratization in the Late Twentieth Century* (Norman: University of Oklahoma Press, 1991); Larry Diamond and Marc Platter, eds., *The Global Resurgence of Democracy* (Baltimore: Johns Hopkins University Press, 1993); and Juan J. Linz and Alfred Stepan, *Problems of Democratic Transition and Consolidation: Southern Europe, South America and Post-Communist Europe* (Baltimore: Johns Hopkins University Press, 1996).

7. See Kenneth Newton, "Social Capital and Democracy," *American Behavioral Scientist* 40 (March/April 1997) and Jean Cohen, "Trust, Voluntary Association and Workable Democracy," in Mark Warren, ed., *Democracy and Trust* (New York: Cambridge University Press, 1999).

8. Sheri Berman, "Civil Society and the Collapse of the Weimar Republic," *World Politics* 49, No. 3 (1997).

9. See Morris P. Fiorina, "Extreme Voices: A Dark Side of Civic Engagement," in Theda Skocpol and Morris Fiorina, eds., *Civic Engagement in American Democracy* (Washington: Brookings Institution Press, 1999) and Laurence Whitehead, "Bowling in the Bronx: The Uncivil Interstices between Civil and Political Society," in Robert Fine and Shirin Rai, eds., *Civil Society: Democratic Perspectives* (London: Frank Cass, 1997).

10. Margaret Levi, "Social and Unsocial Capital: A Review of Robert Putnam's *Making Democracy Work*," *Politics and Society* 24 (March 1996).

11. The classic statement on political institutionalization and democratization remains Samuel Huntington, *Political Order in Changing Societies* (New Haven: Yale University Press, 1968).

12. The dynamics of regime change from authoritarianism to democracy in Spain and Brazil also share a number of important similarities. This explains why many

cross-national studies of democratization politics incorporating the Southern European and South American experiences have relied upon empirical evidence from these two cases to illuminate a variety of political phenomena. In both cases authoritarian rule was a lengthy and relatively stable political affair and it unraveled not as a consequence of the defeat or collapse of the authoritarian regime but rather as a state-controlled process of democratic transformation. For comparisons of democratization politics in Spain and Brazil see: Scott Mainwaring and Donald Share, "Transition Through Transaction: Democratization in Brazil and Spain," in Wayne A. Selcher, ed., *Political Liberalization in Brazil: Dynamics, Dilemmas and Future Prospects* (Boulder: Westview Press, 1986); Margaret Keck, *The Workers' Party and Democratization in Brazil* (New Haven: Yale University Press, 1992); Guillermo O'Donnell, "Transitions, Continuities and Paradoxes," in Scott Mainwaring, Guillermo O'Donnell and J. Samuel Valenzuela, eds., *Issues in Democratic Consolidation: The New South American Democracies in Comparative Perspective* (Notre Dame, Ind.: University of Notre Dame Press, 1992); and Peter McDonough, Doh C. Shin and José Álvaro Moisés, "Democratization and Participation: Comparing Spain, Brazil and Korea," *The Journal of Politics* 60 (November 1998).

13. Linz and Stepan, *Problems of Democratic Transition and Consolidation*, p. 87.
14. Richard Gunther, P. Nikiforos Diamandouros and Hans-Jürgen Puhle, "Introduction," in Gunther et al., eds., *The Politics of Democratic Consolidation: Southern Europe in Comparative Perspective* (Baltimore: Johns Hopkins University Press, 1995), p. 4.
15. Adam Przeworski, *Democracy and the Market: Economic and Political Reforms in Eastern Europe and Latin America* (New York: Cambridge University Press, 1991), p. 8.
16. See, especially, Peter McDonough, Samuel Barnes and Antonio López Pina, *The Cultural Dynamics of Democratization in Spain* (Ithaca, N.Y.: Cornell University Press, 1998) and Omar G. Encarnación, "Civil Society and the Consolidation of Democracy in Spain," *Political Science Quarterly* 116 (Spring 2001).
17. The best portrayal of Brazil's resurgent civil society around the time of the democratic transition is found in Alfred Stepan, ed., *Democratizing Brazil: Problems of Transition and Consolidation* (New York: Oxford University Press, 1989).
18. Frances Hagopian, "Democracy and Political Representation in Latin America in the 1990s: Pause, Reorganization or Decline? in Felipe Agüero and Jeffrey Stark, eds., *Fault Lines of Democracy in Post-Transition Latin America* (Miami: University of Miami North-South Center Press, 1998), p. 124.
19. Linz and Stepan, *Problems of Democratic Transition and Consolidation*, pp. 166–167.
20. Frances Hagopian, "Democracy by Undemocratic Means? Elites, Politics and Regime Transition in Brazil," *Comparative Political Studies* 23 (July 1990), p. 147.
21. Peter R. Kingstone and Timothy Power, "Still Standing or Standing Still? The Brazilian Democratic Regime since 1985," in Peter R. Kingstone and

Timothy Power, eds., *Democratic Brazil: Actors, Institutions and Processes* (Pittsburgh: University of Pittsburgh Press, 2000), p. 13.

22. Linz and Stepan, *Problems of Democratic Transition and Consolidation*, pp. 166–167.

23. A more extended discussion of the term social concertation is included in chapter 4.

24. The present study draws upon the following works: Omar G. Encarnación, "Civil Society and the Consolidation of Democracy in Spain," *Political Science Quarterly* 116 (Spring 2001); "Civil Society Resurgence and Democratization: Cautionary Lessons from Brazil," Paper presented at the Annual Meeting of the American Political Science Association, Washington, D.C., September, 2001; and "Tocqueville's Missionaries: Civil Society and the Promotion of Democracy," *World Policy Journal* 17 (Spring 2000).

2 The Revival of Civil Society

1. Fareed Zakaria, "Bigger than the Family and Smaller than the State: Are Voluntary Groups What Makes Countries Work?" *The New York Times Book Review* 13 (August 1995), p. 1.

2. Robert Putnam, *Making Democracy Work: Civic Traditions in Modern Italy* (Princeton: Princeton University Press, 1993). These reviews of Putnam's work are taken from the book's back cover.

3. See Robert Putnam, "Bowling Alone: America's Declining Social Capital," *Journal of Democracy* 6 (1995). See also by Putnam, *Bowling Alone: The Collapse and Revival of American Community* (New York: Simon & Schuster, 2000).

4. Putnam has recently amended his warning about the crisis in American civil society. In his view, the terrorist attacks of September 11, 2001 have awakened Americans' interest in volunteer work—from participation in the national volunteer service (Americorps) to local soup kitchens. Such developments have lead Putnam to ponder whether an unintended outcome of September 11 will be the restocking of America's sense of civic community. If so, he argues, the senseless horror of September 11 will have at least one positive legacy. See Robert Putnam, "Bowling Together," *The American Prospect* 13 (February 11, 2002).

5. *Democracy in America* was originally published in French and in two volumes: the first one in 1835 and the second one in 1840. Multiple versions of this highly cited work are available. The one used for this study is the two-volume Vintage Classics paperback published by Alfred A. Knopf (New York) in 1990. For contextual and philosophical analyses of Tocqueville's writings see: Jack Lively, *The Social and Political Thought of Alexis de Tocqueville* (Oxford: Clarendon, 1962) and "Democracy in the World: Tocqueville Reconsidered," Special Issue of *Journal of Democracy* 11 (January 2000).

6. Tocqueville was hardly the first scholar to pay attention to civil society. The history of the concept of civil society dates back to Roman days and the works of

philosophers such as Cicero. In the ancient Roman tradition, civil society stood for a civilized community that drew no distinction between the state and society and between the governors and the governed. A legal code, municipal arrangements, commercial activity and the arts were thought to hold this community together. This conceptualization of civil society would undergo a dramatic transformation during the mid-late eighteenth century, a period widely acknowledged as critical in the development of the modern foundations of civil society. For some of the leading figures of the Anglo-European Enlightenment (Adam Ferguson, David Hume and Adam Smith, to name just a few), civil society was the space of associational life that existed outside of the state in which individuals gathered voluntarily to pursue their values and desires. This idea about the existence of a civil society rested on the primacy of the individual as an autonomous agent and the sense of belonging of that individual in a shared public sphere permeated by a commonly held conception of community, citizenship and rights. For a more detailed view of the development of the concept of civil society see: Adam Seligman, *The Idea of Civil Society* (Princeton: Princeton University Press, 1992) and Robert Fine, "Civil Society Theory, Enlightenment and Critique," in Robert Fine and Shirin Rai, eds., *Civil Society: Democratic Perspectives* (London: Frank Cass, 1997).

7. Tocqueville, *Democracy in America*, Vol. 2, p. 123.

8. Putnam, *Making Democracy Work*, p. 182.

9. Carlos Forment, *Democracy in Latin America: Public Life and the Colonial Legacy in Mexico and Peru*, unpublished manuscript, p. 9.

10. "Democracy in the World: Tocqueville Reconsidered," *Journal of Democracy* 11 (January 2000), p. 9.

11. Robert Packenham, *Liberal America and the Third World: Political Development Ideas in Foreign Aid and Social Science* (Princeton: Princeton University Press, 1973).

12. See Victor Pérez-Díaz, *The Return of Civil Society: The Emergence of Democratic Spain* (Cambridge, Mass.: Harvard University Press, 1993); Michael Bernhard, "Civil Society and Democratic Transition in East Central Europe," *Political Science Quarterly* 108 (1993) and Grzegortz Ekiert and Jan Kubik, *Rebellious Civil Society: Popular Protest and Democratic Consolidation in Poland, 1989–1993* (Ann Arbor: University of Michigan Press, 1999).

13. See Margaret E. Keck and Kathryn Sikkink, *Activists Beyond Borders: Advocacy Networks in International Politics* (Ithaca, N.Y.: Cornell University Press, 1998).

14. See Milton J. Esman and Norman T. Uphoff, *Local Organizations: Intermediaries in Rural Development* (Ithaca, N.Y.: Cornell University Press, 1984); John Clark, *Democratizing Development: The Role of Voluntary Organizations* (West Hartford, Conn: Kumarian Press, 1990); Roger Riddell and Mark Robinson, *NGO's and Rural Poverty Alleviation* (Oxford: Oxford University Press, 1996); Anthony Bebbington and Diana Mitlin, *Workshop Report: The NGO Sector and Its Role in Strengthening Civil Society and Securing Good Governance* (London: International

Institute for Environment and Development, 1997); Thomas F. Carroll, *Intermediary NGO's: The Supporting Link in Grassroots Development* (West Hartford, Conn.: Kumarian Press, 1992) and Gary Hensen, *Constituencies for Reform: Strategic Approaches to Donor-Supported Civic Advocacy Programs* (Washington, D.C.: USAID, 1996) and Charles Reilly, ed., *New Paths to Democratic Development in Latin America: The Rise of NGO-Municipal Collaboration* (Boulder: Lynne Rienner, 1995)

15. See Bruce P. Kennedy and Ichiro Kawachi, "The Role of Social Capital in the Russian Mortality Crisis," *World Development* 26, No. 11 (1998).

16. Ernest Gellner, *Conditions of Liberty: Civil Society and Its Rivals* (New York: The Penguin Press, 1994) and Ashutosh Varshney, *Ethnic Conflict and Civic Life: Hindus and Muslims in India* (New Haven: Yale University Press, 2002).

17. See Elizabeth Jelin and Eric Hershberg, eds., *Constructing Democracy: Human Rights, Citizenship and Society in Latin America* (Boulder: Westview Press, 1996); Larry Diamond, *Developing Democracy* (Baltimore: Johns Hopkins University Press, 1999); Laura McDonald, *Supporting Civil Society: The Political Role of Non-Governmental Organizations in Central America* (New York: St. Martin's Press, 1997) and Blair Harry, "Civil Society and Building Democracy: Lessons from International Donor Experience," in Amanda Bernard, Henry Helmrich and Percy B. Lehning, eds., *Civil Society and International Development* (Paris: North-South Centre of the Council of Europe and Development Centre of the Organization for Economic Cooperation and Development, 1998); and Axel Hadenius and Frederick Uggla, "Making Civil Society Work, Promoting Democratic Development: What Can States and Donors Do?" *World Development* 24 (1996).

18. A brief discussion of the concept of democratic consolidation is offered later in this chapter.

19. For overviews of civil society and the democracy aid industry see Alison Van Rooy, ed., *Civil Society and the Aid Industry* (London: Earthscan, 1998); Amanda Bernard, Henry Helmrich and Percy B. Lehning, eds., *Civil Society and International Development* (Paris: North-South Centre of the Organization for Economic Cooperation and Development, 1998); Kevin Quigley, *For Democracy's Sake: Foundations and Democratic Assistance in Central Europe* (Baltimore: Johns Hopkins University Press, 1997); Thomas Carothers, *Aiding Democracy Abroad: The Learning Curve* (Washington, D.C.: Carnegie Endowment for International Peace, 1999); and Omar G. Encarnación, "Tocqueville's Missionaries: Civil Society and the Promotion of Democracy," *World Policy Journal* 17 (Spring 2000).

20. Diamond, *Developing Democracy*, p. 221.

21. Alison Van Rooy and Frank Robinson, "Out of the Ivory Tower: Civil Society Assistance and the Aid System," in Alison Van Rooy, ed., *Civil Society and the Aid Industry*, table 2.1.

22. Carothers, *Aiding Democracy Abroad*, p. 50.

23. John Keane, *Civil Society: Old Images, New Visions* (Stanford, Calif.: Stanford University Press, 1998), p. 7.

24. Theda Skocpol and Morris P. Fiorina, "Making Sense of the Civic Engagement Debate," in Skocpol and Fiorina, eds., *Civic Engagement in American Democracy* (Washington, D.C.: Brookings Institution Press, 1999), p. 7.

25. Ibid., p. 8.

26. This conventional wisdom about American politics can now be questioned. Post–September 11 polling suggests that trust in government is the highest it has been in decades. An October 12, 2001 poll conducted by the Gallup organization reveals that September 11 has transformed the public's wariness of the federal government and the role it should play in the nation's daily life. At the present time, six out of ten Americans say they trust their government, a level not seen since 1968. Today Americans also want more not less government. According to the Gallup poll, more than half of Americans want a government that provides more in services, even if it cost more in taxes. This percentage is the highest it has been in the nine years that Gallup has been tracking public perceptions about government. Only time will tell for how long this new faith in government will endure.

27. Morris P. Fiorina, "Extreme Voices: A Dark Side of Civic Engagement," in Skocpol and Fiorina, eds., *Civic Engagement in American Democracy*, p. 395.

28. Daniel Bell, "American Exceptionalism Revisited: The Role of Civil Society," *The Public Interest* 95 (1989), p. 65.

29. Skocpol, "How Americans Became Civic," in Skocpol and Fiorina, eds., *Civic Engagement in American Democracy*, p. 33.

30. Samuel Huntington, *The Third Wave: Democratization in the Late Twentieth Century* (Norman: University of Oklahoma Press, 1991).

31. Diamond and Platter, "Introduction," in Diamond and Platter, eds., *The Global Resurgence of Democracy*.

32. Ibid., Introduction.

33. In an attempt to link these disparate democratic transitions, Huntington has argued that the Third Wave was occasioned by the following factors: unprecedented economic growth and crisis in many developing countries, the delegitimation of nondemocratic regimes, the pro-democracy foreign policies of the United States, other Western countries and the Vatican and "snowbolling," or nations simply copying each other.

34. Thomas Carothers, "Civil Society," *Foreign Policy* (Winter 1999–2000), p. 19.

35. Vaclav Havel, *The Power of the Powerless* (London: Hutchinson, 1995).

36. Michael Walzer, "The Concept of Civil Society," in Michael Walzer, ed., *Toward a Global Civil Society* (Providence, R.I.: Berghahn Books, 1998), p. 21.

37. Ibid., p. 21.

38. On Solidarity see Roman Laba, *The Roots of Solidarity: A Political Sociology of Poland's Working Class Democratization* (Princeton: Princeton University Press, 1991); Michael Bernhard, *The Origins of Democratization in Poland: Workers, Intellectuals and Oppositional Politics 1976–1980* (New York: Columbia University Press, 1993) and Grzegortz Ekiert and Jan Kubik, *Rebellious Civil Society: Popular Protest and Democratic Consolidation in Poland, 1989–1993* (Ann Arbor: University of Michigan Press, 1999).

39. Michael Bernhard, "Civil Society and Democratic Transition in East Central Europe," *Political Science Quarterly* 108 (1993), p. 325.

40. On Latin American conceptualizations of civil society in the struggle against military rule see: O. Fals Borda, "Social Movements and Political Power in Latin America," in Arturo Escobar and Sonia A. Alvarez, eds., *The Making of Social Movements in Latin America: Identity, Strategy and Democracy* (Boulder: Westview Press, 1992) and Manuel A. Garretón, "Popular Mobilization and the Military Regime in Chile: The Complexities of the Invisible Transition," in Susan E. Eckstein, ed., *Power and Popular Protest: Latin American Social Movements* (Berkeley: University of California Press, 1989).

41. Bob Edwards and Michael W. Foley, "Civil Society and Social Capital beyond Putnam," *The American Behavioral Scientist* 42 (1998), p. 125.

42. On *Las Madres* and their role in Argentine democratization see Marysa Navarro, "The Personal is Political: Las Madres de la Plaza de Mayo," in Susan Eckstein, ed., *Power and Popular Protest: Latin American Social Movements* (Berkeley: University of California Press, 1989).

43. See Arturo Escobar and Sonia A. Alvarez, eds., *The Making of Social Movements in Latin America.*

44. See Scott Mainwaring, *The Church and Politics in Brazil, 1916–1985* (Standford, Calif.: Stanford University Press, 1986) and Ralph Della Cava, "The People's Church, the Vatican and the Abertura," in Alfred Stepan, ed., *Democratizing Brazil* (New York: Oxford University Press, 1989).

45. On the emergence (and eventual decline) of social movements in Chile and Uruguay see Patricia Hipsher, "Democratization and the Decline of Urban Social Movements in Chile and Spain," *Comparative Politics* 27 (April 1996) and Eduardo Canel, "Democratization and the Decline of Urban Social Movements in Uruguay," in Alvarez and Escobar, eds., *The Making of Social Movements in Latin America.*

46. Alison Van Rooy, "Civil Society as Idea: An Analytical Hatstand?" in Alison Van Rooy, ed., *Civil Society and the Aid Industry*, p. 6.

47. Ibid., p. 6.

48. See Charles Taylor, "Modes of Civil Society," *Public Culture* 3 (Fall 1990); Adam Seligman, *The Idea of Civil Society* (Princeton: Princeton University Press, 1992); Jean Cohen and Andrew Arato, *Civil Society and Political Theory* (Cambridge, Mass.: MIT Press, 1992); Ernest Gellner, "Civil Society in Historical Context," *International Social Science Journal* 43 (August 1991); John Hall, ed., *Civil Society: Theory, History and Comparison* (Cambridge: Polity Press, 1995); Gordon White, "Civil Society, Democratization and Development (I): Clearing the Analytical Ground," *Democratization* 1 (Autumn 1994); and John Keene, *Civil Society: Old Images, New Visions* (Stanford, Calif.: Stanford University Press, 1998).

49. Diamond, *Developing Democracy*, p. 221.

50. Michael Walzer, "The Concept of Civil Society," in Michael Walzer, ed., *Toward a Global Civil Society* (Providence, R.I.: Berghahn Books, 1995), p. 7.

51. Diamond, *Developing Democracy*, p. 221.
52. Nancy Bermeo, "Civil Society after Democracy: Some Conclusions," in Nancy Bermeo and Philip Nord, eds., *Civil Society before Democracy: Lessons from Nineteenth Century Europe* (Lanham, Md.: Rowman & Littlefield, 2000), p. 238.
53. Putnam, *Making Democracy Work*, p. 173.
54. Diamond, *Developing Democracy*, pp. 227–229.
55. Tocqueville, *Democracy in America*, Vol. 2, p. 110.
56. Ibid., p. 110.
57. Sheri Berman, "Civil Society and the Collapse of the Weimar Republic," *World Politics* 49, No. 3 (1997), p. 403.
58. Ibid., p. 403.
59. Ibid., p. 404.
60. See James Coleman, *Foundations of Social Theory* (Cambridge, Mass.: Harvard University Press, 1990), p. 302.
61. Putnam, *Making Democracy Work*, p. 173.
62. Robert Putnam, "Tuning In, Tuning Out: The Strange Disappearance of Civic America," *PS: Political Science and Politics* 27 (December 1995), p. 665.
63. Putnam, *Making Democracy Work*, p. 170.
64. Ibid., p. 171.
65. Ibid., pp. 89–90.
66. See Edward Banfield, *The Moral Basis of a Backward Society* (Glencoe, Ill.: Free Press, 1958). Banfield lived in the impoverished Italian village of Montegrano during the 1950s and found that the most remarkable thing about this place was the almost complete absence of associations. "Amoral familism" refers to a situation in which the only moral obligations that the residents of Montegrano felt were to others in their families. This social handicap to trust others outside of the family, in Banfield's view, rendered the residents of Montegrano incapable of coming together to organize their community and efficiently run its institutions.
67. For critiques of Putnam's work see Sidney Tarrow, "Making Social Science Work Across Space and Time: A Critical Reflection on Robert Putnam's Making Democracy Work," *American Political Science Review* 90 (June 1996) and Margaret Levi, "Social and Unsocial Capital: A Review of Robert Putnam's Making Democracy Work," *Politics and Society* 24 (March 1996).
68. Putnam, *Making Democracy Work*, p. 183.
69. Linz and Stepan, *Problems of Democratic Transition and Consolidation*, p. 5.
70. For theoretical discussions of the growing literature on democratic consolidation see Omar G. Encarnación, "Beyond Transitions: The Politics of Democratic Consolidation," *Comparative Politics* 32 (July 2000) and Ben Ross Schneider, "Democratic Consolidations: Some Broad Comparisons and Sweeping Arguments," *Latin American Research Review* 30 (1995).
71. Linz and Stepan, *Problems of Democratic Transition and Consolidation*.
72. Larry Diamond, "Development, Democracy and Civil Society," *Working Paper* (Madrid: Instituto Juan March, June 1996), p. 3.

73. Diamond, "Rethinking Civil Society: Toward Consolidation," *Journal of Democracy* 5 (1994), p. 5.
74. Diamond, *Developing Democracy*, p. 124.
75. Ibid., p. 227.
76. Ibid., p. 208.
77. Ibid., p. 208.
78. Ibid, pp. 239–250.
79. Francis Fukuyama, *Trust: The Social Virtues and the Creation of Prosperity* (New York: Free Press, 1995).
80. Unless otherwise noted, quoted passages in this section come from pages 55–56.
81. Ibid., p. 54.
82. Following Putnam, Fukuyama highlights the bifurcated nature of the development of civil society in Italy: strong in the North and weak in the South.
83. In making these assertions about Latin Catholic societies, Fukuyama, like Putnam's analysis of the Italian south, relies upon Edward Banfield's theories of "amoral familism."
84. Fukuyama, *Trust*, p. 361.
85. Ibid., p. 362.
86. Carothers, *Aiding Democracy Abroad: The Learning Curve*, p. 212.
87. Axel Hadenius and Fredrik Uggla, "Making Civil Society Work, Promoting Democratic Development: What Can States and Donors Do?" *World Development* 24, No. 10 (1996), p. 1622.
88. Ibid., p. 1628.
89. Bob Edwards and Michael W. Foley, "Civil Society and Social Capital beyond Putnam," *The American Behavioral Scientist* 42 (September 1998), p. 130.
90. Ibid., p. 130.
91. Ibid., p. 131.
92. Ibid., p. 129.
93. Ibid., p. 135. The reference to the 1950s is to the civic culture model.
94. Sheri Berman, "Civil Society and Political Institutionalization," *The American Behavioral Scientist* 40 (March/April 1997), p. 565.
95. Ibid., p. 565.
96. Berman, "Civil Society and the Collapse of the Weimar Republic."
97. Levi, "Social and Unsocial Capital: A Review of Robert Putnam's Making Democracy Work."
98. Jean Cohen, "Trust, Voluntary Association and Workable Democracy: The Contemporary American Discourse of Civil Society," in Mark Warren, ed., *Democracy and Trust* (New York: Cambridge University Press, 1999), footnote 15.
99. Laurence Whitehead, "Bowling in the Bronx: The Uncivil Interstices between Civil and Political Society," in Robert Fine and Shirin Rai, eds., *Civil Society: Democratic Perspectives* (London: Frank Cass, 1997), pp. 109–110.
100. Ibid., p. 111.

101. See Theda Skocpol, "Advocates Without Members: The Recent Transformation of American Civic Life," in Skocpol and Fiorina, eds., *Civic Engagement in American Democracy*.

102. Kenneth Newton, "Social Capital and Democracy," *The American Behavioral Scientist* 40, No. 5 (March/April 1997), p. 579.

103. Ibid., p. 579.

104. Ibid., p. 577.

105. Ruth Berins Collier, *Paths towards Democracy: The Working Class and Elites in Western Europe and South America* (New York: Cambridge University Press, 1999)

106. On this dominant theme in the democratization literature see: O'Donnell and Schmitter, *Transitions from Authoritarian Rule: Tentative Conclusions about Uncertain Democracies*; Giuseppe Di Palma, *To Craft Democracies: An Essay on Democratic Transitions* (Berkeley: University of California Press, 1990); Richard Gunther and John Higley, eds., *Elites and Democratic Consolidation in Latin America and Southern Europe* (New York: Cambridge University Press, 1992) and Josep Colomer, *Strategic Transitions: Game Theory and Democratization* (Baltimore: Johns Hopkins University Press, 2000).

107. Philippe Schmitter, "Interest Systems and the Consolidation of Democracies," in Gary Marks and Larry Diamond, eds., *Re-examining Democracy* (Newbury Park, Calif.: Sage Publications, 1992), pp. 158–159.

108. In fairness to Putnam, his analysis is specifically concerned with democratic performance rather than democratic consolidation. But this is not the case of other scholars who have adopted his model and applied it to the study of democratization.

109. Kenneth Newton, "Social Capital and Democracy," *American Behavioral Scientist* 40, No. 5 (March/April 1997), p. 578.

110. On this point see Kathleen Thelen and Sven Steinmo, "Historical Institutionalism in Comparative Politics," in Sven Steinmo, Kathleen Thelen and Frank Longstrech, eds., *Structuring Politics* (New York: Cambridge University Press, 1992).

111. Ronald Inglehart, "Trust, Well-being and Democracy," in Mark Warren, eds., *Democracy and Trust* (New York: Cambridge University Press, 1999), p. 89.

3   Spanish Civil Society in Transition Politics

1. José Amodia, *Franco's Political Legacy* (London: Penguin, 1977), p. 203.

2. Juan J. Linz, "A Century of Interest Politics in Spain," in Suzanne Berger, ed., *Organizing Interests in Western Europe* (Cambridge: Cambridge University Press, 1981), p. 367.

3. Peter McDonough, Samuel H. Barnes and Antonio López Pina, *The Cultural Dynamics of Democratization in Spain* (Ithaca, N.Y.: Cornell University Press, 1998).

4. Ibid., p. x.

5. Ibid., p. 1.
6. These estimates about associational life in Spain, Brazil and South Korea from the study of McDonough et al. roughly correspond with the findings of the *World Values Survey* (*WVS*). In the WVS, the percentage of respondents belonging to one or more associations are: for Spain, 23%, for Brazil, 43% and for South Korea, 61%.
7. The data for this section are drawn from McDonough, Doh C. Shin and José Álvaro Moisés, "Democratization and Participation: Comparing Spain, Brazil, and Korea," *The Journal of Politics* 60 (1998).
8. Victor Pérez-Díaz, "Economic Policies and Social Pacts in Spain During the Transition," *European Sociological Review* 2 (May 1986), p. 6.
9. Patricia L. Hipsher, "Democratization and the Decline of Urban Social Movements in Chile and Spain," *Comparative Politics* 27 (April 1996).
10. Ibid., p. 288.
11. Ibid., p. 291.
12. On the Spanish labor movement during the transition to democracy see José M. Maravall, *Dictadura y disentimiento político: Obreros y estudiantes bajo el franquismo* (Madrid: Ediciones Alfaguara, 1978); Victor Pérez-Díaz, *Clase obrera, orden social y conciencia de clase* (Madrid: Fundación del Instituto National de Industria, 1980); José M. Zufiaur, "El sindicalismo español en la transición y la crisis," *Papeles de Economía Española* 22 (1985); Robert Fishman, *Working Class Organization and the Return to Democracy in Spain* (Ithaca, N.Y.: Cornell University Press, 1990); and Omar G. Encarnación, "Labor and Pacted Democracy: Post-Franco Spain in Comparative Perspective," *Comparative Politics* 33 (April 2001).
13. Zufiaur, "El sindicalismo español en la transición y la crisis," pp. 206–207.
14. In less conventional ways, Spanish labor does not appear so weak, as suggested by its capacity to mobilize the working class, its participation in collective bargaining and the role played by the unions in negotiating social agreements with both the state and the employers. None of the factors, however, distract from the fact that associational levels remain exceptionally low in Spanish unions and that it is the internal, social interaction that unions provide that civil society theorists value most about such organizations.
15. Fishman, *Working Class Organization and the Return to Democracy in Spain*, p. 97. For an overview of the labor movement under Franco see Fernando Morcillo Almendros, Enrique Jiménez-Asenjo, Francisco Pérez Amorós and Eduardo Rojo Torrecillo, *El sindicalismo de clase en España, 1939–1977* (Barcelona: Ediciones Península, 1978).
16. Katrina Burgess, "Unemployment and Union Strategies in Spain," in Nancy Bermeo, ed., *Unemployment in Southern Europe: Coping with the Consequences* (London: Frank Cass, 2000), p. 4.
17. Jose M. Maravall, *The Transition to Democracy in Spain* (New York: St. Martin's Press, 1977), p. 9.

18. Ibid., p. 9.

19. Ibid, p. 14.

20. Fishman, *Working Class Organization and the Return to Democracy in Spain*, p. 34.

21. Joaquín Estefanía and Rodolfo Serrano, "Diez años de relaciones industriales en España," in Angel Zaragoza, ed., *Pactos sociales, sindicatos y patronal en España* (Madrid: Siglo XIX, 1988), p. 36.

22. Roger G. McElrath, "Trade Unions and the Industrial Relations Climate in Spain," Multinational Industrial Relations Series, Industrial Research Unit, No. 10 European Studies, The Wharton School, University of Pennsylvania (1989), p. 114.

23. Ibid., pp. 110–114.

24. Ibid., pp. 110–114.

25. Encarnación, "Labor and Pacted Democracy," p. 348.

26. Philippe Schmitter, "Organized Interests and Democratic Consolidation in Southern Europe," in Richard Gunther, P. Nikiforos Diamandouros and Hans-Jürgen Puhle, eds., *The Politics of Democratic Consolidation: Southern Europe in Comparative Perspective* (Baltimore: Johns Hopkins University Press, 1955), 294.

27. Larry Diamond, *Developing Democracy: Toward Consolidation* (Baltimore: Johns Hopkins University Press, 1999), pp. 228–229.

28. On this period in Spanish history see Juan J. Linz, "From Great Hopes to Civil War: The Breakdown of Democracy in Spain," in Juan J. Linz and Alfred Stepan, eds., *The Breakdown of Democratic Regimes* (Baltimore: Johns Hopkins University Press, 1979).

29. On the CNCA see: J. J. Castillo, *La subordinación política del pequeño campesino* (Madrid: Ministerio de Agricultura, 1979).

30. Gerald Meaker, "Anarchists Versus Syndicalists: Conflicts Within the Confederación Nacional de Trabajadores, 1917–1923," in Stanley G. Payne, ed., *Politics and Society in Twentieth Century Spain* (New York: Viewpoints, 1976), p. 29.

31. Ibid., p. 43.

32. Benjamin Martin, *The Agony of Modernization: Labor and Industrialization in Spain* (Ithaca, N.Y.: Cornell University Press, 1990), p. 215.

33. José M. Maravall and Julián Santamaría, "Crisis del franquismo: transición política y consolidación de la democracia en España," *Sistema* (November 1985), p. 105.

34. Ibid., p. 105.

35. See Felipe Agüero, "Democratic Consolidation and the Military in Southern Europe and South America," in Richard Gunther, P. Nikiforos Diamandouros and Hans-Jürgen Puhle, eds., *The Politics of Democratic Consolidation: Southern Europe in Comparative Perspective*.

36. See McDonough et al., *The Cultural Dynamics of Democratization in Spain*, chapter 6, footnote 9.

37. The classic statement on these issues is Edward C. Banfield's *The Moral Basis of a Backward Society* (Glencoe, Ill.: Free Press, 1958).

38. Francis Fukuyama, *Trust: Societal Virtues and the Creation of Prosperity* (New York: Free Press, 1995), p. 56.

39. See Miguel Requena and Jorge Benedicto, *Relaciones interpersonales: Actitudes y valores en la España de los ochenta* (Madrid: Centro de Investigaciones Sociológicas, 1988) and Félix Requena Santos, "Redes de amistad, felicidad y familia," *Revista Española de Investigaciones Sociológicas* 66 (1994).

40. McDonough et al., *The Cultural Dynamics of Democratization in Spain*, p. 203.

41. J. Jimenez and L. Toharia, *Unemployment and Labour Market Flexibility: Spain* (Geneva: International Labour Office, 1994), pp. 1 and 21. For a broader view of the political impact of the unemployment crisis in Spain see Nancy Bermeo, ed., *Unemployment in Southern Europe: Coping with the Consequences* (London: Frank Cass, 2000).

42. According to McDonough et al., the percentage of women in Spain defined as economically active is 22% compared with 30% for Brazil and 40% for Korea.

43. Ibid., p. 3.

44. On religion and democratization politics in Spain see Juan J. Linz, "Church and State in Spain from the Civil War to the Return of Democracy," *Daedalus* (Summer 1991); Rafael Díaz Salazar, *Iglesia, dictadura y democracia: Catolicismo y sociedad en España, 1953–1979* (Madrid: HOAC, 1981); Stanley Payne, *Spanish Catholicism* (Madison: University of Wisconsin Press, 1984); and Victor Pérez-Díaz, "The Church and Religion in Contemporary Spain," *Working Paper* No. 19, Centro de Estudios Avanzados en Ciencias Sociales, Instituto Juan March (1991).

45. McDonough et al., *The Cultural Dynamics of Democratization in Spain*, p. 2.

46. Linz, "A Century of Interest Politics in Spain," p. 365. For a broader examination of this issue see also by Linz, "Early State-Building and Late Peripheral Nationalism against the State: The Case of Spain," in S. N. Eisenstandt and S. Rokkan, eds., *Building Nations and States* (Beverly Hills, Calif.: Sage, 1973).

47. Salvador Giner and Enrique Sevilla, "Spain after Franco: From Corporatism to Corporatism," in Allan Williams, ed., *Southern Europe Transformed* (London: Harper and Row, 1986), p. 130.

48. On the Franco regime see Stanley Payne, *The Franco Regime, 1936–75* (Madison: University of Wisconsin Press, 1987).

49. Pérez-Díaz, "Economic Policies and Social Pacts in Spain During the Transition: The Two Faces of Neo-Corporatism," p. 6.

50. Amodia, *Franco's Political Legacy*, p. 26.

51. On organic corporatism in Iberian-Latin countries see Alfred Stepan, *State and Society: Peru in Comparative Perspective* (Princeton: Princeton University Press, 1979).

52. Amodia, *Franco's Political Legacy*, p. 137.

53. In undertaking this project, Spain appears to have more in common with the post-Communist world than with its sister authoritarian regimes in South America. It is generally thought that while authoritarian regimes tolerated membership in many forms of groups, Communist ones sought to repress all kinds of autonomous civil society organization and forced the citizenry to belong to mandatory, state-controlled organizations. This difference between authoritarian and communist regimes is often used to explain lower levels of civil society density in the post-Communist world than in formerly authoritarian societies (see Marc Morje Howard, "The Weakness of Post-Communist Civil Society," *Journal of Democracy*, Vol. 13 (January 2002), pp. 159–160). The Spanish case suggests the need to account for the peculiarity of Francoist authoritarian rule with respect to the development of civil society. It also highlights the general point that authoritarian rule can in fact incorporate social indoctrination and forced societal participation in state-sponsored organizations.

54. Ibid., p. 180.

55. On the OSE see Manuel Ludevid, *Cuarenta años de sindicato sindical: Aproximación a la organización sindical española* (Barcelona, 1976).

56. Amodia, *Franco's Political Legacies*, p. 204.

57. Juan J. Linz, "Europe's Southern Frontier: Evolving Towards What?" *Daedalus* 128, No. 1 (Winter 1979).

58. "Preface," in Gunther et al., *The Politics of Democratic Consolidation: Southern Europe in Comparative Perspective*, p. xiii.

59. For a broader view of the Spanish transition see José M. Maravall, *The Transition to Democracy in Spain* (London: Croom Helm, 1982); John Coverdale, *The Political Transformation of Spain after Franco* (New York: Praeger, 1979); Raymond Carr and Juan Pablo Fussi, *Spain: From Dictatorship to Democracy* (London: George, Allen and Unwin, 1986); and José Félix Tezanos, Ramón Cotarelo and Andrés de Blas, eds., *La transición democrática española* (Madrid: Sistema, 1989).

60. Juan J. Linz and Alfred Stepan, *Problems of Democratic Transition and Consolidation* (Baltimore: Johns Hopkins University Press, 1996), p. 108.

61. Adam Przeworski, *Democracy and the Market* (New York: Cambridge University Press, 1991), pp. 7–8.

62. McDonough et al., *The Cultural Dynamics of Democratization in Spain*, p. ix.

63. Ibid., p. 42.

64. Source of data: Linz and Stepan, *Problems of Democratic Transition and Consolidation*, pp. 108–109. For a broader view of Spaniards' attitudes toward democracy and the democratic transition see Juan J. Linz., ed., *Informe sociológico sobre el cambio político en España, 1975–1981* (Madrid: Fundación Foessa, 1981).

65. For modernization-inspired accounts of Spanish democratization see José Casanova, "Modernization and Democratization in Spain," *Social Research* 50 (1993); Edward Malafakis, "Spain and its Francoist Legacy," in John H. Hertz, ed., *From Dictatorship to Democracy: Coping with the Legacies of Authoritarianism*

and Totalitarianism (Westport, Conn.: Greenwood Press, 1983); and José Félix Tezanos "Cambio social y modernización en la España actual," *Revista Española de Investigaciones Sociológicas* 28 (1984).

66. See Joseph Harrison, *The Spanish Economy: From the Civil War to the European Community* (London: Macmillian Press, 1993).

67. See Paloma Aguilar, *Memoria y olvido de la guerra civil española* (Madrid: Alianza, 1996).

68. See Geoffrey Pridham, ed., *Encouraging Democracy: The International Context of Regime Transition in Southern Europe* (London: Leicester University Press, 1991) and Geoffrey Pridham, "The International Context of Democratic Consolidation: Southern Europe in Comparative Perspective," in Richard Gunther et al., eds., *The Politics of Democratic Consolidation: Southern Europe in Comparative Perspective*.

69. Richard Gunther, "The Spanish Socialist Party," in Stanley Payne, ed., *The Politics of Democratic Spain* (The Chicago Council on Foreign Relations, 1986), p. 26.

70. Ibid., p. 26.

71. Juan J. Linz and Alfred Stepan, "Democratic Transition and Consolidation in Southern Europe," in Richard Gunther et al., *The Politics of Democratic Consolidation: Southern Europe in Comparative Perspective*, p. 88.

72. Carlos Huneeus, "La transición a la democracia en España: dimensiones de una política consociacional," in Julián Santamaria, ed., *Transición a la democracia en el sur de Europa y la América Latina* (Madrid: Centro de Investigaciones Sociológicas, 1982), p. 224.

73. Ibid., p. 224.

74. See Juan J. Linz and Alfred Stepan, *Problems of Democratic Transition and Consolidation*; Richard Gunther, "Spain: The Very Model of the Modern Elite Settlement," in John Higley and Richard Gunther, eds., *Elites and Democratic Consolidation in Latin America and Southern Europe* (New York: Cambridge University Press, 1992); and Donald Share, *The Making of Spanish Democracy* (New York: Praeger, 1986).

75. This widely accepted account of the Spanish transition is not without its critics. See, e.g., Ruth Berins Collier, *Paths Towards Democracy: The Working Class and Elites in Western Europe and South America* (New York: Cambridge University Press, 1999).

76. See, especially, Guillermo O' Donnell and Philippe Schmitter, *Tentative Conclusions about Uncertain Democracies* (Baltimore: Johns Hopkins University Press, 1986).

77. A full examination of the politics of social concertation in Spain is beyond the scope of this book. Fortunately, this subject has generated a vast literature, a reflection of its importance to post-transition Francoist politics. For transcripts of the Moncloa pacts and other social pacts see Luis Enrique de la Villa, *Los grandes pactos colectivos a partir de la transición democrática* (Madrid: Ministerio de Trabajo y Seguridad Social, 1985). For analyses of the factors aiding in the rise

of social pacts and their legacies see: Omar G. Encarnación, "Social Concertation in Democratic and Market Transitions: Comparative Lessons from Spain," *Comparative Political Studies* 30 (August 1997) and Joe Foweraker, "Corporatist Strategies and the Transition to Democracy in Spain," *Comparative Politics* 24 (1987). For assessments of the economic legacies of the social pacts see Enrique de la Villa and Juan Antonio Sargadoy Bengoechea, "Social Concertation in Spain," *Labour and Society* 12 (1987) and Angel Zaragoza, ed., *Pactos sociales, sindicatos y patronal en España* (Madrid: Siglo XXI, 1988). For analyses of the end of social pacts in Spain see: Omar G. Encarnación, "A Casualty of Unemployment: The Breakdown of Social Concertation in Spain," in Nancy Bermeo, ed., *Unemployment in Southern Europe: Coping with the Consequences* (London: Frank Cass, 2000) and Sebastián Royo, *From Social Democracy to Neo-liberalism: The Consequences of Party Hegemony in Spain, 1992–1996* (New York: St. Martin's Press, 2000).

78. Author's interview with Mr. Fuentes Quintana (Madrid: February 28, 1994).

79. Although labor as a whole was a supporter of the social pacts, the individual unions reacted quite differently to the practice of "pacting." The CCOO was a far stronger supporter of Moncloa than the UGT. Only the CCOO publicly endorsed this accord and actively promoted it among the workers. The UGT, by contrast, refrained from publicly attacking the accord but made it known that it was not bounded by it. The explanation for these divergent responses rests within the unions' connection to the party system. The CCOO's response to Moncloa was shaped by the Communist party's desire to emphasize its moderation in order to continue to play a role in democratization politics. The UGT, by contrast, expected to win the 1979 elections and did not see many benefits from explicitly supporting the political program of the UCD.

80. Jordi Jusmet Roca, "Los pactos sociales en el estado español," *Crónica de Información Laboral* (1985, No. 32), p. 4.

81. Ramón Tamanes, *The Spanish Economy* (London: C. Hurst, 1986), p. 230.

82. Nancy Bermeo with José García Durán, "Spain: Dual Transition Implemented by Two Parties," in Stephan Haggard and Steven B. Webb, eds., *Voting For Reform: Democracy, Political Liberalization and Economic Adjustment* (New York: Oxford University Press, 1991), p. 94.

83. Royo, *From Social Democracy to Neo-Liberalism*, p. 103.

84. This comparison is also interesting because democracy in Spain and Argentina was initiated by center-right governments facing opposition from parties in control of the labor movement (the PSOE and the PCE in Spain and the Peronist party in Argentina).

85. Ibid., p. 104.

86. Centro de Investigaciones Sociológicas (Madrid: 1994).

87. Pérez-Díaz, "Economic Policies and Social Pacts in Spain During the Transition: The Two Faces of Neo-Corporatism," p. 4.

88. For a broader examination of this point see: Jordi Capo Giol, "Estrategias para un sistema de partidos," *Revista de Estudios Políticos* 23 (September–October

1981) and Mario Caciagli, "Spain: Parties and the Party System in the Transition," in Geoffrey Pridham, ed., *The New Mediterranean Democracies: Regime Transition in Spain, Greece and Portugal* (London: Frank Cass, 1984).
89. McElrath, "Trade Unions and the Industrial Relations Climate in Spain," p. 170.
90. See Royo, *From Social Democracy to Neo-liberalism*.
91. Estefanía and Rodolfo Serrano, "Diez años de relaciones industriales en España," p. 17.
92. I am thankful to Sebastián Royo for highlighting this particular insight.

4 Political Institutions and Democratization in Spain

1. Peter McDonough, Samuel H. Barnes and Antonio López Pina, *The Cultural Dynamics of Democratization in Spain* (Ithaca, N.Y.: Cornell University Press, 1998), pp. 167–168.
2. See Charles T. Powell, *El piloto del cambio: El rey, la monarquía y la transición a la democracia* (Barcelona: Editorial Planeta, 1991) and Joel Podolny, "The Role of Juan Carlos I in the Consolidation of the Parliamentary Democracy," in Richard Gunther, ed., *Politics, Society and Democracy: The Case of Spain* (Boulder: Westview Press, 1993).
3. José M. Maravall, *The Transition to Democracy in Spain* (New York: St. Martin's Press, 1977), p. 10.
4. Stanley Payne, "Introduction," in Stanley Payne, ed., *The Politics of Democratic Spain* (The Chicago Council on Foreign Relations, 1986), p. 4.
5. On the growth of political legitimacy in democratic Spain see McDonough et al., *The Cultural Dynamics of Democratization in Spain*, chapter 1.
6. Ibid., p. 6.
7. Payne, "Introduction," p. 5.
8. Ibid., p. 92.
9. Juan J. Linz, "Innovative Leadership in the Transition to Democracy," manuscript, Yale University (1992), p. 4.
10. Edward Malefakis, "Contours of Southern European History," in Richard Gunther et al., eds., *The Politics of Democratic Consolidation: Southern Europe in Comparative Perspective* (Baltimore: Johns Hopkins University Press, 1995), p. 75.
11. The source of this quote from Suárez is Juan J. Linz and Alfred Stepan, *Problems of Democratic Transition and Consolidation* (Baltimore: Johns Hopkins University Press, 1996), p. 93.
12. Carlos Fernández, *Los militares en la transición* (Barcelona: Argos Vergara, 1982), p. 105.
13. Linz and Stepan, *Problems of Democratic Transition and Consolidation*, p. 97. The quote comes from a collection of speeches given by Suárez between 1976–1978. See *Un nuevo horizonte para España* (Madrid: Imprenta del Boletín Official del Estado, 1978).

14. Linz and Stepan, *Problems of Democratic Transition and Consolidation*, p. 96.
15. Javier Tussell Gómez, "The Democratic Center and Christian Democracy in the Elections of 1977 and 1979," in Howard R. Penniman and Eusebio Mujal-León, eds., *Spain at the Polls: 1977, 1979 and 1982* (Durham, N.C.: Duke University Press, 1985), p. 95.
16. Ibid., p. 95.
17. Eusebio Mujal-León, "Spanish Politics: Between the Old Regime and the New Majority," in Penniman and Mujal-León, eds., *Spain at the Polls*, p. 286.
18. Eventually, the conservatives and the business community abandoned the UCD in droves prompting a disastrous performance by the party in the 1982 elections.
19. *El País* (Madrid, January 14, 1977).
20. On Spanish business during the transition see Victor Pérez Díaz, "Los empresarios y la clase política," *Papeles de Economía Española* 22 (1995).
21. Omar G. Encarnación, "Federalism and the Paradox of Corporatism," *West European Politics* 22 (April 1999), p. 96.
22. Enrique Fuentes Quintana, "Economía y política en la transición democrática española: fundamentos y enseñanzas de una experiencia," *Pensamiento Iberoamericano* 1 (1980).
23. Author's interview with Mr. Fuentes Quintana (Madrid: February 28, 1994).
24. "Programa de saneamiento y reforma económica," in *Los Pactos de la Moncloa* (Madrid: Servicio Central de Publicaciones de la Secretaría General Técnica de la Presidencia del Gobierno, 1977).
25. Fuentes Quintana, "Economía y política en la transición democrática española: fundamentos y enseñanzas de una experiencia," p. 155.
26. Author's interview with José Folgado Blanco, chief economist, CEOE (Madrid: June 1992).
27. On the technocratic pragmatism of the late Franco period see Richard Gunther, *Policy-Making in a No-Party State: Spanish Planning and Budgeting in the Twilight of the Franquist Era* (Berkeley: University of California Press, 1980) and Nancy Bermeo, "The Politics of Public Enterprise in Portugal, Spain and Greece," in Ezra Suleiman and John Waterbury, eds., *The Political Economy of Public Sector Reform and Privatization* (Boulder: Westview Press, 1990).
28. Ibid.
29. Jordi Capo Giol, "Estrategias para un sistema de partidos," *Revista de Estudios Políticos* 23 (September–October 1981), p. 159.
30. Bonnie N. Field, "Continuity and Collaboration? Pacting and the Consolidation of Democracy: The Spanish and Argentine Democracies Compared," paper presented at the 2001 meeting of the Latin American Studies Association, Washington, D.C., September 6–8, 2001.
31. Ibid., p. 1.
32. José M. Zufiaur, "El sindicalismo español en la transición y la crisis, *Papeles de Economía Española* 22 (1995), p. 213.
33. Luis Enrique de la Villa and Juan Antonio Sagardoy y Bengoechea, "Social Concertation in Spain," *Labour and Society* 12 (September 1998), p. 387.

34. For a broader discussion of this point see Andrea Bonime-Blanc, *Spain's Transition to Democracy: The Politics of Constitution-Making* (Boulder: Westview Press, 1987).

35. Interview with the author (Madrid: February 1994).

36. Linz and Stepan, *Problems of Democratic Transition and Consolidation*, p. 114.

37. It is important to note that support for the constitution was not unanimous among all political forces in Spain. The leading regional party in the Basque country (the PNV) did not support the constitution nor was the constitution approved by the majority of Basques.

38. Linz and Stepan, *Problems of Democratic Transition and Consolidation*, p. 115.

39. Charles W. Anderson, *The Political Economy of Modern Spain: Policy-Making in an Authoritarian Regime* (Madison: University of Wisconsin Press, 1970), p. 223.

40. Joseph Harrison, *The Spanish Economy: From the Civil War to the European Community* (London: Macmillan, 1993), p. 18.

41. Ibid., p. 12.

42. Ibid., p. 19.

43. Felipe Agüero, "Democratic Consolidation and the Military in Southern Europe and South America," in Richard Gunther et al., eds., *The Politics of Democratic Consolidation: Southern Europe in Comparative Perspective*, p. 125.

44. Ibid., p. 132.

45. On the rise of the Opus Dei within the Franco regime see Stanley Payne, *The Franco Regime*, 1936–75 (Madison: University of Wisconsin Press, 1987).

46. On this point see Bermeo, "The Politics of Public Enterprise in Portugal, Spain and Greece," p. 148.

47. Richard Gunther, "Spanish Public Policy: From Dictatorship to Democracy," *Working Paper* (Madrid: Instituto Juan March, 1997), p. 13.

48. Robert Fishman, *Working Class Organization and the Return to Democracy in Spain* (Ithaca, N.Y.: Cornell University Press, 1990), p. 94.

49. The discussion in this section borrows from Joe Foweraker, "Corporatist Strategies and the Transition to Democracy in Spain," *Comparative Politics* 20 (October 1986).

50. The Franco regime's toleration of "economic" strikes explains why by the late 1960s Spain was one of Europe's most contentious industrial settings despite the country's authoritarian regime. The ability of the Franco regime to accommodate strikes into its structures also explains the economic gains made by the workers during the late Franco period. For a broader view of strikes in Spain in the last three decades see Encarnación, "Labor and Pacted Democracy."

51. For a broader view of collective bargaining under Franco see Jon Amsden, *Collective Bargaining and Class Conflict in Spain* (London: Weidenfeld and Nicholson, 1972).

52. For a broader view of the works councils in Spain see Juan N. García Nieto, *Workers' Participation in Management in Spain* (Barcelona: Institute of Labour Studies, 1978) and Modesto Escobar, "Works or union councils? The

Representative System in Medium and Large Spanish Firms," *Working Paper* (Madrid: Instituto Juan March, 1993).

53. Foweraker, "Corporatist Strategies and the Transition to Democracy in Spain," p. 64.

54. Fishman, *Working Class Organization and the Return to Democracy in Spain*, p. 48.

55. Pérez-Díaz, *Clase Obrera, orden social y conciencia de clase*, p. 99.

56. Ibid, pp. 101–103.

57. Fishman, *Working Class Organization and the Return to Democracy in Spain*, p. 33.

58. Edward Malefakis, "Southern Europe in the 19th and 20th Centuries: An Historical Overview," *Working Paper* (Madrid: Instituto Juan March, 1992), p. 69.

59. Gunther, "Spanish Public Policy: From Dictatorship to Democracy," p. 8.

60. Ibid., p. 22.

61. Ibid., p. 6.

62. Ibid., p. 22.

63. Peter McDonough and Antonio López Pina, "Continuity and Change in Spanish Politics," in Russell J. Dalton, Scott Flanagan and Paul Allen Beck, eds., *Electoral Change in Advanced Industrial Democracies* (Princeton: Princeton University Press, 1984), p. 392.

64. Malefakis, "Southern Europe in the 19th and 20th Centuries: An Historical Overview," p. 2.

65. See José Félix Tezanos, *Crisis de la conciencia obrera* (Madrid: Editorial Mezquita, 1982).

66. Pérez-Díaz, *Clase obrera, orden social y conciencia de clase*, pp. 101–103.

67. Ibid., p. 24.

68. Fishman, *Working Class Organization and the Return to Democracy in Spain*, p. 232.

69. Ibid., p. 232.

70. Leonardo Morlino and José R. Montero, "Legitimacy and Democracy in Southern Europe," in Richard Gunther et al., eds., *The Politics of Democratic Consolidation: Southern Europe in Comparative Perspective* (Baltimore: Johns Hopkins University Press, 1995), p. 259.

71. Ibid., p. 257.

72. For a more extensive treatment of Spain's party system since 1977 see Richard Gunther, Giacomo Sani and Goldie Shabad, *Spain After Franco: The Making of a Competitive Party System* (Berkeley: University of California Press, 1986).

73. See Huneeus, *La Unión de Centro Democrático y la transición a la democracia en España*.

74. On the CEOE see Harry Rijnen, "La CEOE como organización," *Papeles de Economía Española* 22 (1985).

75. Even though business was the UCD's principal source of electoral support, over the course of UCD administrations, relations between the government and the

business community grew to be quite tense. Much of the conflict centered on the perception by business that the UCD took employers' support for granted. For example, during the making of the Moncloa accords, the UCD leadership largely kept the emergent CEOE at bay for fears of alienating the Left and the unions. After 1981, business began to support *Alianza Popular*, a right-wing party led by former Francoist leaders, a contributing factor in the collapse of the UCD in the elections of 1982.

76. Juan J. Linz, *The Breakdown of Democratic Regimes: Crisis, Breakdown and Reequilibration* (Baltimore: Johns Hopkins University Press, 1978), p. 36.

77. For an overview of the role of the PCE in promoting clandestine groups before the transition see Guy Hermet, *Los comunistas en España* (Paris: Ruedo Ibérico, 1972).

78. On the PCE in the transition to democracy see Eusebio Mujal-León, *Communism and Political Change in Spain*, (Bloomington, Ind.: Indiana University Press, 1983).

79. Gunther, "The Parties in Opposition," in Stanley Payne, ed., *The Politics of Democratic Spain*, p, 92. The quoted passage is taken from Mujal-León's research on the Spanish Communist party.

80. Patricia Hipsher, "Democratization and the Decline of Urban Social Movements in Chile and Spain," *Comparative Politics* 27 (April 1996), p. 288.

81. David Gilmore, *The Transformation of Spain* (London: Quarter Books, 1985), p. 93.

82. Collier, *Paths toward Democracy*, p. 127.

83. Ibid., p. 291.

84. *El País* (May 21, 1976).

85. Eusebio Mujal-León, "The Spanish Communists and the Search for Electoral Space," in Howard R. Penniman and Eusebio Mujal-León, eds., *Spain at the Polls, 1977, 1979, 1982*, p. 162.

86. Manuel Contreras, *El PSOE en la II República: Organización e ideologia* (Madrid: Centro de Investigaciones Sociológicas, 1981).

87. José M. Maravall, "The Socialist Alternative: The Policies and Electorate of the PSOE," in Penniman and Mujal-León, eds., *Spain at the Polls*, p. 147.

88. For a more expansive view of the role of the PSOE in advancing a state-sponsored feminist agenda see: Monica Therelfall, "State Feminism or Party Feminism? Feminist Politics and the Spanish Institute of Women," *European Journal of Women's Studies* 5 (1998) and Monica Therelfall, ed., *Feminist Politics and Social Transformation in Spain* (London: Verso, 1996).

89. On the strength and coherence of the PSOE during the implementation of economic reform see Nancy Bermeo, "Sacrifice, Sequence and Strength in Successful Dual Transitions: The Lessons from Spain," *Journal of Politics* 56 (1994).

90. Unemployment figures come from Omar G. Encarnación, "A Casualty of Unemployment: The Breakdown of Social Concertation in Spain," in Nancy Bermeo, ed., *Unemployment in Southern Europe: Coping with the Consequences* (London: Frank Cass, 2000), p. 32.

91. Sebastian Balfour, *Dictatorship, Workers and the City: Labour in Greater Barcelona* (Oxford: Clarendon Press, 1989), p. 248.

92. José M. Maravall, *Regimes, Politics and Markets: Democratization and Economic Change in Southern and Eastern Europe* (New York: Oxford University Press, 1997), p. 95.

93. Morlino and Montero, "Legitimacy and Democracy in Southern Europe," p. 257.

94. Adam Przeworski, *Democracy and the Market* (New York: Cambridge University Press, 1991), p. 187.

95. Victor Pérez-Díaz, "The Scale of Governance: Mesogovernments in Spain," *Working Paper* (Madrid: Juan March Institute, 1992), p. 64.

96. McDonough et al., *The Cultural Dynamics of Democratization in Spain*, p. 91.

97. Guillermo de La Dehesa, "Spain," in John Williamson, ed., *The Political Economy of Economic Reform* (Washington, D.C.: Institute of International Economics, 1994), p. 136.

5 Brazilian Civil Society in Transition Politics

1. Scott Mainwaring, "Urban Popular Movements, Identity, and Democratization in Brazil," *Comparative Political Studies* 20 (July 1987), p. 134.

2. Alfred Stepan, "Introduction," in Alfred Stepan, ed., *Democratizing Brazil* (New York: Oxford University Press, 1989), p. xii.

3. Alfred Stepan, *Rethinking Military Politics: Brazil and the Southern Cone* (Princeton: Princeton University Press, 1988), p. 5.

4. Mainwaring, "Urban Popular Movements, Identity, and Democratization in Brazil," p. 132.

5. Timothy J. Power and J. Timmons Roberts, "A New Brazil? The Changing Demographic Context of Brazilian Democracy," in Kingstone and Power, eds., *Democratic Brazil: Actors, Institutions and Processes* (Pittsburgh: University of Pittsburgh Press, 2000), p. 256.

6. Peter McDonough, Doh C. Shin and José Álvaro Moisés, "Democratization and Participation: Comparing Spain, Brazil and Korea," *Journal of Politics* 60 (November 1998), p. 919.

7. Renato R. Boschi, "Social Movements and the New Political Order in Brazil," in J. D. Wirth, Edson de Oliveira Nunes and Thomas E. Bogenschild, eds., *State and Society in Brazil: Continuity and Change* (Boulder: Westview Press, 1987), p. 180.

8. Ibid., p. 174.

9. See John Burdick, "Rethinking the Study of Social Movements: The Case of the Christian Base Communities in Urban Brazil," in Arturo Escobar and Sonia A. Alvarez, eds., *The Making of Social Movements in Latin America: Identity, Strategy and Democracy* (Boulder: Westview Press, 1992); Ralph Della Cava, "The People's Church, the Vatican and the Abertura," in Stepan, ed., *Democratizing Brazil*; Thomas Bruneau, *The Political Tranformation of the Brazilian Church* (New York: Cambridge University Press, 1974); Emanuel De Kadt, *Catholic Radicals* (London: Oxford University Press, 1970); and Scott Mainwaring, *The Church*

and Politics in Brazil, 1916–1985 (Stanford, Calif.: Stanford University Press, 1986).

10. Della Cava, "The People's Church, the Vatican and the Abertura," in Stepan, ed., *Democratizing Brazil,* p. 144.

11. The source of data for this section comes from: Helmut K. Anheier and Lester M. Salomon, *The Nonprofit Sector in the Developing World: A Comparative Analysis* (Baltimore: Johns Hopkins University Press, 1998), box 1.2, and Timothy J. Power and J. Timmons Roberts, "A New Brazil? The Changing Sociodemographic Context of Brazilian Democracy," in Kingstone and Power, eds., *Democratic Brazil: Actors, Institutions and Processes,* pp. 225–226.

12. Kathryn Hochstetler, "Democratizing Pressures from Below? Social Movements in the New Brazilian Democracy," in Kingstone and Power, eds., *Democratic Brazil: Actors, Institutions and Processes,* pp. 178–179.

13. Ibid., p. 179.

14. Sonia A. Alvarez, "Politicizing Gender and Engendering Democracy," in Stepan, ed., *Democratizing Brazil,* p. 205.

15. Sonia Alvarez, *Engendering Democracy in Brazil: Women's Movements in Transition Politics* (Princeton: Princeton University Press, 1990), p. 66.

16. Ibid., p. 228.

17. Ibid., p. 230.

18. Ibid., p. 230.

19. On gay and lesbian movements in Brazil see Edward MacRae, "Homosexual Identities in Transitional Brazilian Politics," in Escobar and Alvarez, eds., *The Making of Social Movements in Latin America*; on Afro-Brazilian movements see Carlos Hasenbalg, "Racial Inequalities in Brazil and Throughout Latin America," in Elizabeth Jelin and Eric Hershberg, eds., *Constructing Democracy: Human Rights, Citizenship, and Society in Latin America* (Boulder: Westview Press, 1996) and Michael Hanchard, eds., *Racial Politics in Contemporary Brazil* (Durham, N.C.: Duke University Press, 1999).

20. MacRae, "Homosexual Identities in Transitional Brazilian Politics," in Escobar and Alvarez, eds., *The Making of Social Movements in Latin America,* p. 201.

21. Power and Roberts, "A New Brazil? The Changing Sociodemographic Context of Brazilian Democracy," in Kingstone and Power, eds., *Democratic Brazil,* p. 255.

22. On Brazil's labor movement prior to the transition to democracy see Victor Alba, *Politics and the Labor Movement in Latin America* (Stanford, Calif.: Stanford University Press, 1968); Hobart A. Spalding, Jr., *Organized Labor in Latin America: Historical Case Studies of Workers in Dependent Societies* (New York: New York University Press, 1977); Kenneth P. Erickson, *The Brazilian Corporative State and Working Class Politics* (Berkeley: University of California Press, 1977); and Paul Drake, *Labor Movements and Dictatorship: The Southern Cone in Comparative Perspective* (Baltimore: Johns Hopkins University Press, 1996).

23. Alba, *Politics and the Labor Movement in Latin America,* p. 259.

24. Anthony W. Pereira, "Working for Democracy: Brazil's Working Class in Comparative Perspective," *International Labor and Working Class History* 49 (1997), p. 94.

25. For a more extensive view of the formation of the CUT see Iram J. Rodrigues, *Sindicalismo e politica: A trajectoria da CUT* (São Paulo: Stritta, 1997).

26. Maria Helena Moreira Alves, "Trade Unions in Brazil: A Search for Autonomy and Organization," in Edward Epstein, ed., *Labor, Autonomy and the State in Latin America* (Boston: Unwyn Hyman, 1989), p. 50.

27. John Humphrey, *Capitalist Control and Workers' Struggle in the Brazilian Auto Industry* (Princeton: Princeton University Press, 1982), p. 195.

28. Kenneth Mericle, "Corporatist Control of the Working Class in Brazil," in James Malloy, ed., *Authoritarianism and Corporatism in Latin America* (Pittsburgh: University of Pittsburgh Press, 1977), p. 325.

29. Source of data on the CUT: Jeffrey B. Sluyter-Beltrao, "Media Limelight and The Institutionalization of Brazilian Organized Labor, 1980–1997," paper presented at the 1997 American Political Science Association, Washington, D.C., August 27–31, 1997, p. 13.

30. On rural unions in Brazil see Peter P. Houtzager, "State and Unions in the Transformation of the Brazilian Countryside, 1964–1979," *Latin American Research Review* 33 (1998).

31. Adalberto Moreira Cardoso, "Brazilian Central Union Federations at the Crossroads," paper presented at the conference National Labor Confederations in Brazil and South Korea, Berkeley, Calif., May 13–15, 1989, p. 5.

32. On strikes in democratic Brazil see Luis Flavio Rainho and Osvaldo Martinez Bargas, *As lutas operarias e sindicais dos metalurgicos em São Bernardo, 1977–79* (São Bernardo, SP: Sociedade Cultural, 1983); Amneris Maroni, *A estrategia da recusa: analise das greves de maio/78* (São Paulo: Brasiliense, 1982); Eduardo Noronha, *Brasil: relatório sobre a situaçao social do pais* (São Paulo: Núcleo de Estudos de Política Públicas de Universidade Estadual de Campinas, 1988); Ricardo Antunes, *A rebeldia do trabalho* (Campinas, SP: Editora da UNICAMP, 1988); and A. M. Salvador Sandoval, *Social Change and Labor Unrest in Brazil* (Boulder: Westview Press, 1993) and Adalberto Moreira Cardoso, "Brazilian Central Union Federations at the Crossroads," paper presented at the conference "National Labor Confederations in Brazil and South Korea," University of California, Berkeley, May 13–14, 2000.

33. Pereira, "Working for Democracy," p. 98.

34. Stepan, "Introduction," in Stepan, ed., *Democratizing Brazil*, p., xi.

35. On this point see Bolivar Lamounier, "Authoritarian Brazil Revisited: The Impact of Elections on the *Abertura*," in Stepan, ed., *Democratizing Brazil*.

36. McDonough, Shin and Moisés, "Democratization and Participation," p. 930.

37. Ibid., p. 930.

38. Thomas Skidmore, "Brazil's Slow Road to Democratization: 1974–1985," in Alfred Stepan, ed., *Democratizing Brazil*, p. 33.

39. It is interesting to note that in the study by McDonough, Shin and Álvaro Moisés, the Church is the principal variable in explaining divergent levels of participation in voluntary groups in South Korea, Brazil and Spain.

40. Della Cava, "The People's Church, the Vatican and the Abertura," in Stepan, ed., *Democratizing Brazil*, p. 146.

41. Ibid., p. 146.

42. Margaret Keck, "The New Unionism in the Brazilian Transition," in Stepan, ed., *Democratizing Brazil*, p. 261.

43. Ibid., p. 274.

44. See Kenneth P. Serbin, "The Catholic Church, Religious Pluralism, and Democracy in Brazil," in Kingstone and Power, eds., *Democratic Brazil*.

45. Ibid., p. 154.

46. Ibid., p. 154.

47. See Antônio Flávio de Oliveira and Reginaldo Prandi, eds., *A realidade social das religiões no Brasil: Religião, sociedade, e política* (São Paulo: HUCITEC).

48. On the Brazilian democratic transition see Maria Helena Moreira Alves, *State and Opposition in Brazil* (Austin, University of Texas Press, 1985); Bernardo Kucinski, *Abertura: a historia de uma crise* (São Paulo; Brasil Debates 1982); Thomas Skidmore, *The Politics of Military Rule in Brazil, 1964–1985* (New York: Oxford University Press, 1987); Frances Hagopian, *Traditional Politics and Regime Change in Brazil* (New York: Cambridge University Press, 1996); and Thomas Bruneau, "Brazil's Political Transition," in Higley and Gunther, eds., *Elites and Democratic Consolidation in Latin America and Southern Europe* (New York: Cambridge University Press, 1992).

49. To be sure, this is not the only (or even the most important) reason that accounts for the vigor of Brazilian labor in the contemporary period. A provocative thesis set forth by Anthony W. Pereira is the lateness of Brazilian industrialization relative to that of other Southern Cone countries such as Chile and Argentina. See Pereira, "Working for Democracy."

50. *Veja* (January 16, 1985).

51. See, in particular, Ruth Corrêa Leite Cardoso, "Popular Movements in the Context of the Consolidation of Democracy in Brazil," in Escobar and Alvarez, eds., *The Making of Social Movements in Latin America*.

52. MacRae, "Homosexual Identities in Transitional Brazilian Politics," in Escobar and Alvarez, eds., *The Making of Social Movements in Latin America*, p. 185.

53. Philippe Schmitter, "Transitology: The Science or Art of Democratization?" in Joseph Tulchin and Bernice Romero, eds., *The Consolidation of Democracy in Latin America* (Boulder: Lynne Rienner Publishers, 1995).

54. By almost any measure Brazil's new democracy is a vast improvement over the one established in 1964. Participation of the public in the "old" democracy was quite limited since illiterates lacked the right to vote, a barrier lifted by the new democracy. After 1947, the Communist party was banned; by contrast one of the first decisions made after 1985 was to legalize this party. The old democratic

regime also faced serious succession crises and multiple military rebellions. On democratic politics in Brazil prior to 1985 see Thomas Skidmore, *Politics in Brazil, 1930–1964: An Experiment in Democracy* (New York: Oxford University Press, 1976). For an insightful comparison of democratic politics in Brazil between 1946 and 1964 and after 1985 see: Kurt Wayland, "The Growing Sustainability of Brazil's Low-Quality Democracy," paper presented at the conference "Advances and Setbacks in the Third Wave of Democratization in Latin America," Kellogg Institute, University of Notre Dame, April 23–24, 2001.

55. Linz and Stepan, *Problems of Transition and Consolidation*, p. 166.

56. Frances Hagopian, "Democracy by Undemocratic Means? Elites, Political Pacts and Regime Transition in Brazil," *Comparative Political Studies* 23 (1990), p. 155.

57. Scott Mainwaring, "Grassroots Popular Movements and the Struggle for Democracy," in Stepan, ed., *Democratizing Brazil*, p. 196.

58. Ibid., pp. 196–197.

59. Ruth Berins Collier, *Paths Toward Democracy: The Working Class and Elites in Western Europe and South America* (New York: Cambridge University Press, 1999), p. 134.

60. Bruneau, "Brazil's Political Transition," in Higley and Gunther, eds., *Elites and Democratic Consolidation in Latin America and Southern Europe*, p. 260.

61. Ibid., p. 260.

62. In contrast to Spain and Brazil, the transition to democracy in Portugal was accompanied by the collapse of the state, allowing for a process of regime change orchestrated from below as well as for the radicalization of civil society, especially the labor movement.

63. Joan Dassin, ed., *Torture in Brazil* (New York: Vintage, 1986).

64. This is a summary of Dassim's study provided by Craig Arceneaux, *Military Regimes and Democratization in the Southern Cone and Brazil* (University Park, Penn.: Penn State Press, 2001), p. 170.

65. For a broader view of human rights politics in contemporary Brazil see: Gilberto Dimenstein, *Democracia em pedaços: Direitos humanos no Brasil* (São Paulo: Companhia das Letras, 1996).

66. A truth commission was finally organized in Brazil by President Cardoso in 1996, ten years after the formal end of military rule, the outcome of an electoral promise to investigate human rights abuses by the military. This was aided to some degree by Cardoso's own past as a victim of the military dictatorship. The military took away his professorship at the University of São Paulo for political reasons and he was forced into exile for several years.

67. The information contained in this section is culled from a variety of reports on Brazil from Freedom House.

68. Anthony W. Pereira, "An Ugly Democracy? State Violence and the Rule of Law in Brazil," in Kingstone and Power, eds., *Democratic Brazil*, p. 218.

69. For general statistics about crime and violence in Brazil (especially state-sponsored) see *Policy Abuse in Brazil* (New York: Americas Watch Committee,

1987), *Brasil* (London: Amnesty International, 1989) and *Rural Violence in Brazil* (New York: Americas Watch Committee, 1991); and *Urban Violence in Brazil: Torture and Police Killings in São Paulo and Rio de Janeiro after Five Years* (New York: Americas Watch Committee, 1993).

70. Ibid., p. 235.

71. Teresa P. R. Caldeira, *City of Walls: Crime, Segregation and Citizenship in São Paulo* (Berkeley: University of California Press, 2000), p. 176.

72. Steven Dudley, "Deadly Force: Security and Insecurity in Rio," *NACLA Report*, Vol. XXXII (November/December 1998), p. 32.

73. The military police is not responsible for all of these assassinations. Many of them have been carried out by such groups as the UDR, the landowners' movement, in its attempt to use violence to systematically suppress popular mobilization.

74. Pereira, "An Ugly Democracy? State Violence and the Rule of Law in Brazil," p. 230.

75. Elisa P. Reis, "Modernization, Citizenship, and Stratification: Historical Processes and Recent Changes in Brazil," *Daedalus: Special Issue: Brazil: The Burden of Its Past; The Promise of Its Future* 129 (2) (Spring 2002), p. 17.

76. Paul Chevigny, *Edge of the Knife: Police Violence in the Americas* (New York: New Press, 1995).

77. Teresa P. R. Caldeira, "Crime and Individual Rights: Reframing the Question of Violence in Latin America," in Elizabeth Jelin and Eric Hershberg, eds., *Constructing Democracy: Human Rights, Citizenship, and Society in Latin America*, p. 198.

78. "The 2000 Freedom House Survey," *Journal of Democracy* 12 (January 2001), p. 90.

79. Dudley, "Deadly Force: Security and Insecurity in Rio," p. 32.

80. Ibid., p. 32.

81. Caldeira, *City of Walls: Crime, Segregation and Citizenship in São Paulo.*

82. Caldeira, "Crime and Individual Rights: Reframing the Question of Violence in Latin America," p. 198.

83. Linz and Stepan, *Problems of Democratic Transition and Consolidation*, p. 172.

84. Marta Lagos, "Between Stability and Crisis in Latin America," *Journal of Democracy* 12 (January 2001), p. 138.

85. Scott Mainwaring, "Party Systems in the Third Wave," *Journal of Democracy* 9 (1998), p. 68.

86. William R. Nylen, "Testing the Empowerment Thesis: The Participatory Budget in Belo Horizonte and Betim, Brazil," *Comparative Politics* 34 (January 2002), p. 170.

87. Ibid., p. 170

88. Ibid., p. 170

89. *The New York Times* (July 25, 1993).

90. Linz and Stepan, *Problems of Democratic Transition and Consolidation*, p. 173. For a more extensive look at this survey see: Judith Muszynski and Antonio Manuel

Teixera Mendes, "Democratização e opinião pública no Brasil," in Bolivar Lamounier, ed., *De Geisel a Collor: O balanço da transição* (São Paulo: Editora Sumaré, 1990), p. 71.

91. Ibid.

92. Power and Roberts, "A New Brazil? The Changing Sociodemographic Context of Brazilian Democracy," p. 248.

93. *The New York Times* (July 25, 1993).

94. See Power and Roberts, "A New Brazil? The Changing Sociodemographic Context of Brazilian Democracy," in Kingstone and Power, eds., *Democratic Brazil*.

95. It should be made clear that my intention in this section is not to fault civil society organizations for failing to solve Brazil's grave social problems and injustices. Rather my sole purpose is to show how assumptions about the powers of vibrant and robust civil societies fall short when exported to the Brazilian context. Of course, this same criticism can be applied to the United States, where discrimination and injustice persists despite its possession of the most famous of vibrant civil societies.

96. See Hasenbalg, "Racial Inequalities in Brazil and Throughout Latin America," in Jelin and Hershberg, eds., *Constructing Democracy: Human Rights, Citizenship, and Society in Latin America*.

97. Reis, "Modernization, Citizenship, and Stratification: Historical Processes and Recent Changes in Brazil," p. 8. For a broader overview of the much examined issue of inequality in democratic Brazil see Jane Souto de Oliveria, ed., *O Traço da Desigualdade Social no Brasil* (Rio de Janerio: IBGE, 1993); Maria Regina Soares de Lima and Zario Borges Cheibub, *Elites Estratégicas e Dilemas de Desenvolvimento* (Rio de Janerio: IUPERJ, 1994) and Kurt Wayland, *Democracy Without Equity: Failures of Reform in Brazil* (Pittsburgh, Pa.: University of Pittsburgh Press, 1996).

98. See *O crimen anti-homosexual no Brasil* (Editora Grupo Gay da Bahia, 2001).

99. Reported by Freedom House in its 1999 country profile of Brazil.

100. Hasenbalg, "Racial Inequalities in Brazil and Throughout Latin America," p. 171.

101. See Margaret Keck, "The New Unionism in the Brazilian Transition," in Alfred Stepan, ed., *Democratizing Brazil and The Workers' Party and Democratization in Brazil* (New Haven: Yale University Press, 1992); also Armando Boito, Jr., "The State and Trade Unionism in Brazil," *Latin American Perspectives* 80 (Winter 1994).

102. Wendy Hunter, *Eroding Military Influence in Brazil: Politicians Against Soldiers* (Chapel Hill, N.C.: University of North Carolina Press, 1997), p. 81.

103. Linz and Stepan, *Problems of Democratic Transition and Consolidation*, p. 169.

104. Renato Boschi, *A arte da associaçao: Politica de base e democracia no Brasil* (São Paulo Vertice, 1987).

105. Kathryn Hochstetler, "Democratizing from Below? Social Movements in the New Brazilian Democracy," in Peter R. Kingstone and Timothy J. Power, eds., *Democratic Brazil*, pp. 162–163.

106. Ibid.
107. Gianpaolo Baiocchi, "Participation, Activism and Politics: The Porto Alegre Experiment and Deliberative Democratic Theory," *Politics and Society* 29 (March 2001), p. 55.
108. Marta Lagos, "Latin America's Smiling Mask," *Journal of Democracy* 8 (July 1997), p. 133.
109. This section borrows from Adalberto Moreira Cardoso, "Brazilian Central Union Federation at the Crossroads," paper presented at the conference "National Labor Confederations in Brazil and South Korea," Berkeley, Calif. May 13–14, 2000.
110. A social pact in Brazil may well finally happen, given the huge popular mandate Lula gained with the elections and his party's connections to the labor movement. Employers may also wish to participate in a social pact if only to secure a formal role in the forging of the new government's economic agenda.
111. On business associations in democratic Brazil see Ben Ross Schneider, "Organized Business Politics in Democratic Brazil," *Journal of Inter-American Studies and World Affairs* 39 (Winter 1997–1998).
112. Ibid., p. 100.
113. Ibid., p. 111.
114. Luis F. Andreade, "The Labor Climate in Brazil," Multinational Industrial Relations Series No. 4, Philadelphia: Industrial Research Unit, The Wharton School, University of Pennsylvania, p. 91.
115. Moreira Cardoso, "Brazilian Central Union Federation at the Crossroads," p. 19.
116. *Folha de São Paulo* (November 28, 1991).
117. *Folha de São Paulo* (November 25, 1988). For a broader view of the CUT"s assessment of attempts at pact-making in Brazil see CUT, "Negociacão ou pacto social?" (São Paulo, 1991).
118. Sluyter-Beltrao, "Media Limelight and the Institutionalization of Brazilian Organized Labor, 1980–1997," p. 18. On these characterizations of the CUT see *Jornal do Brasil* (August 3, 1986).
119. CUT, "Negociaçao ou pacto social?" (São Paulo, 1991).
120. Rolando Munck, "Workers, Structural Adjustment and *Concertación Social*," *Latin American Perspectives* 82 (1992), p. 94.
121. Arturo Bronstein, "Societal Change and Industrial Relations in Latin America: Trends and Prospects," *International Labour Review* 134 (1995), p. 181.

6 *Political Institutions and Democratization in Brazil*

1. See, e.g., the outstanding collection of essays in Peter R. Kingstone and Timothy Power, eds., *Democratic Brazil: Actors, Institutions and Processes* (Pittsburgh: University of Pittsburgh Press, 2000).
2. Thomas Skidmore, *The Politics of Military Rule in Brazil, 1964–1985* (New York: Oxford University Press, 1998), p. 175.

3. Craig L. Arceneaux, *Bounded Missions: Military Regimes and Democratization in the Southern Cone and Brazil*, (University Park, Penn.: Penn State Press, 2001), p. 171.

4. Thomas Skidmore, "Brazil's Slow Road to Democratization, 1974–1985," in Alfred Stepan, ed., *Democratizing Brazil* (New York: Oxford University Press, 1989), p. 15.

5. Ibid., p. 15.

6. Arceneaux, *Bounded Missions: Military Regimes and Democratization in the Southern Cone and Brazil*, p. 173.

7. Scott Mainwaring, *Rethinking Party Systems in the Third Wave of Democratization: The Case of Brazil* (Stanford, Calif.: Stanford University Press, 1999), p. 90.

8. Ibid., p. 90.

9. Skidmore, "Brazil's Slow Road to Democratization," pp. 28–29.

10. Juan J. Linz and Alfred Stepan, *Problems of Democratic Transition and Consolidation* (Baltimore: Johns Hopkins University Press, 1996), p. 168.

11. Scott Mainwaring, "Grassroots Popular Movements and the Struggle for Democracy," in Alfred Stepan, ed., *Democratizing Brazil*, p. 195.

12. A survey of January 16, 1985, by the Brazilian magazine *Veja* found that 66% of Brazilians thought that Neves would make an effective leader.

13. Linz and Stepan, *Problems of Democratic Transition and Consolidation*, p. 168.

14. Maria Do Carmo Campello De Souza, "The Brazilian New Republic: Under the Sword of Damocles," in Alfred Stepan, ed., *Democratizing Brazil*, p. 361.

15. Maria Helena Moreira Alves, "Trade Unions in Brazil: The Search for Autonomy," in Edward C. Epstein, ed., *Labor Autonomy and the State in Latin America* (Boston: Unwin Hyman, 1989), p. 61.

16. Scott Mainwaring, Rachel Meneguello and Timothy J. Power, "Conservative Parties, Democracy and Economic Reform in Brazil," in Kevin Middlebrook, ed., *Conservative Parties, the Right, and Democracy in Latin America* (Baltimore: Johns Hopkins University Press, 2000), p. 177.

17. Ibid., p. 177.

18. Thomas Bruneau, "Brazil's Political Transition," in John Higley and Richard Gunther, eds., *Elites and Democratic Consolidation in Latin America and Southern Europe* (New York: Cambridge University Press, 1992), p. 266.

19. Wendy Hunter, "Civil-Military Relations in Argentina, Brazil and Chile," in Felipe Agüero and Jeffrey Stark, eds., *Fault Lines of Democracy in Latin America* (Miami: University of Miami North South-Center Press, 1998), p. 303.

20. See, e.g., Alfred Stepan, *Rethinking Military Politics: Brazil and the Southern Cone* (Princeton: Princeton University Press, 1986). More recent accounts of military politics in Brazil have challenged Stepan's analysis by contending that over time civilian governments have effectively eroded military prerogatives. See, e.g., Wendy Hunter, *Eroding Military Influence in Brazil: Politicians Against Soldiers* (Chapel Hill, N.C.: University of North Carolina Press, 1997).

21. For a more detailed view of the influence of the military on the policies of the new democracy from agrarian reform to the constitution see: Eliézer Rizzo de Oliveira, "O papel das forces armadas na nova constituição e no futuro da democracia no Brasil," *Vozes* 82 (July–December 1988).

22. Linz and Stepan, *Problems of Democratic Transition and Consolidation*, p. 169.

23. Felipe Agüero, "Democratic Consolidation and the Military in Southern Europe and South America," in Richard Gunther et al., eds., *The Politics of Democratic Consolidation: Southern Europe in Comparative Perspective* (Baltimore: Johns Hopkins University Press, 1995), p. 134.

24. The creation of a civilian-led ministry of defense was finally accomplished under President Cardoso in 1999. Presumably, this has helped in the ongoing effort to establish civilian control over the military.

25. Agüero, "Democratic Consolidation and the Military in Southern Europe and South America," p. 135.

26. Linz and Stepan, *Problems of Democratic Transition and Consolidation*, p. 169.

27. Ibid., p. 169.

28. Frances Hagopian, "Democracy by Undemocratic Means? Elites, Politics and Regime Transition in Brazil," *Comparative Political Studies* 23 (July 1990), p. 156.

29. *The New York Times* (July 25, 1993).

30. On the political economy of democratization in Brazil see Stephan Haggard and Robert Kaufman, *The Political Economy of Democratic Transitions* (Princeton: Princeton University Press, 1995), pp. 341–342.

31. Linz and Stepan, *Problems of Democratic Transition and Consolidation*, p. 168.

32. On the Collor de Mello administration see, in particular, Luiz Carlos Bresser Pereira, *Os tempos de Collor: Adventuras da modernidade e desvesturas da ortodoxia* (São Paulo: Nobel, 1991).

33. On Collor's removal from office see the government report "Relatório Final da Comissão Mista de Inquérito" (Brasilia: Congreso Nacional, August 1992).

34. See Kurt Weyland, "The Rise and Fall of President President Collor de Mello and Its Impact on Democracy," *Journal of Inter-American Studies and World Affairs* 35 (1993).

35. Linz and Stepan, *Problems of Democratic Transition and Consolidation*, p. 170.

36. In 1989 Collor created his own political party, the Party of National Re-construction (PRN).

37. Frances Hagopian, "Democracy and Political Representation in Latin America in the 1990s," in Agüero and Stark, eds., *Fault Lines of Democracy in Post-Transition Latin America*, p. 104.

38. Linz and Stepan, *Problems of Democratic Transition and Consolidation*, p. 170.

39. See *Veja* (April 28, 1993).

40. Linz and Stepan, *Problems of Democratic Transition and Consolidation*, p. 188.

41. Gilberto Dimenstein and Josias de Souza, *A Historia Real: Trauma de una Sucessão* (São Paulo: Editora Ática), pp. 110–111, 138–143.

42. *The Economist*, "Special Report: Brazil's Elections" (October 5–11, 2002), p. 25.

43. Ibid., p. 25.

44. Power, "Political Institutions in Democratic Brazil," in Kingstone and Power, eds., *Democratic Brazil: Actors, Institutions and Processes*, p. 35.

45. Stepan, "Introduction," in Alfred Stepan, ed., *Democratizing Brazil*, p. 209.

46. Frances Hagopian, "The Compromised Consolidation: The Political Class in the Brazilian Transition," in Scott Mainwaring et al., eds., *Issues in Democratic Consolidation: The New South American Democracies in Comparative Perspective* (Notre Dame, Ind.: University of Notre Dame Press, 1992).

47. See Richard Graham, *Patronage and Politics in Nineteenth Century Brazil* (Stanford, Calif.: Stanford University Press, 1990).

48. Ibid., p. 248.

49. Human Rights Watch, *World Report 1997* (New York: Human Rights Watch, 1996), p. 82.

50. Kurt Wayland, The Brazilian State in the New Democracy," in Kingstone and Power, eds., *Democratic Brazil*, p. 43.

51. Mainwaring, *Rethinking Party Systems in the Third Wave*, p. 177.

52. Ibid., p. 208.

53. Kathryn Hochstetler, "Democratizing Pressures from Below? Social Movements in the New Brazilian Democracy," in Kingstone and Power, eds., *Democratic Brazil: Actors, Institutions and Processes*, p. 165.

54. Ibid., p. 179.

55. Ibid., p. 181.

56. See, e.g., John Burdick, "Rethinking the Study of Social Movements: The Case of Christian Base Communities in Urban Brazil," in Arturo Escobar and Sonia A, Alvarez, eds., *The Making of Social Movements in Latin America: Identity, Strategy and Democracy* (Boulder: Westview Press, 1992).

57. Kurt Wayland, "The Growing Sustainability of Brazil's Low-Quality Democracy," paper presented at the conference "Advances and Setbacks in the Third Wave of Democratization in Latin America," Kellogg Institute, University of Notre Dame, April 23–24, 2001, p. 13.

58. Kenneth P. Serbin, "The Catholic Church, Religious Pluralism, and Democracy in Brazil," in Kingstone and Power, eds., *Democratic Brazil: Actors, Institutions and Processes*, p. 158.

59. Ibid., p. 156.

60. See Ben Ross Schneider, *Politics within the State: Elite Bureaucrats and Industrial Policy in Brazil* (Pittsburgh: University of Pittsburgh Press, 1991).

61. Source of Data: Freedom House country profile on Brazil, 1999.

62. *Folha de São Paulo* (January 1, 1997).

63. Teresa Caldeira, *City of Walls: Crime, Segregation, and Citizenship in São Paulo* (Berkeley: University of California Press, 2000), p. 15.

64. Guillermo O'Donnell, "Micro escenas de la privatización de lo público en São Paulo," *Working Paper* No.121, Helen Kellogg Institute for International Studies,

University of Notre Dame (1989) and "Why Should I Give a Shit? Notes on Sociability and Politics in Argentina and Brazil," in O'Donnell, *Counterpoints: Selected Essays on Authoritarianism and Democratization* (Notre Dame: University of Notre Dame Press, 1999).

65. Ibid., p. 314.
66. Steven Dudley, "Deadly Force: Security and Insecurity in Rio," *NACLA Report*, Vol. XXXII, No. 3 (November/December 1998), p. 34.
67. Anthony W. Pereira, "An Ugly Democracy: State Violence and the Rule of Law in Postauthoritarian Brazil," in Kingstone and Power, eds., *Democratic Brazil: Actors, Institutions and Processes*, p. 230.
68. Ibid., p. 34.
69. Ibid., p. 34.
70. Ibid., p. 34.
71. Alves, "Trade Unions in Brazil: The Search for Labor Autonomy," p. 47.
72. See, especially, John Humphrey, *Capitalist Control and Workers' Struggle in the Brazilian Auto Industry* (Princeton: Princeton University Press, 1982).
73. See David Collier, ed., *The New Authoritarianism in Latin America* (Princeton: Princeton University Press, 1979).
74. Ian Roxborough, "Inflation and Social Pacts in Mexico and Brazil," *Journal of Latin American Studies* 24 (1992), footnote 27.
75. Paul Singer, "Democracy and Inflation in Brazil," in William L. Canak, ed., *Lost Promises: Debt, Austerity and Development in Latin America* (Boulder: Westview Press, 1989), p. 43.
76. Ibid., p. 43.
77. Robert Kaufman, "Stabilization and Adjustment in Argentina, Brazil and Mexico," in Joan Nelson, eds., *Economic Crisis and Policy Choice* (Princeton: Princeton University Press, 1990), p. 78.
78. Ibid., p. 50.
79. "Interview with Lula," *Latin American Perspectives* 33 (Fall 1979), p. 90.
80. Scott Mainwaring, "Brazilian Party Under-development in Comparative Perspective," *Political Science Quarterly* 107 (No. 4 1992–1993), p. 681.
81. Scott Mainwaring and Timothy Scully, eds., *Building Democratic Institutions: Party Systems in Latin America* (Stanford, Calif.: Stanford University Press, 1995).
82. Ibid, p. 374.
83. Power, "Political Institutions in Democratic Brazil," p. 30.
84. Wayland, "The Growing Sustainability of Brazil's Low-Quality Democracy," p. 13.
85. Ibid., p. 14.
86. Mainwaring, "Brazilian Party Under-development in Comparative Perspective," p. 679.
87. Mainwaring et al., "Conservative Parties, Democracy and Economic Reform in Contemporary Brazil," p. 219.
88. Hagopian, "Democracy and Political Representation in Latin America in the 1990s," p. 125. This data is based on a study by Maria D' Alba Gil.

89. Alessandro Pizzorno, "Interests and Parties in Pluralism," in Susanne Berger, ed., *Organizing Interests in Western Europe: Pluralism, Corporatism and the Transformation of Politics* (New York: Cambridge University Press, 1981).

90. Mainwaring, *Rethinking Party Systems in the Third Wave of Democratization: The Case of Brazil*, p. 5.

91. Mainwaring, "Grassroots Popular Movements and the Struggle for Democracy," p. 191.

92. Ibid., p. 191.

93. Stepan, *Rethinking Military Politics*, p. 7.

94. Mainwaring, *Rethinking Party Systems in the Third Wave of Democratization*, p. 126.

95. Ibid., p. 127.

96. Ibid., p. 127.

97. Ibid., p. 127.

98. Mainwaring, "Grassroots Popular Movements and the Struggle for Democracy," p. 193.

99. Campello de Souza, "The Brazilian New Democracy," p. 380.

100. Keck, "The New Unionism in the Brazilian Transition," in Alfred Stepan, ed., *Democratizing Brazil*, p. 281.

101. On the PT see Margaret Keck, *The Workers' Party and Democratization in Brazil* (New Haven: Yale University Press, 1992); Isabel Ribeiro de Oliveira, *Trabalho e politica* (Petropolis: Vozes, 1988); Moacir Gadotti and Octaviano Pereira, *Pra que PT: origem, projeto e consolidaçao do partido dos trabalhadores* (São Paulo: Cortez, 1989); and Raquel Meneguello, *PT: A formaçao de um partido* (Rio de Janeiro: Paz e terra, 1989).

102. Keck, "The New Unionism in the Brazilian Transition," in Alfred Stepan, ed., *Democratizing Brazil*, p. 274.

103. On "non-party parties" in Latin America see Borda, "Social Movements and Political Power in Latin America," in Sonia A. Alvarez and Arturo Escobar, eds., *The Making of Social Movements in Latin America*.

104. Mainwaring, *Rethinking Party Systems in the Third Wave*, p. 91.

105. See William Nylen, "The Making of Loyal Opposition Party: The Workers' Party and the Consolidation of Democracy in Brazil," in Kingstone and Powers, eds., *Democratic Brazil*.

106. Rebecca Abers, "From Clientelism to Cooperation: Local Government, Participatory Policy and Civic Organizing in Porto Alegre, Brazil," *Politics and Society* 26 (December 1998), p. 511.

107. Marta Lagos, "Latin America's Smiling Mask," *Journal of Democracy* 8 (July 1997), p. 125.

108. Skidmore, "Brazil's Slow Road to Democratization," p. 32.

109. Ibid., p. 32.

110. Leigh Payne, "Working Class Strategies and the Transition to Democracy in Brazil," *Comparative Politics* (January 1991), p. 229.

111. *Folha de São Paulo* (July 9, 1986).

112. Caldeira, *City of Walls*, p. 355.

113. Source of data: James Petras, "The Rural Landless Workers' Movement," *Z Magazine* (March 2000); "The New Revolutionary Peasantry," *Z Magazine* (October 1998); and *Jornal Sem Terra* (various issues), the MST's official publication.

114. See Hochstetler, "Democratizing Pressures from Below? Social Movement in the New Brazilian Democracy," in Kingstone and Power, eds., *Democratic Brazil*, p. 177.

7 Civil Society Reconsidered

1. Sidney Tarrow, "Making Social Science Work Across Space and Time: A Critical Reflection on Robert Putnam's Making Democracy Work," *American Political Science Review* 90 (June 1996).

2. Ibid., p. 392.

3. Ibid., p. 293.

4. Ibid., p. 394.

5. Interestingly enough, the widely held impression of the post-Communist world as a barren associational landscape is not borne out by the empirical evidence provided by the *World Values Survey*. See appendix.

6. Laurence Whitehead, "Bowling in the Bronx: The Uncivil Interstices between Civil and Political Society," in Robert Fine and Shirin Rai, eds., *Civil Society: Democratic Perspectives* (London: Frank Cass, 1997), p. 109.

7. Peter Reddaway, "Civil Society and Soviet Psychiatry," *Problems of Post-Communism* XL (July–August, 1991), p. 42.

8. Pauline Jones Luong and Erika Weinthal, "The NGO Paradox: Democratic Goals and Non-Democratic Outcomes in Kazakhtan," *Europe-Asia Studies* 51 (1999), p. 1275.

9. Martin Aberg, "Putnam's Social Capital Theory Goes East: A Case Study of Western Ukraine and L'viv," *Europe-Asia Studies* 52 (2000), p. 293.

10. Ibid., p. 312.

11. Thomas Carothers, "Civil Society," *Foreign Policy* (Winter 2000/2001), p. 26.

12. Samuel Huntington, *Political Order in Changing Societies* (New Haven: Yale University Press, 1968), p. 10.

13. Ibid., p. 2.

14. For a more extended discussion of the events discussed in this section see Omar G. Encarnación, "Venezuela's Civil Society Coup," *World Policy Journal* 19 (Summer 2002).

15. Sheri Berman, "Islamism, Revolution and Civil Society," unpublished manuscript, 2003, p. 9.

16. Ibid., p. 17.

17. See Juan Linz and Alfred Stepan, *The Breakdown of Democratic Regimes* (Baltimore: Johns Hopkins University Press, 1979).

18. For example, the government of Spain's Second Republic adopted an atheist constitution, despite the nation's overwhelmingly Catholic population. Allende sought to nationalize the Chilean economy.

19. Huntington, *Political Order in Changing Societies*, p. 28.

20. Sheri Berman, "Civil Society and Political Institutionalization," in Bob Edwards, Michael W. Foley and Mario Diani, eds., *Beyond Tocqueville: Civil Society and the Social Capital Debate in Comparative Perspective* (Hanover, N.H.: University of New England Press, 2001), p. 39.

21. Ibid., p. 39

22. Tocqueville, *Democracy in America*, Vol. II, p. 116.

23. Tocqueville, quoted by Rahn, Brehm and Carlson, "National Elections as Institutions for Generating Social Capital," in Skocpol and Fiorina, eds., *Civic Engagement in American Democracy*, p. 122. Tocqueville also focused on elections as a source of democratic socialization and trust by political institutions. He writes that despite "the dishonorable means often used by candidates and the calumnies spread by their enemies," the "eagerness to be elected may, for the moment, make particular men fight each other, but in the long run, this same aspiration induces mutual helpfulness on the part of all; and while it may happen that the accident of an election estranges two friends, the electoral system forges permanent ties between a great number of citizens who might otherwise have remained forever strangers to one another."

24. Keith E. Whittington, "Revisiting Tocqueville's America, *American Behavioral Scientist* 42 (September 1998), p. 25.

25. Ibid.

26. Larry Diamond, *Developing Democracy: Toward Consolidation* (Baltimore: Johns Hopkins University Press, 1999), p. 250.

27. Ibid.

28. Thomas Carothers, "Democracy Assistance: The Question of Strategy," *Democratization* 4 (Autumn 1997), p. 117.

29. Tocqueville, *Democracy in America*, p. 190.

30. This was arguably the case in Venezuela, where USAID money channeled through the trade unions may have been used in the failed attempt to topple the Chávez government. See Encarnación, "Venezuela's Civil Society Coup," p. 45.

Appendix

1. Larry Diamond provides a useful classification of countries based on the Freedom House averages. Countries with averages of 1.0–3.0 are qualified as "liberal democracies," those with averages of 3.5–6.5 are rated as "non-liberal electoral democracies" and "pseudo-democracies," and those with averages beyond 6.5 as "authoritarian regimes." See Larry Diamond, *Developing Democracy: Toward Consolidation* (Baltimore: Johns Hopkins University Press, 1999), appendix.

2. For an overview of the intellectual foundations of the *World Values Survey* see: Ronald Inglehart, *Modernization and Post-modernization: Culture, Economic and Political Change in 43 Societies* (Princeton: Princeton University Press, 1997).

3. This organizational cumulative percentage has come under some criticism. A common complaint is the overwhelming "Western" orientation of the *World Values Survey* since many of its categories make little sense outside of the Western experience.

4. Arthur M. Schlesinger, "Biography of a Nation of Joiners," *American Historical Review* 50 (1944).

5. Inglehart, *Modernization and Post-modernization*, p. 189.

6. See Juan J. Linz and Alfred Stepan, *Problems of Democratic Transition and Consolidation* (Baltimore: Johns Hopkins University Press, 1996).

7. The civil society density average for Uruguay comes form the WVS of 1995–1997. This case was not included in the original survey that provided the empirical basis for Inglehart's *Modernization and Post-Modernization*. In the 1995–1997 survey Spain and Uruguay are listed as having the same level of civil society density, this time calculated in the form of an organizational membership per person average (1.39).

8. Edward N. Muller and Mitchell A. Selligton, "Civic Culture and Democracy: The Question of Causal Relationships," *American Political Science Review* 88 (September 1994).

9. Inglehart, *Modernization and Post-modernization*, p. 174.

10. Ronald Inglehart, "Trust, Well-being and Democracy," in Mark Warren, eds., *Democracy and Trust* (New York: Cambridge University Press, 1999), p. 89.

11. The cases of Spain and Japan appear to challenge this assumption. In both cases the consolidation of democracy has not created a dense civil society.

Index